THE SUSTAINABLE TEACHER

THE

SUSTAINABLE

TEACHER

PRACTICAL WAYS TO
A BETTER BALANCE

MELISSA KENNEDY

amba
press

Published in 2023 by Amba Press, Melbourne, Australia
www.ambapress.com.au

Cover design: Tess McCabe
Internal design: Amba Press
Editor: Rica Dearman

ISBN: 9781922607829 (pbk)
ISBN: 9781922607836 (ebk)

A catalogue record for this book is available from the National Library of Australia.

CONTENTS

INTRODUCTION

Teaching is fun, frustrating and totally absorbing all in the space of 15 minutes on a random Tuesday afternoon. I like it because I love people, puzzles and learning. Teaching is a never-ending jigsaw of helping people to find their possibilities in life, as they help you to find yours. The challenge is that, like most fabulous things in life, it's hard. It can suck up every ounce of energy, thought and humour so that before you know it, you're burned out, feeling resentful and you want to scream.

After 20-odd years of practice, I'd like to share some ideas about how to create a sustainable teaching life so you're more likely to scream in excitement than frustration. Just like a folder of files in your Dropbox or OneDrive, which you can click on whenever you need some advice, some empathy or the knowledge that someone else has made a bigger mistake than you just did and survived! It's a place with tips and tricks to conserve your energy and avoid the crash and burn. There's so much information about teaching and education out there that it can be overwhelming as you wonder who's worth paying attention to. I get it. Plenty of times I've sifted through all the white noise of educational advice to focus on the essentials. In this book I've curated advice and strategies based on my experience as a practising teacher. Maintaining a balance in the ecosystem of your teaching life is possible, as we design new ways to connect and learn.

> **"To be sustainable is to conserve an ecological balance by avoiding depletion of natural resources"**
> **– Oxford Dictionary**

In teaching, those natural resources are energy, patience, compassion, resilience, enthusiasm and health. In the world of education there are plenty of things that drain your natural resources: writing programs, lesson preparation (with seemingly 15+ levels of differentiation), teaching lessons, developing classroom management resources and strategies, endless piles of marking, counselling students, meetings, phone calls to parents, mediating student conflicts, extracurricular responsibilities, writing reports, maintaining accreditation, making and curating resources, excursions, sport trips, professional learning, reading government education directives and... you get the idea. It's a lot to do. Much of it you can't directly influence. What you can do is navigate these demands on your time in sustainable ways, so you stay healthy, happy and balanced. Only then can you give your best to your students and colleagues.

Teaching is the business of developing people. It's about people and the relationships you grow with them. At its core it's about persuading another person that the concept, idea or skill you want them to know is worth learning about. It's developing their trust in you, each other and themselves. It's capturing and keeping their attention using your personality, voice, movement, print and digital resources, humour, games and whatever works best in the moment. It's understanding how they learn, so you can work with them to find a technique that sparks that flash of insight. It's building their confidence as people and learners in our beautifully complex world. It's about building connections with your colleagues, parents and the wider community as we all embrace change. It's about supporting them to know and be confident in the most authentic version of themselves.

Hope is the most valuable superpower you can give your students. Teaching is a profession that has the power to impact the future through tiny little moments of hope shared daily through your words and actions. Life is messy and often dark for some young people, and your hope – in them and the possibilities their life holds – will help them to move forward.

I've had more than a few moments of feeling awkward and insecure about sharing the ideas in this book because I have an allergy to the 'guru-isation' of education. I don't see myself as an 'expert teacher'. I'm experienced, sure, and I have lots of tricks and tips to share. I become 'expert' at teaching the young people in my class through practise as I get to know them during the year. And then I get new classes the following year and the process begins again as I learn and make mistakes in the process of becoming a more effective and sustainable teacher. What works one year might be a complete face-plant experience the next. It's a good thing I feel nervous every time I meet a new class, or I get worried about whether an activity will work or stress about how a student is doing. It means I care and will keep reflecting on how to get better at this teaching gig.

This book is an invitation to start a conversation about how to be a more sustainable teacher, whether you have been teaching for two days, two weeks or 20 years. All sections are relevant for early career teachers, and those who are more experienced may like to read a few sections for a different perspective or for ideas to mentor colleagues. It is informed by educational research and you can dig deeper, if you choose, via the reference list.

This is not a training manual. There are so many different school contexts and so many ways to teach – you know your students best. I'm here to ask questions and suggest strategies for making your teaching life more sustainable, which you can then build upon. I explore some Principles of Sustainable Teaching, which I encourage you to add to and modify to suit yourself, your students and school communities. Share them with me, if you like, on Instagram @sustainableteacherfiles or email me at sustainableteacherfiles@gmail.com.

Principles of Sustainable Teaching

1. **Plan intentionally** – Be clear about what, how and why you're doing something. Avoid planning more than you need to.

2. **Be prepared** – Organise yourself so the time and energy you spend on a task is matched with an equal benefit for your students.

3. **Conserve time** – Create systems and processes to ensure you never waste time voluntarily.

4. **Cultivate joy** – Find and celebrate fun, happy and goofy moments. They're the glue that keeps you and others motivated.

5. **Prioritise skilfully** – Do tasks in the priority they deserve, always putting people before admin.

6. **Respect boundaries** – Respect your boundaries and those of other people because crossed wires and over-commitment suck time and energy.

7. **Communicate clearly** – Communicate clearly and concisely so people get what you mean the first time. Transparency saves time and energy.

8. **Collaborate** – Work together. It's faster, more fun and avoids duplication of effort.

9. **Reflect** – Take time to think about what worked and what didn't to avoid making the same mistake twice.

10. **Recalibrate** – Take what you learned from reflection and make a change.

It's a fact that teaching has become increasingly complex, there is a significant recruitment shortage and more teachers are leaving the profession. The Gallop Inquiry (2021) into the teaching profession investigated these issues in detail, showing what has led to a challenging situation for our profession and suggesting strategies for improvement. Changes will take time to implement and it can feel disheartening to watch politicians and bureaucrats take so long to make structural change in the education system. Join your teaching union, speak up and get active because teachers' working conditions are students' learning conditions. While we are doing that, I feel we can also make change from within. That's why I'm sharing these ideas from my experience teaching and leading in government, independent, Catholic, Christian and international schools. In each school I was supported by teams – of students, colleagues, parents and community members. They taught me that teaching is a team sport, not an individual pursuit. It is netball not tennis, soccer not swimming. It is about the team working together to educate the individual and the group, guiding them to find the best versions of themselves in the most surprising ways and at the most unexpected of moments – a flash mob of learners, tap dancing into their future.

PART 1
PLAN

Over-planning is a thing. And it can lead to burnout. It's common in those who are so keen to impress and inspire students that they work themselves to the bone. It's also common in those who are on temporary or casual teaching contracts and trying to secure a permanent position. Often, they're teachers in their first five years of teaching. You can spend hours planning what you believe is a brilliant lesson that will have your students totally immersed in engaging activities; only for something to happen that explodes all your hard work into a mess of missed opportunities, confusion and incomplete learning tasks. And then you feel a mix of frustration, disappointment and stupidity because you worked until stupid o'clock when you could have spent that time bingeing on Netflix or hanging with friends at the pub. I've done it. More than once!

I've learned that effective planning involves skilfully prioritising what you need to do, when you need to do it and, most importantly, WHY you're doing it in the first place. Sheryl Sandberg, Chief Operating Officer of Facebook, in an interview with CNN, declared the importance of learning to "ruthlessly prioritise". She explored ideas about productivity and living in her 2013 book *Lean In*. 'Ruthless' is a bit harsh for me, so I prefer the term 'skilfully prioritise'. Sandberg says that prioritisation is doing the BEST thing for your business, whatever that may be.

> **In teaching, your business is people and their learning experiences. For me, that means the students and teachers and their needs come first.**

The data collection, compliance measures, accountability checks and administrivia follow on from that depending on time and perceived urgency. Sometimes I receive an email in which I'm told that some administration or compliance task needs to be completed ASAP. But I've learned not to take on other people's sense of urgency as my own. I've learned the importance of prioritising my time.

Being well-planned and organised is on a continuum and it looks different for each teacher. I like to think of it as the Goldilocks continuum. Like the 'just right' porridge she consumed, you can be organised and respond flexibly to changes that may arise in a teaching day. Then you could be a 'hot mess' in complete chaos. On the other side, you could always be in 'cool control': super-organised, but find it difficult to adapt to changes in a day.

The Goldilocks organisation continuum

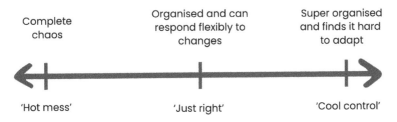

You can be organised in some areas of your teaching life more than others. And neat doesn't always mean organised. I consider myself an organised person, but my desk is one of the messiest in our staffroom.

So… what does it look like to be an organised teacher?

To be organised is to:

- Prepare for an activity or event and have contingencies in place for when things go differently to how you expected. That's 70–90% of the time!
- Use a diary/calendar and consult schoolwide bulletins regularly for changes that will impact you and your students.
- Prepare teaching programs and lesson sequences in advance.
- Book alternative learning spaces in advance.
- Factor in the impact of the swimming carnival on your lesson planning for the week.
- Know when and where you have playground duty and turn up on time.
- Use folders and filing rules in your email inbox, so when the email flood arrives you don't drown in a digital sea!
- Use your teaching program as a dynamic tool in which you register your lessons regularly.
- Develop systems and processes for marking and storing student work samples.

- Handle incoming email correspondence only once.
- Create deadlines and work within them to avoid the dreaded snowball effect of a mountain of work either midterm or end of term.
- Store resources and activities for use next time you teach a topic or concept.

What organised teachers have in common is that they project an aura of calm, which inspires people. They have established expectations and routines so that when life throws a curveball everyone, has confidence in them and their capacity to face the challenges and guide people through. Organisation is the breeding ground for confidence, which builds trust. Trust encourages people to take risks in their learning.

When we take risks, we grow.

CURRICULUM

Know what to teach

What you teach, when and how sounds simple enough, but it helps to know exactly how the whole thing works with our different levels of government in Australia. It saves a lot of time and energy and avoids you accidentally teaching something you don't need to from an old syllabus.

If you don't have a good working knowledge of the curriculum you're teaching and you just pick up a teaching program that people have been using for a while or lesson ideas you found on the internet, you risk teaching the wrong thing and wasting lots of time and energy in the process. If you teach the wrong thing in Years 11 and 12, you risk students being unprepared for their Senior state-wide exams, like the HSC or VCE. In New South Wales, individual schools have ended up on the front page of *The Daily Telegraph* or *The Sydney Morning Herald* for doing just that.

Always locate the right syllabus or curriculum and the right version and check that whichever teaching program you're using aligns with it. In New South Wales, all syllabuses are updated online and announcements about updates are made via their Official Notices. A curriculum is designed by a range of people to explain what our society views as essential knowledge, skills, values and attitudes our young people need to learn to become healthy, active people who can do good things in the world. School education is not listed in the Australian Constitution as a federal responsibility, so it's actually the role of state and territory governments to make laws about how schools are organised and administered. The federal government has a role in school education through funding channels and agreements with the states and territories. In 2019, state and federal politicians met to create *The Alice Springs Declaration (Mparntwe)*. It states the vision and framework for national education, building on the *Melbourne Declaration on Educational Goals for Young Australians*, signed in 2008, which led to the creation of a national curriculum by an organisation called The Australian Curriculum and Reporting Authority (ACARA).

Australian Curriculum implementation

AUSTRALIAN CURRICULUM (currently v. 9.0)

NSW VIC QLD SA WA NT TAS ACT

All use the Australian Curriculum flexibly
according to their law, policies and procedures

The tricky thing is that this Australian Curriculum filters through to students in varied forms depending on where they live, because each state or territory implements it slightly differently, according to their legislation, educational practices, standards and how much money they have in their education budget. In New South Wales, the Education Act of 1990 says syllabuses are developed for each course of study that include, "aims, objectives and desired outcomes in terms of knowledge and skills". In New South Wales, we call the overall design of the learning experience a curriculum and the subject or course-specific learning roadmap a syllabus. We teach from the curriculum and syllabuses, developed during a consultation process, that incorporate the Australian Curriculum content descriptions and achievement standards repackaged in the form of outcomes and content statements. It's kind of like each state buys ACARA brand name lollies and then repackages them in party bags with their own logos, including chocolates and small toys only found in their own state or territory.

These documents are updated every five to 10 years as discoveries are made, knowledge shifts and society changes. When I was in primary school, we learned that Pluto was a planet and we recited a rhyme to remember the order in which the planets orbit around the sun: Mercury, Venus, Earth, Mars, Jupiter, Saturn, Uranus, Neptune and Pluto. In 2006, scientists announced that Pluto was no longer classified as a planet but a 'dwarf planet', so now primary school students stop at Neptune when reciting the planets of the solar system. This new knowledge meant the curriculum needed to be changed to reflect a new understanding of the world. This also happens with teaching strategies and techniques. When I learned how to write essays in high school, we were taught never, ever times one billion to use 'I' or 'my' in our essays. Now, I mark HSC English essays in which students are encouraged to express their informed, personal opinion and nobody's head is chopped off for using a personal pronoun. Ideas, values and approaches change as time passes.

The holy grail for what you need to teach, why, when and in what sequence is in your state or territory's curriculum documents which, thankfully, are all online, so are easy to access anytime, anywhere. All other sources of information are supplementary and you always need to double-check what someone tells you with the relevant curriculum. In Australia, all states and territories use the Australian Curriculum in some way; they incorporate it slightly differently depending on the education laws of their state or territory. South Australia, the Northern Territory and the Australian Capital Territory all use the Australian Curriculum pretty much as it is. When you go to their curriculum websites you are linked back to the Australian Curriculum site. In New South Wales, you will find all you need to know at the NESA curriculum and syllabuses sites, and in Victoria, at the Victorian Curriculum F–10 site.

In Queensland and Western Australia, they have two different sites for their curriculum to Year 10, and then the Senior secondary years. It can also be confusing when there are syllabus changes and you're working with both the existing and new syllabuses across multiple websites, depending on the year group and/or learning area. It can be frustrating as some of these sites aren't easy to navigate and could do with some design help. But you need to know how to navigate them and you need to visit your relevant site often to check for syllabus news and updates. My advice is to bookmark each relevant site in your preferred web browser and visit them regularly.

Know your syllabus seems kind of an obvious thing to say. But too often I've seen teachers become incredibly stressed and overwhelmed because they are trying to teach content, skills and knowledge that aren't in the current curriculum or they are emphasising aspects that students already know. They try to teach what they think is the curriculum and struggle because it's too much, not relevant to their students or not effectively sequenced. At the risk of stating the heart-wrenchingly obvious, teaching is a busy profession. It's full-on, with lots of information that is catapulted at you from various sources on a daily basis. And this means you can feel overwhelmed, especially when you start a new job, a new syllabus is released or you're implementing a new teaching approach.

I've discovered that sometimes teachers are using outdated programs. At other times they find resources, programs and activities on teacher websites that may not be relevant to their state or territory's curriculum. And then there are the times when teachers receive advice from people on teaching social media sites, such as Facebook groups, which is actually a 'syllabus myth' rather than a 'syllabus fact'. The people that give such advice have the best intentions in the world, but they don't necessarily have the updated information nor are they necessarily the best people to ask for advice in your particular context.

Accreditation

Knowing the content and skills of what you teach students sounds simple enough. When you apply to university to study an undergraduate or master's degree in teaching, part of the application process involves the university checking that you have the required knowledge to teach the subject/s. In addition, to be accredited as a teacher, the education authorities in your state or territory check that you have the necessary subject knowledge before they grant you your conditional teaching accreditation. The four career stages of the Australian Teaching Standards are described along a continuum of increasing expertise, skill and quality – Graduate, Proficient, Highly Accomplished and Lead Teacher.

In New South Wales, the levels of accreditation are:

- **Conditional** – You can apply for conditional accreditation if you have completed a substantial part of an accredited undergraduate or graduate teaching degree and meet the requirements specified in the *NSW Teacher Accreditation Manual 2022*.
- **Provisional** – You move from conditional to provisional accreditation when you have completed an approved teaching degree and made an application for accreditation through the New South Wales Education Standards Authority (NESA) website.
- **Proficient** – In your first three years of full-time teaching, or longer if you are in part-time or casual employment, you work towards proficient accreditation.

Optional:

- **Highly Accomplished** – This is an optional level of accreditation. Teachers who apply need to show evidence they have achieved the Teaching Standards at the Highly Accomplished level, proving they are making an impact on their students, colleagues and wider school community. You must pay an application fee and go through a process that involves online assessments, collection of evidence and teaching observations.
- **Lead Teacher** – This is the next level of optional accreditation. Teachers who apply need to show evidence they have achieved the Teaching Standards at the Lead Teacher level, proving they are making a significant impact at a school, education sector and wider community level. Head Teachers and Deputies are most likely to apply for this level of accreditation. It also involves paying a fee and undertaking a similar application process as those who apply for Highly Accomplished accreditation.

WHO, HOW and WHY, before WHAT

I used to think it would be obvious that a teacher would have a passion for what they teach and not just the people they teach. I mean, it's our job to excite students about their learning, so if we don't like the topic then how will they? And then I met Reality. Reality is a confronting beast. I was 23 and working in London. The English call it 'supply teaching'.

There, I taught anything. The Australian dollar was worth approximately 40 British pence, so if I was going to travel in Europe, I needed money, and if I only waited for English or History teaching jobs, either day-to-day or temporary contracts, then it would take a long time to save all those pounds for my planned European adventures. So, I taught French, PE, Maths, Kindergarten, Years 4–6, English, History, Science, Geography, Economics, Art, Drama… whatever I was offered, I accepted. Please know that I struggled to develop a passion for teaching Economic Theory, and Rounders – an English sporting game – is frankly kind of boring, especially when you're the teacher. So, I honed my acting skills and tried to persuade a young group of strangers that they were in for a fun period or day (if it was primary school) of learning with me.

> **I recognised that my focus is and always should be on the WHO (students) and HOW (strategies) and WHY (engage, enlighten, empower) over the WHAT (content).**

There were times when I had the privilege of teaching something that I thought was dry and boring to young people who had been through more than I could ever imagine. And they thanked me? This blew me away every time. On one occasion, I recall teaching a Year 4 class in North London. I spent over an hour teaching a young boy, whose family had fled civil war in Serbia, how to tell the time in English using analogue and digital clocks. Even now I feel goose bumps on my arms as I think of how hard he worked to understand something in what I later learned was his third language.

When I returned from overseas, I accepted a temporary teaching job in a small country town, which involved teaching a range of subjects, including Senior Physics, Junior Maths and Science. The 7–10 Science didn't faze me at all as I had studied Chemistry for two and a half years in my undergraduate degree, as well as English Literature and History. What did worry me was Senior Physics. I mean, it's Physics. I knew basic theorems like speed = distance/time. I knew Newtown's Third Law of Motion that every action has an equal and opposite reaction. After all, hadn't I tried to master that one in the classrooms of East London as I learned the fine art of supply teaching?

I had no passion for Physics; instead, I was scared of it. How could I teach it? I could and did by focusing on the who, how and why, before the what. I also got pragmatic and asked for help. I studied Chemistry at uni, but Physics, to me, was like playing major league baseball when I'd been playing in a local competition. I needed a job and this one offered a guaranteed term's employment. I also had the benefit of a Science teacher dad as a mentor, great colleagues, brilliant executive leadership who would help me and there was a textbook! A nerd by trade and a goody two-shoes by design, I had always done my homework and so I dove in. I survived and quite enjoyed the experience. I realised my 'intense curiosity' for Physics could easily masquerade as passion and I like to think and/or hope I didn't damage the students' future scientific careers in the process. Sometimes you don't feel a passion for what you are teaching and that is OK. I have met English teachers who don't much like Shakespeare and primary teachers who aren't so fond of teaching Science or PDHPE.

> **What matters most is that you love working with young people, you ask for help when you need it, you're curious about learning and you create learning experiences that infect young people with this curiosity.**

Scope and sequences and teaching programs

A scope and sequence is a document that shows the depth and breadth of what students will learn over a time period, usually a year or stage. In New South Wales, it will show the weeks of a term, the hours a week for this subject, the outcomes students are working towards achieving and an outline of each unit of work, including assessment activities and any key requirements of the syllabus, for example, fieldwork.

A teaching program is a unit of work that focuses on a particular topic or inquiry question. In New South Wales it includes sections for outcomes, content points, teaching, learning and assessment activities and resources. Many education sectors and schools have their own templates. A register is required to prove what you have taught, when, how and why. It shows how you have differentiated for the students in your class. They help you and your team of teachers to reflect and decide what strategies worked well and what needs to be adjusted next time to improve students' learning experiences and help them to achieve better outcomes.

Creating all these documents involves lots of paperwork if you don't devise a smooth workflow. A more sustainable approach is, to paraphrase the Pet Shop Boys, 'Go digital (for) together we will learn and teach'. I believe it's easier to go all digital – from the syllabus, the scope and sequence and program to the register. There's no need to keep paper copies of absolutely everything. Store everything on the school intranet, in a Google shared drive or whichever cloud storage your school uses. Some people like to type these documents and then print and store them. My theory is that this takes more time and energy, let alone storage space, than needed. Planning documents need to be flexible and easily modified as the year progresses, so digital creation, version control, curation and storage is the key to more sustainable teaching.

Sustainable workflow

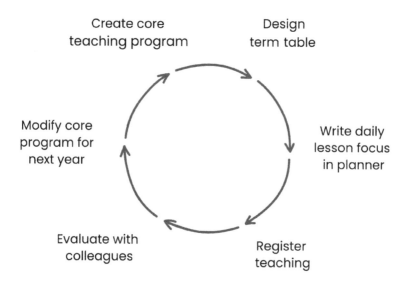

Create core teaching program

Design term table

Modify core program for next year

Write daily lesson focus in planner

Evaluate with colleagues

Register teaching

There are many ways to make and store digital scope and sequences and programs. You can use an online programming tool or you can use a live collaborative document in Google Drive or Microsoft Teams. I highly recommend sharing the load and creating these core or master documents in writing teams of two or three. Then you each export a version to use as your day-to-day teaching program and regularly use it as a planning and registration tool by crossing out, adding in and commenting on what was/was not achieved by the students and why. You then use that program, with its annotations, to 'register' what your class has done that term, upload it to a central faculty or stage file for your supervisor and colleagues, and then you can all evaluate your programs at the next faculty/stage meeting and make any changes for the next year in your master documents. Minimise paper shuffling and maximise lesson planning time: it's the sustainable way to go.

Program and register

Digital storage systems for curriculum documents, resources and registers will save you lots of administration time, as will a folder- and file-naming protocol. A naming protocol is useful to ensure all curriculum and resource files are easy to share and find. For example:

Year group_term_file description

(if relevant)   (if relevant)

e.g.:

8_T1_program (Year 8 Term 1 program)

T3_examprocedures (Term 3 exam procedures)

Depending on your sector and school requirements, you will have a scope and sequence and teaching program for each class. You teach that program and make modifications to it, using your professional judgement, to meet the needs of your students. The modifications you make are annotated on the program and then registered.

Registration is a process stating what you taught, how, why and to whom in a certain period of time, for example, a five- or 10-week block. New South Wales public school teachers use the 'Implementation document for Curriculum Planning and Programming, Assessing and Reporting to Parents K-12 policy'. Section 1.4.2 states for Years 7–10 that, "a scope and sequence and associated learning programs for each course, including teaching activities mapped against NESA syllabus outcomes and content and including registration and evaluation" are required documents. And for 11–12, the same requirement is stated in section 1.4.3. It's technically possible to write a teaching program and say you have taught all the activities in it, but in 20-odd years of teaching, I have never seen a teaching program taught as written verbatim in the time available for every class in a year group. Why?

1. **People are so different.** Each individual and class has different skills, needs and experience/s. So, no matter what and how you intend to teach, it will change as the unit of work progresses.

2. **Life happens.** The swimming carnival is rescheduled to the day you plan an exciting hook lesson featuring a guest speaker. But she can't attend again for months because she is so busy, so your lesson sequence needs to be changed. You discover that half your class have already mastered a skill you plan to teach, so you need to modify your lessons so you can differentiate effectively to ensure each half of the class is engaged and learning.

3. **New ideas spring up as you teach.** Frequently, you plan a fabulous activity when you write a teaching program but then, during the unit, someone shows you a great resource you hadn't seen until now or you see a TV show that inspires a different approach, or a colleague introduces you to a new idea that you think will work better than your original plan as outlined in your teaching program.

Teaching programs are 'living' documents. They're messy.

They evolve as you teach. To record all this, you need to register what you did, when, why and how for each program. You also must include an evaluation. When I first started teaching, evaluations were considered as 'tick-a-box' type compliance measures and people tended to write vague statements like, 'All students enjoyed the unit. Some students found it hard to understand X, so I changed my approach to use Y strategy. Next year I'll try to use that strategy earlier.' This style of evaluation is a waste of time because it doesn't help the students, you or your colleagues. Evaluations have a purpose, which is: improvement. Improvement of the:

*   Quality and relevance of the teaching program
*   Quality and relevance of the teaching strategies

- Students' skills, knowledge and understanding
- Teachers' skills, knowledge and understanding

Evaluations are used to adjust the programs to improve the quality of the teaching and learning experience for all students as we teach and for the next time, we teach this unit of work. It's a cyclical process.

Teacher tips

- "Bookmark in your internet browser the relevant state/territory website with the curriculum link." Alex W – English teacher
- "Break the syllabus documents into chunks and use these with your students, particularly Seniors, in every lesson to help them become familiar with syllabus terms and how they link directly to each lesson." Clarinda O – Deputy Principal and PDHPE teacher
- "Never ask yourself, 'What did I do wrong?.' We always do things with good intentions. Sometimes it works, other times not as well as we planned. When reflecting, ask yourself, 'How can I do better next time?'." Frank G – Mathematics Head Teacher

SCHOOL

School policies and procedures

Each school system and school is unique. Some people think all public schools or all Catholic schools basically run in the same way. That's not true at all: context is key. I've taught in numerous public schools in the same city and I was surprised by how differently they operated in practice, even though they all followed the New South Wales Department of Education's policies.

> Schools run differently because of their unique social, cultural and economic environments. These policies are put in practice in ways that best meet the differing needs of each school's students, teachers, families and wider community.

Start researching your school's context as early as possible. One of the first things I do before starting at a new school is to explore its website. You'll find lots of information about how the school functions and its processes for supporting students and teachers. If you're a student teacher on a professional experience placement, a casual teacher or newly appointed to a position, ask for a copy of the teacher handbook. It will include such boring but essential basics as a school map, bell times, names of key staff and their responsibilities, the canteen menu and outlines of policies and procedures.

One of the most important documents is the school behaviour management plan. This plan is guided by the school sector's plan, if a school is part of one, such as the New South Wales Department of Education's Student Behaviour policy. One of the common schoolwide approaches to behaviour management is Positive Behaviour for Learning. It's a whole-school approach, which does what it says on the label: it addresses student behaviour through systems that create a positive learning environment for everyone. It provides a structured approach for interventions and guiding students to make more positive behaviour choices. It is evidence-based, practical and in my experience, very useful. There are lots of other approaches for managing student behaviour within a school.

> **Remember, you're never alone in managing student behaviour. Whatever structure is in place, the school leadership and your colleagues are there to support you to teach your students.**

Timetables are the backbone of a high school. Your timetable will be etched in your brain, so much so that on a random Tuesday afternoon during the holidays you'll suddenly find yourself thinking of Year 9, because that's the class with whom you usually spend the next hour.

Timetables come in all shapes and sizes. Most high schools run a fortnightly timetable. This means the classes you teach are timetabled over a 10-day period. Some schools have 50-minute learning periods, others 60 and a few use 75-minute periods. Whatever yours has, use it to plan your lessons carefully because time of the day and time of the week matter a lot. Students' focus, energy and willingness to participate in an activity you created will be very different Period 1, Monday in Week 2 to Period 6, Friday in Week 8 of the same term. If you take that into account in your planning, you will save yourself lots of time, energy and frustration. Also, be kind to the Period 5 or 6 teachers. If you regularly load up students with lots of new concepts and skills earlier, they can be very tetchy by the day's end.

Example of the first week of a colour-coded fortnightly timetable

Time (Mon/Tue)	Monday	Tuesday	Time (Wed)	Wednesday	Thursday	Time (Thu)	Friday	Time (Fri)
AM 7:25 – 8:25		Ext1English (11EX1) Room: D12 M KENNEDY	AM 7:25 – 8:25		Ext2English (12EX21) Room: D12 M KENNEDY	AM 7:25 – 8:25	Ext1English (11EX1) Room: D12 M KENNEDY	AM 7:25 – 8:25
RC 8:25 – 8:35			RC 8:25 – 8:50			RC 8:25 – 8:34		RC 8:25 – 8:35
1 8:35 – 9:35	English Standard (11ENS2) Room: D15 M KENNEDY	English (9ENG3) Room: E04 M KENNEDY	1 8:50 – 9:45	English (8ENG4) Room: D14 M KENNEDY	English (7ENG2) Room: D14 M KENNEDY	1 8:34 – 9:23	English (9ENG3) Room: E04 M KENNEDY	1 8:35 – 9:35
2 9:35 – 10:35	English (7ENG2) Room: D14 M KENNEDY		2 9:45 – 10:40	English (8ENG4) Room: D14 M KENNEDY	English Standard (11ENS2) Room: D15 M KENNEDY	2 9:23 – 10:12	Wellbeing (11WEL3) M KENNEDY	2 9:35 – 10:35
3 10:35 – 11:35		English (7ENG2) Room: D14 M KENNEDY	3 10:40 – 11:35	English (9ENG3) Room: E04 M KENNEDY		R 10:12 – 10:32	English (7ENG2) Room: D14 M KENNEDY	3 10:35 – 11:35
L1 11:35 – 11:55	Duty (Oval 1)		L1 11:35 – 11:55			3 10:32 – 11:21		L1 11:35 – 11:55
L2 11:55 – 12:15			L2 11:55 – 12:15		Duty (Quad)	4 11:21 – 12:10		L2 11:55 – 12:15
4 12:15 – 13:15	English (9ENG3) Room: E04 M KENNEDY		4 12:15 – 13:15			L1 12:10 – 12:30	English Standard (11ENS2) Room: D15 M KENNEDY	4 12:15 – 13:15
R 13:15 – 13:35			R 13:15 – 13:35			L2 12:30 – 12:50		R 13:15 – 13:35
5 13:35 – 14:35			5 13:35 – 14:35	English Standard (11ENS2) Room: D15 M KENNEDY		Sport 12:50 – 14:35		5 13:35 – 14:35
PM 14:35 – 15:35	Staff Meeting		PM 14:35 – 15:35			PM 14:35 – 15:35		PM 14:35 – 15:35

Your Head Teacher or Head of Department works with the timetabling team to ensure that you teach the required number of classes and have a 'balanced load', which hopefully means you get a range of classes. For example, teaching only Years 7 and 8 can be tedious and doesn't give you much of a chance to develop your skills; the more experience you have in teaching different year groups and courses, the better.

Usually, you get a print copy of your timetable, and you can download it from your school's learning management system (LMS). I like to download my timetable to my Outlook and/or iCal calendars. You can customise each class using a different colour. More of an old-school but equally useful idea is to use different coloured highlighters to indicate each class on a print copy of your timetable and stick it up on your desk at work. That way, everyone knows where you are, at a glance, if they need to find you during the day. The colours help see the visual flow of a week and make it easier to plan and adjust lessons quickly, as unexpected events, like a guest speaker or a last-minute sports excursion, pop up.

Lesson planning

I'm a big fan of online planning. Digital is simple, easy-to-transfer information and accessible anytime, anywhere. A few years ago, I made the jump and I've never looked back. Many of the companies that make print teacher planners also have online versions. Some schools pay for a print diary for their teachers and some schools pay for online versions. If you buy one yourself you can claim it on tax.

There are bucket-loads of pretty teacher planners and cool online tools. You can spend hours making them look good and writing up all sorts of information. The thing is, you can also waste time duplicating information and transcribing from print to digital form. With most schools using an LMS, much of what we used to keep in print is now reliably online, like class rolls, assessment records and student records. Your mobile device (laptop, tablet and/or smartphone) is the portal to access all these records. When it comes to lesson planning, what you need are two basic personal organisation systems:

1. Day-to-day planning tool/s
2. Strategy for registering programs

For each class, I have:

- Word or Google Doc version of that term's program, which becomes my register. I annotate it as I teach it, evaluate it at the end of the term and save it in our faculty registration folder.
- Table for each class, per term, which summarises the focus of each lesson and is drawn from the detail in the term program. It also includes events like sporting carnivals, public holidays, excursions and assessment dates.
- A5 daily diary, which I can easily slip into a bag. This is my only print organiser. Sometimes I need to make notes in a meeting and it seems rude to sit there and type on a laptop when I'm chatting with people. If I have a touchscreen and stylus, then I will handwrite digitally.

Cloud storage is the Willy Wonka Chocolate Factory of digital bliss for a teacher. It means that you can store all your files to be accessible anytime, anywhere, on any device. Cloud storage allows you to save any file, retrieve it with ease, maintain version control and backup all your files with (hopefully!) minimal drama. It's always worth keeping a hard drive or USB backup of any crucial documents. File storage is like investing, it always pays to have a diverse portfolio of options to spread the risk when something goes wrong.

Cloud storage options

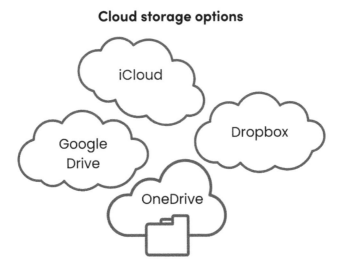

There are a smorgasbord of possibilities including Google Drive, OneDrive and Dropbox. The trick is to make the most cost-effective and time-effective choice for your needs. In some schools or school systems you are told which one to use. I have used Dropbox for about 10 years, across multiple schools, and when Google Classroom became such an easily accessible tool in my school system, I also began to use Google Drive. Its search functions are brilliant, so I can easily find files from years ago and adapt them as needed. This saves me time and energy.

An LMS is a place you can do things like upload files, embed videos, set student tasks, share quizzes for self-assessment and provide feedback. They're usually closed systems where you invite students to join your 'class'. You can organise the material in topics and subtopics. There are many different types of LMS and, as a teacher, you usually don't have a choice of which one to use as it's a whole-school or sector decision. To save time and energy, I suggest learning everything you can about the strengths and weaknesses of your school's LMS as fast as you can.

Spaces

You may have been lucky and scored a classroom space all your own. If so, we're all jealous. What a gift it is to have a space to organise just how you want for the needs of you and your students without having to negotiate seating configurations, display space on walls, cupboard space for storing resources and who replenishes stationery supplies. In a high school, learning spaces involve high-level negotiation and diplomacy skills worthy of United Nations membership.

So, if you have scored a classroom of your own, then get to it and organise away! Ensure your seating configuration is flexible for the needs of your different classes, stick your negotiated classroom expectations on the wall, check that your digital resources are in working order, organise display space for student work, find some posters about your subject area and put them on the wall, create a positive learning habits display to encourage a growth mindset, put everyday stationery like pens, loose-leaf paper and workbooks in an easily accessible cupboard and store tissues and hand sanitiser in the same place.

But if you didn't win the classroom of your own lottery, don't despair. You now have a chance to practise your diplomacy and negotiation skills. Firstly, most Head Teachers and Deputies involved in timetabling will do their best to ensure that you teach your classes in the minimum number of classrooms possible. Timetabling in a high school is an ecosystem that relies on everybody doing their bit and taking their share of what I refer to as the 'compromise load'. Sharing a classroom/s has provided me with many chances to learn from my colleagues and the students they teach.

Work out how many classrooms you are in for each class you teach, for example, if you teach high school, you may teach five classes in three classrooms. Locate a rooming timetable and find out which teachers also teach in those classrooms. Chat to them personally about seating configurations. This is often one of the most contentious issues when sharing a classroom with another teacher. Some teachers are 'rows' people, others swear by 'pairs', a few are double 'U-shaped' diehards, some prefer 'groups', while others are 'flexible' seating arrangers who always like to mix it up! I started as a 'groups' person, moved to become a double 'U-shaped' diehard and then spent time as a 'flexible' seating arranger. I work with the other teacher/s who use the space to find the best solution for all of us and our students, and that often changes as the year progresses. A set seating configuration means you can make a seating plan, which helps to reduce distractions and to develop sound learning habits.

Seating configuration ideas

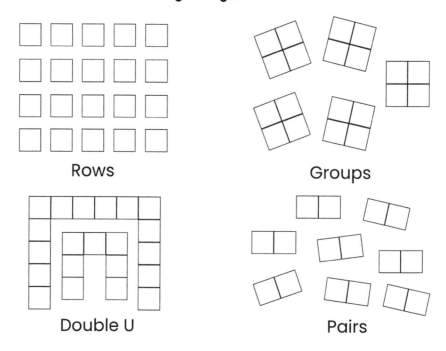

Rows

Groups

Double U

Pairs

Cupboard space is our next point of negotiation. For my Year 7–10 classes I usually require more cupboard space than for the Seniors. I use it to store stationery, books and general resources. Usually, I ask to have at least two shelves and I label them for my classes. Yes, I am one of those label-maker people!

I always find it best to negotiate expectations beforehand, so in the middle of term when the inevitable stressors crop up, you don't want to murder each other over who dumped these books on my shelf or who didn't replace the supply of pens/spare paper/textas/pencils, etc. It may seem over-organised, but a quick five-minute conversation at the beginning of the year in which you organise the seating configuration, cupboard space and anything else that crops up makes a world of difference.

Taking the time to create an environment that is conducive for learning and wellbeing will pay off big time for you and the young people you teach.

Meetings

A meeting can be a fabulously productive time to discuss issues, plan projects and achieve lots with your colleagues. It can also be a gigantic time sucker where you spend the hour (or more) planning lessons in your head and feeling frustrated about what you could be achieving if only you weren't in this meeting. There are many ways to shape a sustainable relationship with meetings, so you can experience more of the time-efficient ones and far fewer of those that feel like you're stuck in a time and space vortex. The trick is knowing what you can control and what you can't. Also, if you're going to attempt to multitask in a meeting, it's best to not get caught by the Senior Executive!

All schools have a meeting schedule of some kind. When I first started in teaching, I didn't manage many meetings, but I did participate in lots that were run by people who had vastly different meeting management styles. The meetings I liked were those run by people who clearly communicated the purpose of the meeting, actively listened, valued each person's time, stuck to the agenda and had the skills to thank someone for their contribution and tell them that their idea would be tabled for further discussion at the next meeting if it looked like they had inadvertently (or intentionally) hijacked the meeting.

When people are passionate about ideas, things can become interesting – they ask lots of questions, disagree with each other and enthusiastically debate an issue. I call this healthy friction. It's great when people ask lots of questions and debate issues because it (usually) means they care. But there is a point in a meeting when a decision needs to be made and things need to move on, otherwise everyone is stuck in meeting quicksand. It's frustration on steroids. Often, people are too polite or too scared to say anything to help the meeting move forward. To avoid that, I've learned how vital it is to worship at the altar of the meeting agenda and the clock. If you're in the meeting, you have a role in ensuring that everyone sticks to the agenda and respects the time allocated. You have the power to politely speak up and to say, "Interesting idea, may we discuss it later and make a decision at our next meeting?" It's not just the role of the chair to keep the meeting on track – everyone present has a part to play.

A whole-school staff meeting can involve up to 60–100 teachers and support staff. These types of meetings are often more like information briefings and it is very tempting to take your laptop and get work done.

Sustainable multitasking is possible if you skilfully prioritise with a smile, a practised look of polite concentration and quick Alt/Tab screen change if someone higher up in the school food chain happens to wander behind you. The challenge is you must be very aware that the Senior Executive knows people will be marking, writing reports or sending emails during the meeting and if you don't want to get caught, you need to be cleverer than that Year 12 student you discovered online shopping while she was meant to be completing a Modern History essay.

I recommend never multitask in any meeting that involves serious issues like health and safety or child protection training. That may send a message that you don't take these issues seriously. And you always need to give these issues 100% of your attention. Next, arrive early and sit as far up the back as possible. If someone is sitting behind you, check they're not the kind to tell others that you were giving less than 40% of your concentration to the meeting. Next, choose a task that only requires 50–60% of your concentration, that may be returning emails, low-stakes class marking or editing a document. You'll still need 10% energy to keep an eye on what's happening around you so you can quickly switch to 100% engagement if the need arises. You may be asked a direct question, so always be at least 30% aware of what's going on in the meeting. In an ideal world, you wouldn't have to multitask in a meeting but, in teaching, time is more precious than gold, so many people feel they have no option. If possible, have a meeting wing-buddy who can alert you that you may be about to get busted for planning other things in a meeting.

Mentors

Plan to make connections with people who will advise and support you. A mentor doesn't have to be an older and/or more experienced teacher. It can be anyone of any age in any role who has some wisdom to share with you. The word 'mentor' means an experienced and trusted adviser and brings to mind pictures of older, greyer people who quietly divulge the secrets of life. Kind of like Gandalf from *The Lord of the Rings*. But truthfully, I think that's a narrow ideal. I've found it helpful to seek advice from whomever is keen to give it, whether that be my dad who has been a high school teacher for over 40 years, my friends' nine-year-old who knows everything possible about Minecraft or girls in my Year 12 class who taught me how I commit the pop-culture sin of being 'cheugy'.[*]

To teach sustainably, you need to have a strong relationship with yourself and those around you. An effective mentor holds a mirror up for you to examine yourself, other people and the way you interact with them. A mentor may be encouraging when you're feeling bruised and tired, and they can also give you truth bombs when you really need someone to point out you're being a bit of an idiot. What's key is that a mentor doesn't necessarily have to be a close friend; sometimes it's hard for people to be a mentor and close friend.

Mentors who help you to learn about a school context and the relationships of the people who work and learn in it are super-helpful. This is especially important when you go to a new school as they can give you an insider's perspective about how things work. It's important to remember, though, that you need to seek mentors who are good with professional boundaries – you don't want to find yourself inadvertently seeking advice from someone who has a grudge against the Principal or the reputation for being a gossip.

Sometimes mentors are other teachers, cleaners, Senior Executive, administration staff, students and/or grounds people. One of the best types of mentors for knowing how people work in a school is the gardener, maintenance person or general assistant. I once had a gardener introduce himself to me at a new school with the line, "Hi, Ms K, remember me? Thanks for not kicking me out of Year 10 English too often." Turns out earlier in my career I'd taught him Year 10 English. He had a habit of avoiding classwork by being disruptive in class and he used to find himself sent to the Deputy's office a little more often than most. He was super-friendly and kind to me and I learned a great deal about how my new school operated through our random chats every week or so.

Before email and social media, it was harder to find a teaching mentor, especially if you were teaching in a country school. Often you were the only qualified teacher in your subject in the school and, if there was only one school, in the whole town. That can be a lonely situation. I know because it's happened to me. What I did was ask for help from a range of

---

[*] Cheugy – According to *The New York Times*, it's someone who is trying too hard and is just a bit out of date.

sources, including teacher friends in other towns and schools. I was also lucky because my parents are teachers and they're good at giving advice, including the tough advice I didn't want to hear. Since the invention of social media, there are lots more ways you can find a mentor if you don't have access to one at your school. A word of caution: read your code of conduct and/or employment contract in relation to the use of social media and follow it carefully. Sometimes, when looking for advice and support, we forget that social media is public and we let slip information about where we teach and issues with students, teachers, parents and/or administration. There may be serious repercussions if you do so. Please be aware of this and avoid using social media about a school issue (or ever) when you are in a state of heightened emotion.

I teach English and History and some of the best mentors I've ever had taught other subjects like Science, PDHPE, Maths and/or different ages like Primary years. Someone once told me to soak up wisdom about teaching from anywhere because I was teaching people first and a subject second. One of my mentors is a friend who teaches Science. She's 10 years younger than me. We rarely see each other at school on a day-to-day basis because we're so busy. But we do belong to the same outdoor fitness group. What really helped me one year, when I had a Year 9 class with students I found quite challenging, was our accidental debriefing sessions as we lifted weights in the park or stretched after a running session. We basically shared the same class. I learned different techniques to manage the students' emotional and social needs and also found out so much more about what was going on in their lives, which I could use to engage them in their learning experiences in English. I received the benefit of my friend's teaching wisdom, kindness, compassion and experiences with these students, so I could help them and myself to better negotiate our learning relationship. We were always super-careful to respect our students' privacy and never reveal any details that could identify them to anyone who may be in the vicinity. I could not have taught that Year 9 class effectively without my friend's wise weekly input.

About 18 years ago, I met a solicitor at a book club in Sydney, whom I call Gilbert Blythe. I call him that because, at the time, his email address was, gilbertblythe@hotmail.com. It's the name of a character from the children's book series by Canadian author Lucy Maud Montgomery. He loves books. He reads a lot. He also swam the English Channel one year. When I met him, I asked him to speak to Year 12 English who were studying the concept 'Journeys'. He did a wonderful job speaking to more than a hundred students and they loved him. I organised for it to be videoed so he could show his parents. He was chuffed because the experience was so unique for him. Gilbert taught me a lot about how to engage boys in reading novels because he hadn't been an avid reader in his early adolescence. We lost contact for about eight years and then rekindled our friendship via email and WhatsApp and the occasional catchup in person as one or both of us lived overseas. What I came to realise is that Gilbert is another accidental mentor. As a solicitor, writer, traveller, filmmaker and photographer, he has a diversity of professional and personal life experiences that he is always happy to share. I learn so much from him.

There is great power in reaching out to people within your social circles and the community as a whole to share their expertise and strengths with young people. Everyone is busy and, at times, it can feel scary to ask for their time but, in my experience, it's worth it.

Teacher tips

- "I survey my students at the start of every year, find out their past experience of the subject, what they are looking forward to and anxious about." Alex W – English teacher

- "Be a bowerbird and find already made resources, you don't need to be a Pinterest teacher." Nadia S – History Head Teacher

- "Be resourceful! Use the many wonderful resources available through colleagues or online. Some people are tremendous resource creators and not all teachers have this strength. Paid resources can be worth it if you see that your own time is money. And a new addition to this is to get familiar with AI and learn how it can be an assistant for you." Christine M – English teacher

CLASS

Building relationships

Building relationships with people is fun, sometimes challenging and occasionally confusing. As a teacher, you will build relationships with colleagues, students, parents and the general community. It's important to have a personal plan about how you will behave and manage the inevitable conflicts that will arise in day-to-day teaching life whether that be student behaviour management or interactions with colleagues and parents. Being proactive beats reactive, hands down, except, of course, in the case of imminent physical danger to a student from a falling meteor or out-of-control basketball heading for your colleague's head as she was too busy talking to that gorgeous Maths teacher to take any notice.

In my experience, it's easy to feel overloaded by what everyone has to say and what they recommend you do. I have gotten myself in a flap on many an occasion worried about whether I'm doing things 'right'. Sometimes I'm unsure of which person to believe and which strategy to try. It can feel like many of these experts have forgotten what it's like to be a new teacher, not knowing where to start in managing young people who are complex, surprising, creative, noisy, wilful and oh, so unpredictable.

You're taught all sorts of things at school and at university about how to interact with other people. There are lots of researchers, academics and writers who give excellent advice, ideas and strategies, like:

- Bill Rogers
- Brené Brown
- Dr Timothy O'Leary
- Dr Hayley Watson
- Paul Dix
- Andrea Downie
- Peps Mccrea
- Tom Bennett
- Simon Sinek

Planning to be an effective teacher with resilient mental health is key. Dr Hayley Watson has an excellent wellbeing program in which she talks about how teachers interact with hundreds of people a day and make thousands of decisions, both big and small, often within highly emotional contexts. As teachers, we need to plan how to effectively manage our interactions with other people and ourselves, without burning out. Decision fatigue is real. Planning ahead helps, as does taking regular time out to recharge.

Andrea Downie's work with Project Thrive explores the value of "eudaimonic wellbeing [which] is about meaning, purpose, authenticity and personal growth". The word 'eudaimonia' derives from Greek and is an abstract noun, which basically means 'well-spirit'. It is the state of being we reach when we're living in accordance with who we are, 'our truest self'. To live in such a way, you need to identify and listen to your values. If you value being brave, kind, curious and flexible, you're off to a sustainable start as a teacher. From here, you build ideas about how to positively manage interactions. You'll make mistakes. We all do. That's when humility comes in handy.

> **The ability to apologise and admit an error is an underrated skill.**

I filter all the great advice from teachers, researchers and academics through the following ideas:

1. Set shared expectations early and firmly and maintain them.
2. Ask questions so you both feel heard.

3. Listen first with the intent to understand, not to respond.

4. Take the emotion out of a situation as soon as possible.

5. Devise a 'win-win' solution, so you both feel there is a path forward.

6. Slow down your thinking, speech and reactions.

I refer to them regularly when I'm feeling frustrated with a determined Year 7 student who believes constant nagging is a sure-fire way to get what they want, or a Year 9 student who has decided that the classroom is theirs to control as they wish. And I just trial different strategies until I hit on one that works for the particular individual or group of students. I'm in beta mode – a constant work in progress! Young people understand what it is to make mistakes, they just want to feel seen, heard and valued by you.

Adapt for your class

So, you have a scope and sequence and a teaching program, and now you need to organise what you will teach and when. Working out the best way to make these decisions can be a little frustrating. You just teach your program sequentially; I mean, that's why you wrote the thing, isn't it? Nope. It's just a plan. You need to build in flexibility, so you can adapt to whatever curveball is thrown at you from left field, on any given day.

What I find super-useful is a Google Sheet or Word table or whatever else serves the same purpose (I'm digitally ecumenical), showing the weeks of the unit of work, day and period for each class and then a summary of the teaching activities planned for that period. It helps me to see the *scope and depth* of the term, when I need to pre-book equipment or library space, where the 'pinch points' may be and to backward-map effectively from any formal assessment task due date or basic skills test, such as the National Assessment Program – Literacy and Numeracy (NAPLAN).

When I create this table, I also include school events, excursions for that year group in other subjects, which mean students will miss our class, public holidays, sports carnivals, guest speakers and anything else that will impact on the learning sequence. As the term progresses, I can adapt this plan as I need to. Sometimes I find that most of the class knows more or less about a topic than I expected, and so I can easily alter the Google table and adjust our direction.

T2, Year 7 | English Overview

Lesson overview table (first five weeks)

Week	Monday	Tuesday	Wednesday	Thursday	Friday
1A	Staff PD day	ANZAC Day	Intro Narrative skills revision task		Athletics Carnival
2B		Vis Ass revision and asst task prep		Vis Ass revision and asst task prep Reading – Trash	Founder's Day
3A	Novel activities – setting	Novel activities – setting	Novel activities – characterisation and perspective		Novel activities – concept and theme
4B		Novel activities – characterisation and perspective		Novel activities – characterisation and perspective	Novel activities – concept and theme
5A	Novel activities – concept and theme	Novel activities – concept and theme	Writing a short story inspired by the novel activities		Writing a short story inspired by the novel activities

When I take this step, I feel more organised and I can manage the inevitable curveballs that come our way without freaking out. Also, being organised means I think, feel and behave in a proactive rather than reactive manner. There is no fear like the terror of making up a lesson as you walk into a room of 30 14-year-olds. Believe me, I've felt it more than once.

Being organised in a classroom is about planning and good habits. I know, how boring, right? Part of me wishes I could spout some impressive-sounding, pseudo-psychological, Insta-worthy advice. But I'd be lying. Organisation within a classroom is about developing and maintaining solid habits for you and the young people in your care to build a culture of trust and consistency that makes people feel safe.

For most people, a classroom is a room within an institution called a school that you were compelled to sit in, on often quite uncomfortable chairs, for periods of time from Monday to Friday, at least 180 days a year. In high schools there are general classrooms and specialised spaces for subjects such as Art, Science and PDHPE. Some schools have multipurpose spaces for learning. During the COVID-19 pandemic, most students learned from home, so the classroom was a virtual one. For students who learn via distance education, due to their remote location, illness or sporting commitments, a virtual classroom is their 'normal.'

A classroom is far more than a physical space: it's a community of people learning and teaching together. A classroom may be what lies behind the door of D12 of the main building, an urban garden undergoing regeneration, an orienteering course through the local streets or a class discussion on Zoom. Planning ahead is key. To be sustainable, you need to:

- Understand the space – physical, experiential and/or virtual.
- Organise the equipment and have it ready at point of need.
- Match the curriculum plans (scope and sequence/program) to the space and the students.
- Develop group habits and processes that promote responsibility for self and others.

Email

Email is an unfortunate but necessary evil in modern teaching life. Tools such as Microsoft Teams are making inroads, but most people still use emails more to communicate about work. It's brilliant at many things, but it will never surpass a face-to-face conversation for quality, efficiency, understanding or building a strong culture. To 'do sustainable email' you must create a plan. I recommend making email rules and sticking to them! Disorganised email practices are time and energy suckers.

I cannot stress enough the need to establish personal boundaries around your use of email, otherwise you will drown in other people's information, requests and expectations. You need to decide when, where and how frequently to check emails. Organising your personal 'email healthy habits' requires making decisions, writing them down, communicating them clearly and following them.

I have worked in schools in which the culture was to check emails numerous times a day, at least every hour. It seemed like the expectation was that we would respond to emails sent during class time. As a result, I fell into the trap of believing that everything was urgent, and I had to respond ASAP. It's not. I didn't. Boundaries. And when you think in this way, you find yourself fuelled by adrenaline and every time an email alert appears you receive a shot of virtual coffee. It's seductive and often exciting because you feel what you're doing is important and urgent and part of a bigger picture within the whole school. But it's unsustainable. And it's dangerous because you will make mistakes, like misreading an email, replying using an emotional tone, clicking 'reply all' instead of 'reply' and/or emailing the wrong person.

Over time I learned to set boundaries. I try (and sometimes fail) to maintain email hours from 7.30am to 5pm only, on weekdays. If a student emails me after these times, I ignore it until the next day. I try to look at emails three to four times a day. I create folders in my inbox and establish rules for my email traffic. Microsoft Outlook has a great How-to Guide, as does Gmail; it refers to the organising structure within Gmail as labels. Instructions explaining how to create 'rules' to filter your email traffic are available for Gmail and Outlook. I don't have the email app on my phone or iPad, which forces me to access it on a laptop or desktop and, as it's more of an effort, it makes it seem more like work and I'm less likely to check it 'just in case'.

Sometimes I've received an email in which a student, parent or colleague expresses their emotions about an issue and I feel worried for them, which stresses me and if I respond, then they may respond and an email trail follows which, nine times out of 10, still doesn't resolve the issue and we can't do anything until the next day anyway. So, I try to conserve my time and energy by avoiding checking emails 'just in case'. On weekends, I try to only check my email if I know there is a reason for doing so, such as a student is sending me an essay for feedback or a teacher needs me to proofread their Year 10 reports.

Those 'just in case' email checks are pointless and stress-inducing. If the issue is serious, one of my colleagues would have already called or texted me. All other emails fall under the category of, 'I can't do anything about it until tomorrow'.

One time, I was leaving school at about 5.05pm to catch the train home and a parent and student saw me in the school grounds. They wanted me to check my emails because the student had sent a draft of their writing and wanted feedback now so they could redraft it and submit it later in the week for an assessment task. They had already missed the deadline for feedback that we had negotiated in class, and they were aware of the times I was able to respond to emails. I politely said I would be happy to do so in the morning and left to catch my 5.20pm train. The next day, I discovered that the student's expectation was that I would read their email, on my iPhone, as I stood there in front of them in the playground. They were stressed and me doing this would relieve their stress. Earlier in my career, I probably would have felt I had no choice but to do so. I have learned the hard way that caring means having boundaries and maintaining them. I need to care for myself before I can care for the students I teach. Sure, they and their parent believed this request was urgent, but I didn't have to share that belief and I didn't have to agree to their request. My, "Happy to help, I can do so tomorrow", response was the healthiest and most useful answer for all of us.

Avoid the guilt trap at all costs. You control your email use within the expectations of your school's policies and its leadership's expectations.

I believe all the ideas I've outlined are possible to put into practice within any school – public, independent or international. I know this because I have taught in these contexts. BUT in some schools, there may be an expectation that you respond to emails more frequently than I have recommended. And if that's a requirement of your employment, you may have little choice.

Laptop and other ICT resources

Planning ahead to ensure your technology works can be tricky. In most independent schools and many public schools, teachers are given a work laptop that is current and includes up-to-date software. If you're in that fortunate situation, the tech aspect of your teaching life is off to a relatively smooth start.

If you're in a school where you get a laptop that is four to five years old, then you may want to invest in a laptop of your own and claim it on tax. A newer laptop that can handle your day-to-day requirements will save you hours of frustration. When you have an older laptop, it's more likely to crash on a regular basis, not work efficiently with other devices, be slower and incompatible with new software. If you buy towards the end of a financial year (May/June), you may get a good deal – and don't forget to claim it on tax!

> Schools are archaeological sites for technology.
> Dig deep enough and you will find an overhead projector somewhere! The nature of school funding means that it is rare for the entire school to switch to a new technology at the same time.

What this means for you, in practice, is that you need to plan ahead so you have access to reliable data projectors, speakers and adaptors. Assume nothing! Always check things work. If you're a Mac user, then you're probably already familiar with the use of adaptors. If you're not, then things can get a little frustrating when you try to connect your laptop or mobile device to a data projector in one room with an HDMI cable, but in the next room there is VGA connection. Some schools have wireless connections to data projectors, but many don't.

My best tip is to invest in a multiport adaptor or travel dock, which will connect you to VGA, HDMI, Ethernet, USB 2.0 and 3.0 ports. This simple piece of technology will make a world of difference in your day, especially if you move between classrooms to teach and need to connect your laptop to a new data projector in each room. I carry my tech with me in coloured bags in a basket. As a high school teacher, some years I teach in five or more different classrooms, and my multiport adaptor is key to my tech organisation. Without it I feel flustered, waste time and it's more likely that the students will be off task as they wait for me to get my act together.

Stationery

Stationery is one of your secret weapons. I'm blushing with embarrassment as I write that because I've managed to sound melodramatic and boringly obvious at the same time. But it's so true. As that 1990s Kellogg's Cornflakes advertisement declared, "The simple things in life are often the best".

With a whiteboard marker you can create a learning activity in seconds, when all your plans have gone out the window because of something beyond your control, like your laptop died, the wi-fi has disappeared or you've unexpectedly had to teach outdoors. When a student says she can't do anything because she hasn't got a pen or a highlighter or a ruler or an eraser or a sharpener or coloured pencils... you can pull out your stationery drawer/box/cupboard and hand it over in no time. Post-it notes are essential kit for so many learning activities, from brainstorming to formative assessment exit-tickets.

Essential stationery: Post-it notes

A consistent stationery supply is essential for sustainable teaching. Organising your stationery and having it readily available each lesson will save you time and hassle. Your stationery needs will vary depending on the year groups and/or subject/s you teach. Most primary teachers and many high school teachers will have a classroom of their own to store everything. For everyone else, a giant pencil case or some sort of carrying container is useful.

Stationery kit ideas:

- Whiteboard markers (× 2 minimum) – try to stick to blue or black for writing; remember, some students will have learning needs that affect their ability to see different colours on a whiteboard
- Pens × 5
- Lead pencils × 2, eraser, sharpener
- Ruler
- Highlighters × 2
- Coloured pencils/textas × 1 packet
- Sharpie permanent marker × 1
- Post-it notepads × 2 minimum
- Ruled writing pads × 2
- A4 blank paper × 30
- Stickers or stamps or stationery rewards

This pencil case is your 'go-to' when you're out and about within the school. Maintaining this supply will ensure you're always organised with whatever you need, in your own Mary Poppins' carpet bag of tricks. This includes if you're a casual teacher who moves between classrooms regularly. Control over your own stationery supply will save you having to beg other teachers for whiteboard markers, which is potentially awkward and embarrassing.

If you're lucky enough to have a classroom of your own, then dedicate a cupboard to stationery. I recommend:

- Blank workbooks or notepads × 10
- Coloured notepads × 3
- Highlighters × 5–10
- Box of pens (blue or black)

- Coloured pencils or textas (three or four packets)
- If you're super-fortunate a spare laptop, although technically not stationery, is also handy

A few years ago, our team created stationery boxes for each of our classrooms, which include all the essential supplies. Label-maker queen me created labels for each box and each item, and a contents list so that restocking is a relatively easy process.

A lack of stationery or the wrong stationery item at the wrong time can cause you to feel like an idiot. Like the time I stood in front of a class of 30 Year 7 students silently urging my whiteboard marker to last a little longer, only to have it stop mid-sentence. Or the time my Year 10s were sitting a test and I miscalculated the number of writing booklets I would need and I didn't have any spare paper anywhere in the room. Both times I felt foolish, frustrated and under time pressure. Thirty sets of eyeballs judging my lack of organisation is intimidating, to say the least. Some people would suggest that I just leave the classroom, go to the staffroom or a classroom next door and get what I need. The problem with that is that I'm legally bound to supervise these students in my care for that period. If I leave them unsupervised and an incident occurs, I'm liable. The better option, if you find yourself in such a situation, is to write a note for one or two students to leave class to find the required stationery supplies because you can't. Then all you need to do is suffer the ignominy of their eye rolls as they mutter under their breath about how you're wasting their time and you really should get your act together. In my case, they had a fair point.

Teacher tips

- "My lesson plans are always succinct, accessible and adaptable or I find they are useless on the day." Rohan R – Special Education teacher
- "Learn the students' interests. Remember them and ask about them to build a connection." Gemma G – Special Education teacher
- "Establish clear expectations at the start of the year and be fair and consistent." Michelle H – Japanese teacher

PART 2

TEACH

Teaching is part psychology, part scholarship, part advertising, part performance and part sharing of your soul. The soil of teaching is relationships. Nobody can learn and grow in a school without strong relationships. To teach well and by that, I mean to be an effective teacher whose efforts make change for young people, you need to be a clear-eyed optimist. Teaching is stepping forward into the future and to do so you need to be hopeful. You need to believe in change – that your students will learn, no matter how many mistakes they make, that colleagues and parents are only human, too, and that you will face-plant quite spectacularly on a regular basis, but you can and will pick yourself up and keep moving forward.

'Clear-eyed' is about being pragmatic.

There's an idealised view of the best teachers being those who sacrifice everything for their students. This idea is also associated with the notion of teaching as a calling, something you are destined to be. I think this is rubbish as it's damaging for the teacher and their students. Teaching is a profession. An excellent profession, but it's a job. If we buy into the idea that teaching is some sort of noble calling, we put pressure on the students and ourselves to live up to unrealistic expectations. You have a chance to be a key person in a young person's life for a year or sometimes more. You can teach well and for a sustained period of time, if you have a full and enriching life yourself. If you try to live up to this notion of teacher as noble do-gooder, then I'd bet money you burn out within five years.

By design, teachers are helpful and caring people. We want to look after others and 'fix' whatever problems we see. The trick is, we need to teach ourselves to accept responsibility for our role and avoid biting off more than we can manage. It's inevitable that we will step outside this philosophy from time to time. We will spend extra lunchtimes helping students catch up on work they miss; we will volunteer to manage more extracurricular activities than is our responsibility; we will take on an extra management role without additional time allowance; and we will spend our Saturday morning coaching sporting teams, to help out. There is nothing wrong with doing any of these activities to support our students and our school community. But if you're doing them because you think you 'should', you're feeling overwhelmed and it's becoming increasingly difficult to switch off, then you need to stop and recalibrate. To be caring, useful and effective for your students, you need to, as they say, put on your own oxygen mask first.

You need to remember that you are just ONE person in a village of people needed to teach, support and grow a young person into their best selves.

There may be people who disagree with my position on this issue and argue that they're the only ones who can help their students, there is nobody else, etc. Perhaps that's true, but I challenge them – and you – to consider that there is always more than just you in a young person's life, and if 'doing extra' at school is causing you to feel overwhelmed, then stop, because the greatest gift you can give them is a healthy, balanced self, who has perspective. An older teacher once summed this up by telling me:

> *"The students survived before you arrived, they will survive despite what you do and they will survive when you leave. Teach them the curriculum, have fun, share your joy and always set personal boundaries."*

There have been times, especially in my first few years of teaching, when I felt like I was drowning, but I learned how to swim – sometimes treading water and sometimes relying on flotation devices thrown by colleagues, friends and family. Now, when things are feeling a bit tough, I just remind myself to stay afloat, I'll swim again when I've rested and recalibrated.

ENGAGE

Be you

Trying to be yourself is actually not as obvious nor as easy as it sounds. There are a couple of layers to this idea. Firstly, you are in a role of authority and you have responsibility for the young people in your care, so the person you do need to be is the responsible adult version of yourself who teaches and nurtures your students, as you do your job. You're friendly and approachable and kind, but you're not their friend.

This is where the next layer comes in. Some teachers think they need to be someone they're not in order to gain respect, be liked by the students and/or maintain control in the classroom. A teacher may try to look, sound and act much younger than they actually are so the students will like them. It is highly likely to backfire, and students describe them as 'a try-hard'. Another teacher may try to be much tougher and stricter and louder in their voice and body language because they are nervous about maintaining control in the classroom. They may be under the impression that you need to be a big person in stature and personality to gain the respect of students. This is also highly likely to backfire. Students just won't take them seriously and, somehow, they will sense that the teacher is trying to be someone they aren't and, more to the point, don't need to be.

One of the most effective teachers I've ever worked with was a petite PDHPE teacher from New Zealand who used a range of verbal and nonverbal strategies to manage student behaviour in an inner-city

London boys' school. She showed me clearly that it's the relationships you build with your students and the strategies that you use rather than your gender or physical size that make a difference.

What is most useful is authenticity. We all have different sides of ourselves that we present to the different people in our lives for various reasons.

> There is no single 'you' but, in teaching, the most relaxed and authentic version of you, for a student audience, is the one that will be most useful in this school context and easiest to sustain.

Young people know when you are 'being real'. They trust you if you are. They are more likely to see you as a complex human who is trying their best for them and will make mistakes, but will also learn from them.

So, who am I? I am enthusiastic. I am awkward. I am a trier. I am loud at times and quiet at others. Brené Brown refers to people like me as 'outgoing introverts'. I like interesting learning activities. I am easily bored, according to my mother and my Year 12 class of 2019. I like interaction and verbal repartee. I talk quickly, too quickly at times. I am a worrier, but I am calm under pressure. I use lots of metaphors when explaining things. I like elegant solutions to problems and I hate duplication of effort. I once overheard a librarian tell someone that I was uncommonly persistent. These are all aspects of my personality and way of looking at the world. Whoever you are and, I believe we are all growing and changing, the best foundation from which to build a sustainable teaching life is to be yourself.

Lead first, manage second

To lead is to motivate students to act, individually and together, to reach a common goal. Leadership involves clear communication, setting shared expectations within the parameters of a school environment, inspiring, motivating and guiding students. It's about walking with them on a learning journey. Managing is about having the responsibility for organisation of processes, logistics, equipment and controlling the learning environment. Managing is commonly referred to as 'being in charge'. Teachers need to have both sets of skills.

> **The trick is that if you lead first, your management load is drastically reduced as students understand what they need to do, why and, most importantly, they trust in you.**

Sometimes teachers will focus more on the management than the leadership side of the equation and this may cause many students to feel frustrated and 'act out' as they don't feel heard or understood. They feel that they are being bossed around and told what to do because an adult has insisted that they do so. Managing conflict within a classroom environment is much easier if you've done the leadership work first. You've got to water the flowers before you start picking out the weeds.

As the leader of our class team, I set the tone for everyone's words and actions. If I have a polite, positive, consistent and, most importantly, calm approach to everything I do, it's more likely that students will respond positively. And when I make mistakes, which happens regularly, because I'm human, I need to be able to reflect and learn from them. There will always be interpersonal issues within a class environment, there will always be students who make choices that aren't positive either for themselves or the people around them and there will always be students who challenge your authority. What you can control is how you respond.

Share status

As a Head Teacher, from time to time I'm asked to assist with conflict resolution after a classroom incident or a student repeatedly choosing not to follow a teacher's instructions. I learned all my negotiation skills as a teacher; I've just refined them as a Head Teacher. The first thing is establishing a connection. If I know the student, I might say, for example:

> *"Hi, Jack, I've heard that something has happened in English. Can you tell me more about it? We need to sort it out for everyone."*

Sometimes I might use a variant of this opening spiel, like:

> *"Morning, Josie, how are you?"*

Pause for a response, which may range from a scowl to a shrug of the shoulders or sometimes a sentence.

Then I'll follow it up with:

> *"I've heard we have a problem with <insert whatever the issue is> and I'm here to help. Can you tell me what's happening from your point of view?"*

Approaching any behaviour management or conflict resolution situation with a negotiation sensibility will always lead to better outcomes for everyone involved.

Sometimes I don't know the student, so I start with:

> *"Hi, I'm Ms Kennedy. We've not met yet. It's Omar, isn't it?"*

Pause for a nod of the head and slight wary confusion as he thought I'd be much crankier than this.

> *"Do you know what my job is?"*

Pause for acknowledgment and sometimes a verbal response that his teacher has asked me to help, as I'm the Head Teacher.

"Yes, my job is to help you with your learning and part of that is that I help your teacher to help you. That's why I'm here. Mr Smith tells me that things haven't been going too well this morning because <insert reason teacher has supplied>. Can you tell me what's been happening from your perspective?"

In all three examples, I am shaping the situation to maximise our chances of developing a 'win: win' solution for everyone. I try to be calm and leave emotion out of it.

De-escalation of people's heightened emotional states is vital before resolving any issue that has arisen.

The Neurosequential Model in Education created by child psychologist Dr Bruce Perry provides scientific basis for why this is so important and great strategies for teachers to achieve this aim, summarised in, 'regulate, relate and reason'. His SXSW Edu 2021 (South by Southwest) interview with Oprah Winfrey provides a quick introduction to the model if you're short on time. Perry and Winfrey cowrote a book called *What Happened to You: Conversations on Trauma, Resilience, and Healing*, which explores this model in action.

I begin politely with a greeting and acknowledging the student by name if I know them or asking them who they are if I don't. I'm friendly and curious as it serves to disarm any defensive aggression that they may use as an armour. I frame the conversation using inclusive pronouns: it's 'we' have an issue to resolve rather than, "What have you done?". It's vital that I listen so the student feels heard and that we can learn the essence of why they chose to behave in the way they did that disrupted their learning and/or the learning of others. The behaviour is information about the student, which can indicate an underlying issue. I mention my job so that they know this isn't personal: it's just part of my role. I am sharing status with them; they are equal to me in our ability to solve this problem together. This focus is important as it acknowledges the power they have in their lives; too often young people feel powerless because of the circumstances in which they live, and it helps to develop self-efficacy – they learn how to be proactive rather than reactive. They always know that I'm the person who has been given the responsibility and power to use my skills and the structures and processes within our school context to resolve the issue. They know that I'm the adult who looks after their welfare and education, and the person who has a moral imperative to help.

What I haven't done is used my authority as a power tool. When you use your authority in this way, the students read the subtext of whatever you are saying as:

> "I am right, you are wrong. I am strong, you are weak. You are one of the bad kids."

They think you're Miss Trunchbull, from Roald Dahl's *Matilda*. Some adults do this because they don't believe kids are 'people' until they become adults; rather, they are sometimes cute and charming and sometimes annoying creatures who need to remember to listen and do what they're told. Other adults do this unwittingly when they are scared, tired or frustrated. If we don't share status with young people to resolve issues but instead choose to wield our authority like a power tool, we don't give them a chance to learn about how actions have consequences, how to make mistakes and move on, how to ask for help, how to listen, how to compromise and how to grow and develop their character. They need lots of practice in low-stakes situations to take ownership over their words, behaviour and learning. At the very least, I'd suggest taking a scientific approach in so far as you're far more likely to experience success in resolving an issue if all parties have an interest in doing so.

Resentment does not encourage cooperation.

Trust is vital in developing connections with students, which leads to positive and productive working relationships. The problem is young people are human, too, they do lie and do break promises, some of them on a regular basis. So, where does that leave you? I guess it's back to that clear-eyed optimist approach I encourage. Your default setting needs to be trust: each student will be reliable and tell the truth. It sets a positive tone and a high expectation that they will work to live up to. If they choose not to for whatever reason, then you work with them to help them earn back your trust. The onus is on them.

> **Disappointment is a positive power tool in a teacher's toolbox of reactions.**

I've been lied to in spectacular ways over the years. I used to get quite upset about it, but I've learned that a quiet expression of disappointment can be a motivating factor for a student to change. For me, expressing disappointment is far less energy zapping than anger.

Some teachers are of the view that students need to earn your trust. I agree to a certain extent but, with a sustainable teaching approach, starting with a positive culture in which you trust everyone means less work for you and a far more pleasant teaching and learning environment. If we start from a position of positivity, a perspective of abundance, then the onus is on students to be who you believe they are – trustworthy, reliable people. If they make a mistake or choose not to be trustworthy, the onus is still on them to earn back your trust. Either way, the emotional work lies where it should: with them, not you.

Set boundaries and expectations

Boundaries and expectations are core to establishing a positive and productive relationship with students, individually or in class groups. Boundaries are healthy; they are reasonable and safe ways of behaving towards each other and an agreed set of processes to follow if these boundaries are not respected. The school has boundaries, which are outlined in a behaviour code for students, and every teacher follows a professional code of conduct. All these boundaries are informed by the sector and schools' ethics and values. In New South Wales public schools, they are listed as: 'fairness, respect, integrity and responsibility'. Every school follows these basic ethics and values, perhaps with different wording or the addition of a few more. In tandem with boundaries come expectations – our beliefs of how we will behave in our words and actions as individuals and as a group. An example is that I have an expectation that, within a class, during direct instruction and/or discussion time, people will be quiet while another person is speaking. This expectation derives from our values of fairness and respect and our boundary that: "Everyone has the right to be heard without interruption." I'm bound by my own context and experience, so I'm not trying to replicate ideas from others; rather, my aim is to share a few strategies I have found invaluable over the years.

Every day you are doing something truly remarkable: you are shaping learning communities from a diverse range of individuals with varied backgrounds and lives.

In your classroom sits a cross-section of society that brings their unique personalities and experiences, different beliefs, values and family lives. For some students the beliefs and values taught at home may be different to those at school. An example is a student who believes he can use his mobile phone in class whenever he likes. He is persistent and loud when he argues about 'his rights'. He values his independence and believes fairness is when he gets what he wants in the timeframe he decides. It may appear that in his home expectations are looser than those at school and that he has developed these behaviour patterns because boundaries are not followed up with consequences as consistently as they are at school. Or he could just be addicted to his mobile phone. It's hard, but it's not our place to judge student home lives or their parents' parenting skills. It's our job to understand why and how students develop behaviour patterns that cause them to react negatively to our shared boundaries and expectations. And then we model and teach the school's values and expectations.

One of the scariest things for students, when they meet a new teacher, is not knowing how to categorise them. Are they nice, strict, funny, sarcastic or cool? They sit there wondering how things will unfold in the first lesson and the many lessons that will follow. Some think positively, others are somewhat wary and reserve the right to not pigeonhole you just yet. After introducing myself, I have learned to be direct by stating:

> "It's great to meet you all. The first thing we're doing today is setting our expectations for us as a class. Hands up if it's a bit scary when you start a new class because you can't figure out what the teacher wants."

Pause for sniggers, some hands raised and some nodding heads.

I then talk about our school values and that we are a learning community that has shared boundaries and expectations. Because I teach high school, I modify this approach depending on which year group I'm teaching. It will look quite different with a Year 7 class to a Year 12 class. With students from Years 7-9, I tend to take a similar approach involving a discussion and the writing of these shared expectations to refer to regularly as the year progresses, and with students from Years 10-12, it's more a discussion and, if needed, I'll ask them to write it down. If possible, with all year groups I'd recommend recording your 'Classroom Expectations' on a poster or display board in the learning space, as a visual reminder.

So, why 'Classroom Expectations' and not 'Class Rules'? For me, it comes down to the basic ideas of trust and positivity. An expectation implies that I trust that you will behave in a certain way, while a rule implies that I don't trust you enough to do something without it. An expectation is easier to phrase positively than a rule.

When I meet a new class, I already know the five to six 'Classroom Expectations' I want us to discuss and record by the end of our conversation, but I prefer to negotiate with the class, so what we end up with will differ slightly in content and wording from class to class. These expectations apply to the students and to me.

An example of possible classroom expectations:

1. Respect other people and their possessions.
2. Be quiet when another person is speaking.
3. Try our best at all times.
4. Be ready for learning.
5. Be kind to other people in what we do and say.

Many teachers use the classroom expectation that students will put their hand up and wait for the teacher to notice them before they speak. That can be very useful with some age groups and classes but, in my experience, in other age groups, it will slow down discussion and interaction. I choose to use it and other 'take your turn' strategies when needed, but I always insist on the expectation that we are quiet when another person is speaking.

If students are late to class, my expectation is that they knock on the door, wait until I can listen because I may be in the middle of speaking with the class, and explain why they are late, apologising if needed. This is a great sustainability strategy as the responsibility is theirs, not mine, and they are learning to actively respect other people's time and energy. My nan called it 'using your manners'.

Students also have expectations of me, as their teacher, such as that I give them feedback on their work as soon as I can. With many class tasks I give feedback during the lesson, if possible, and with longer tasks I try to return any feedback within a week. Assessment tasks, across the year group, we try to return within two weeks. Boundaries can vary more between subjects, classes and teachers. I have a boundary concerning time and punctuality. If a student asks for my help but doesn't turn up to our meeting place or turns up late, without a reason, then I feel like they are not respecting my time or effort. We chat about it and the next time they want my help we negotiate a mutually agreed time. I will wait for them to come collect me from the staffroom, but if they don't turn up, then I have saved time and effort.

In schools, boundaries around physical space are very important. We have a 'no-touch' policy in the school for safety and in high school students this can be a challenge because they may engage in rough play on the playground or choose to vent their frustration at another through pushing, shoving or hitting. Schools have processes for managing such incidents. As a teacher, your job is to remind them of the boundary of respecting others' physical space and the 'no-touch' policy before an incident escalates into something serious.

From time to time, in a high school setting, you will also need to remind students who are in a relationship, or who would like to be, of this boundary. The first time you come across students embracing or kissing in the corridor, it can feel intrusive to be telling them to move apart from each other, as tactfully as possible, of course! They do know this boundary, though, as it's been around since their earliest primary school years. It's all about context, and a school environment, as a work environment, is not the appropriate place for public displays of affection.

Being consistent is hard and takes practice, yet it's essential for the students to build their trust in you.

If you establish a behavioural expectation and then don't apply consequences consistently, you will get yourself a reputation very fast. Within a high school setting, you will soon be known by a nickname that is anything but favourable. Young people value fairness and are aware of any situation in which an expectation isn't upheld equally for all. Despite my best intentions, I've fallen into this trap more times than I would like to admit, accidentally being more lenient on one student than another. It usually revolves around excessive classroom talk.

There are many methods for consistently rewarding positive behaviour and consistently applying consequences for negative behaviour. I've worked in schools that use merit award structures or systems like the Positive Behaviour for Learning rewards. In regard to applying consequences, I most frequently use verbal reminders; Post-it note reminders stuck quietly on a student's desk (kind of like the red card system in soccer); and I also write names on the whiteboard or somewhere central as a reminder about who will be receiving merit awards.

One time, a Year 7 boy, Zach, called an impromptu 'stop work' meeting because I had forgotten to place a cross by one of his classmate's names on the whiteboard as a warning for repeatedly not following instructions, but I remembered to place a cross by his name when he had done the same. As he delivered his stirring speech to the class declaring that I was "the most unfair teacher ever", I burst his balloon of indignation by declaring:

"You are right. I made a mistake. I'm sorry. Let me fix it now."

He was in shock because he wanted a fight. I quickly remedied my error and explained that I try hard to be fair, but I sometimes make mistakes and I was glad he felt confident enough to help me out when I did. I had shown them that I was human, the consequences apply to everyone and if I made a mistake, I was happy to repair it as soon as I could.

Mirror your words and actions

Adults are practised at using masks to manage their emotional states. In many situations we need to put on our 'game face' and get on with the job. That may be when we are at a family function chatting with a relative who bores us or making conversation with a difficult parent at work. Part of being an adult is emotional self-regulation.

When we talk with young people, I have learned how important it is that our words and actions match. It saves you a lot of time and energy if they do. Communication involves words, voice and body language working together to convey a message or idea. If your words or tone of voice don't match your facial expressions, students may think something isn't quite right – maybe you're hiding something.

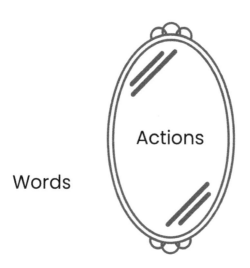

For young people to trust that you're authentic, they need to feel that your words mirror your actions.

Something that can short-circuit that connection is trying too hard to pretend everything is 'fine' with you when it's not. It's a tricky balance to achieve, but I find it time and energy efficient to be honest about my feelings and what's happening in my life, within professional boundaries, of course. The day before my 34th birthday, I was diagnosed with a melanoma. I needed an operation that required 30 stitches and some time away from school. I told my students all about it and explained why I would be absent for two weeks and we chatted about the fact that melanomas can grow on any part of the body, including those rarely, if ever, exposed to sunlight. Mine was on my left rib, so I couldn't show them where it was. We talked about operations and how being sick can be hard.

I found it valuable to be honest and open with them as much as I could, as they saw I was experiencing something significant. Me trusting them with my melanoma story helped to forge a stronger relationship and made it much easier to explain why I was feeling a little fragile.

Sometimes terrible news catapults into your school day and you must share it with teachers and students. In more than 20 years of teaching, there have been a few times when I had to support students after a classmate has passed away. It's hard and I've learned that being honest about my own feelings, within professional boundaries, has given students the space and courage to share their own. It's also important to get professional support yourself from a counsellor or GP, if you feel you need it.

Occasionally, a life irritation can affect your mood. A few years ago, driving home from school, someone ran into the back of my car. It was a shock and an annoyance, but we were both OK. My car was damaged, I could still drive it and I knew I needed to get to the smash repairers the next day. What I didn't know until I was driving home was that the boot alarm had malfunctioned. There was a constant high-pitched beeping sound, which I could do nothing about until I saw a mechanic. I am sensitive to high-pitched sounds, so by the time I arrived at school the next day I was a frazzled mess of nerves. I tried to hold it together, but ended up telling my Period 1 class all about the accident and the beeping sound. They were very supportive and we bonded over phobias and fears. Plus, they laughed at how sensitive my ears are for an old person (defined as: 30+ apparently).

As a profession, teaching has an inbuilt sense of authority. There's an expectation that teachers get things right. Until we get things wrong. I make mistakes because I'm human. Often, they're excruciatingly embarrassing mistakes. What has saved me from many an uncomfortable moment is that I'm a transparent, 'wear my heart on my sleeve' kind of person. I can quickly admit my mistake even though I'm feeling embarrassed and uncomfortable. For me, this is much better than the heavy feeling of guilt I'd carry if I didn't do it as soon as possible.

Young people are amazingly forgiving if you're honest and quick to make amends.

It was about my second year of teaching, in mid-February, that I had to phone a parent about her son's pattern of disruptive behaviour to ask for assistance in helping him to make more positive choices. His name was Jake. This was more than 20 years ago, so student records weren't as easily accessible for teachers as they are now. Maybe I found the parent's number on a school database or perhaps I asked the school office for it. I vividly recall phoning Jake's mum and earnestly relating the strategies I'd been using to help him behave appropriately in class and telling her of his latest escapades. After about five to six minutes, she politely told me:

> *"Ms Kennedy, I appreciate your phone call and I know you're working very hard, but that is not my son you're describing."*

In my super-keen naivety, I thought she was trying to defend him and was about to carefully suggest that maybe he behaves differently in a class of 30 students, when I looked down at my class roll and stopped myself. My heart felt like a kettlebell and I was nauseous. I'd got the wrong Jake. There were two Jakes in the class and I'd phoned the mother of the angelic one. I was mortified. I shook. A thought flashed through my brain that I would be fired. At this point, Jake's Mum realised I had recognised my mistake. She said:

> *"It's OK, sweetheart. I think you meant to call the parents of the other Jake."*

I spluttered:

> *"I'm so sorry! I can't believe I did that. I'm so sorry! Jake is a wonderful young man and a great student. I am so sorry."*

She kindly advised me to relax:

> *"Everyone makes mistakes, honey. Jake tells me he enjoys your History class. You create interesting lessons, apparently. You best go call the other Jake's parents now."*

She was so kind to an earnest and inexperienced me, who had tried hard to do the right thing, but face-planted spectacularly. She could have made a big deal about it and complained to the Deputy or the Principal, but she didn't. It was a valuable lesson for me in admitting my mistake and not trying to cover things up. I apologised to that Jake the next day and he took it just as well as his mother. The other Jake, who is probably a digital entrepreneur by now, with his charm and strong leadership skills, did his lunch detention without any of the drama I was fearing may eventuate. I was lucky.

Teacher tips

- "Adding an element of fun to your lesson is a great way to build relationships with students and, ultimately, engage them in your lesson. There are many online games you can access (Kahoot!, Who Wants to be a Millionaire?) that can be used to test knowledge. Students also love old-school-type group challenges that you can adapt to what you are teaching." Marnie T – English teacher

- "Remember, their behaviour is information about them. It is not about you." Gemma G – Special Education teacher

- "Having simple seating plans helps you to learn names ASAP and getting students working early in lessons will boost your authority and engage students." Antony S – Mathematics teacher

PERSUADE

I'm a professional persuader. In designing lessons, I advertise an educational product to students – a concept, skill or idea. Teenagers may be a reluctant audience, so I need to use all my persuasive muscle to get them to love the product. I've discovered that taking an advertising approach to my lesson design is useful to engage my audience.

At university you learn that students are not 'empty vessels' to be filled with knowledge. They're individuals with their own unique personalities, contexts and experiences. You study education theories like Behaviourism, Cognitive Psychology, Constructivism, Social-Learning Theories and Experiential Learning. They're full of useful ideas about the theory and practice of teaching young people.

> The most important thing I ever learned was to master the art of persuasion and sell my lesson experiences with passion, commitment and authenticity. It is the HOW that matters more than the WHAT.

I know more than 30 years later that 0° Kelvin is -273ºC because Mrs Mahon, my Year 9 Science teacher, made us write science fiction short stories incorporating scientific facts. She knew that teaching us dry facts wasn't going to be anywhere near as engaging as 'selling us' the idea of incorporating them in a short story.

Some may think it's tacky to use the language and techniques of advertising in designing learning experiences. After all, advertising agencies are widely stereotyped as greedy and exploitative organisations that make billions from manipulating the public on behalf of equally dodgy multinational corporations. Right? The TV series *Mad Men* and the media empire drama *Succession* both explore this world. And while there may be some truth in that impression, it's not what I'm suggesting does or should happen in education. Techniques of persuasion are not the sole province of advertising agencies, and they're much older than the modern world of advertising (via TV, websites, social media and print) with which we're all too familiar. I'm talking the ancient Greeks. They knew how to sell a big idea.

Lesson preparation

How much time it takes to prepare lessons is a bit like asking the question: 'How long is a piece of string?'. My favourite analogy is one my nan used: 'If you've got all day to clean the house, you'll take all day'. Creating lessons can be creative, lots of fun and time-consuming. When I first started teaching, we had a dial-up modem – the iPhone was yet to be invented – and researching my lesson plans involved spending time in the library and borrowing print books. I'm in my late 40s, so this wasn't so long ago!

I spent ages planning my first lesson and then only to see it fall apart in front of my eyes, those of 30 young people and my university practicum supervisor. The first thing I had to let go of was the expectation that I could design and deliver the 'perfect' lesson. I could design what I thought was a 'perfect' lesson, creatively and theoretically speaking, I could do everything 'right', but then something outside my zone of influence would affect how it unfolded and the whole thing would result in what I now refer to as a 'scrambled egg lesson'.

This 'perfect' lesson in reality featured students jumping out a (ground-floor) window. I thought I'd definitely failed my practicum, but what the university supervisor told me in our debrief, stuck in my head. She said:

"It's how you pivot back to focus on learning that matters, Melissa."

Like the solid country netballer I was, I'd given myself whiplash pivoting so much in that period. But she was right. I focused most of the class on a learning activity for most of the lesson and I changed strategies at least four or five times, while dealing with window escapees. I could never have planned for such a scenario and I would have been a bundle of nerves if I'd tried.

> **Sustainable lesson planning is about letting go of unrealistic expectations. Perfect lessons will never exist; no matter what any edupreneur or 'star teacher' tries to tell you on social media.**

You also need to let go of any expectation that you may have about designing absolutely everything yourself for a lesson. It's OK to use resources from print books, textbooks, the internet and other sources, always trying to acknowledge your sources and model good copyright practices. We have always used textbooks in schools, to some extent, depending on the subject you are teaching. The internet and AI tools have opened up so many more possibilities.

What you can't let go of is the basic principles of good lesson design, involving understanding your students and how they learn, curating content, prioritising a skill development sequence and differentiating activities to suit the needs of the young people in your care. You can't 'copy and paste' a unit of work from the internet and expect it to work in the classroom without your active input, ideas and critical evaluation. It's not a sustainable practice and I've seen too many people try this approach under the expectation that it'll help them to save time, only to find that it takes far more time than if they just wrote their own or modified an existing unit.

> **The students in your class are unique and they need you to recalibrate the teaching resource (lesson plan, unit of work, activity) to meet their contexts and needs based on the information (data) you have about them.**

Social media is a great resource for teachers to share ideas, lesson plans and units of work. There are professional association Facebook pages for different subject areas and stages of teaching, which are valuable sources of information in preparing lessons. Be aware of the dangers of using such sites without critically evaluating what is being shared by asking yourself questions such as:

- Is this resource (lesson plan, unit of work, activity) linked to the syllabus I am teaching?
- How can I confirm the accuracy of the advice someone is giving me?
- Is this person or group trying to sell me something?
- Does the syllabus support what they are telling me?

People have shared what I call 'edu-myths' online about things such as syllabus requirements, HSC marking and/or assessment processes. They believe they're helping you, but they aren't always correct, and they can inadvertently spread inaccurate information, which causes teachers stress and wastes time. This is not healthy or sustainable for you. Always refer to the syllabus and any official support material from the education authorities in your state – in New South Wales it's the New South Wales Education Standards Authority (NESA) and in Victoria the Victorian Curriculum and Assessment Authority (VCAA) – for up-to-date and accurate information.

Behaviour management

You can't notice everything in a classroom environment, constantly correcting students for their behaviour and not burn out. You need to let some things go for the greater goal of maintaining learning momentum as you're persuading students about the merits of a learning experience. The tricky thing is recognising what to let go and what not to. I want to stress the importance of balance, it's like baking a cake – the right ingredients at the right time matter. A lot.

You and your students know the lesson's learning intentions and that's your roadmap for what you need to achieve in the lesson, which you will measure using the success criteria. The challenge is that there are lots of other ingredients outside your control, which will contribute to the success of a lesson.

You need to understand and use your school's behaviour management processes and policies each and every lesson. A few years ago, our Deputy visited one of my classes regularly to assist me in managing students' behaviour and I relied on my colleagues to help, too. I couldn't do it alone.

> **Consistency matters, giving students confidence and helping them to regulate their own behaviour. But the reality is that they often don't do so, for a multitude of reasons.**

There is a hierarchy of behaviours that we find unacceptable in a school environment. There are behaviours you should never let go that mostly involve issues of harassment, bullying, swearing, violence, dangerous behaviour and cheating that should always be addressed appropriately following the school's behaviour management processes and procedures. With 'minor behaviours', like swinging on a chair in class, the trick is to observe patterns and evaluate the student, their context and whether their behaviour is affecting their engagement or the engagement of those around them in the lesson activities.

For example, most schools have a school expectation/rule that hats are taken off in the classroom. Once, a Year 9 student left his hat on, despite me asking him to take it off more than once. He was not a huge fan of school; he was not disturbing anyone else and he was mostly engaged in the lesson. I was having a busy day, feeling a little stressed and I made a mistake in insisting that he take his hat off. He exploded and we had a 'chat' outside the classroom. He was cranky with me and, in retrospect, rightly so. He had a haircut he was embarrassed about and that's why he didn't want to take his hat off. He felt I should have read the situation better and made an exception for him this time. He was right. And I felt he could have told me this quietly and I wouldn't have pushed the issue. I apologised, he grudgingly said sorry and he kept his hat on for the rest of the lesson.

> **When I first started teaching, I believed I needed to be fair by treating everyone the same, but what I've learned is that I need to be equitable to ensure fairness for all students.**

In this example I didn't read the situation effectively. I relied too heavily on 'rules' without fully assessing the situation and the relationship I'd developed with this student. I risked alienating him, all because of a baseball cap that I stubbornly insisted had to be taken off to ensure I was maintaining standards and treating everyone in the class equally. I didn't find out more information by asking the simple (and oh so obvious) question, "Why won't you take your hat off?"

If I'm tough on the small things, it affects the momentum of the lesson. I forget I'm persuading students to embrace a new idea, skill or understanding. It's like I willingly drive our 4WD of Learning Potential into a muddy bog. I'm doing a Miss Trunchbull; I'm communicating to the students that I value my sense of control more than their learning. People are going to turn off very quickly and become reluctant to engage if you take that approach. That's why it's far more effective to share status with students when addressing an issue about their behaviour. Together you're solving a problem.

I think I was scared that I would lose control of the classroom if I didn't pick up on *everything* and correct students then and there. I was wrong. And I learned to notice patterns instead. When it comes to minor inappropriate behaviours, patterns give more valuable information than a one-off event. It also gives students space to breathe and make safe mistakes.

I learned to trust myself and my ability to make split-second evaluations. I now tend to tactically ignore behaviours that fall in the 'minor behaviour' list but aren't greatly affecting student engagement. I guess I'm doing a cost-benefits analysis on the run. In doing this, I also lessen the load on myself, as a teacher. It's now about all of us engaged in the learning experience together: each responsible for our behaviours. This makes me a more sustainable teacher and a far happier person. I like to see classroom behaviour management as a dance: Year 7 is like a barn dance, Year 8 hip-hop, Year 9 definitely a tap dance, Year 10 jazz and by Year 11 and 12 I hope to be waltzing confidently.

Selling a big idea

Aristotle, the ancient Greek philosopher, created the rhetorical triangle: ethos, pathos and logos. He reasoned that to persuade an audience you, the speaker, need to do three things: convince them of your credibility or character (ethos), use logical and well-reasoned arguments (logos) and appeal to their values and emotions (pathos). Aristotle was taught by another famous philosopher, Plato, enrolling in Plato's Academy when he was just 17. Aristotle spent years honing his craft of rhetoric and teaching it to the select young men of Athens, including the future leader, Alexander the Great. Politicians are professional advertisers as well. It's no accident that many politicians began their professional lives as teachers.

Aristotle's rhetorical triangle

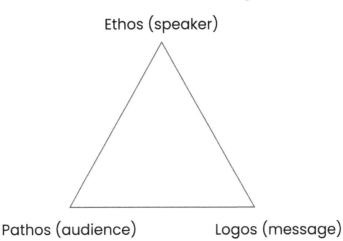

Ethos (speaker)

Pathos (audience)   Logos (message)

Young people use the art of persuasion regularly at home, with their friends and at school. In English, one of the ways we teach students to identify the elements of Aristotle's rhetorical triangle is by selling them the opportunity to script and perform a conversation in which they persuade their parents or carers to buy them something, whether that be KFC for dinner or a mobile phone. It's amazing how quickly they can identify the rhetorical elements and apply them because it's linked to their everyday experiences. This is because we have researched our product and users. In English, our product range revolves around communication, literature, conceptual thinking and reasoning skills. Our users are the young people whom we teach.

> Context is king: knowing the context of the young people I teach will help me immeasurably to sell them a concept, idea, skill, way of thinking and/or communicating.

I've adapted this activity in many ways to suit the context of the students I teach. In a school with a high population of student boarders, they want to persuade you to give them extra food. When it's surfers they want more time on the water, and for many young people it's a new phone. The principle remains the same: in order for them to buy (engage with) what you're 'selling' (learning concept/skill), you must make it relevant for them.

Advertising executives are brilliant at event management. They know how to stage a learning experience to sell a product or service to an often reluctant or sceptical audience. Many teaching methods, such as project-based learning, use techniques like 'hook lessons' to engage the audience of students in an immersive exploration of a new concept or idea. What are product launches, after all, if not 'hook lessons'? One of the most famous exponents of the 'hook lesson' was Steve Jobs, from Apple Inc, who famously launched the iPhone in 2007. Yes, he was good, very good, in fact, and in terms of his presentation style, he taught me a lot about performance, especially the art of the pause to build expectation and excitement about this new product. Pause, as my Speech and Drama teacher Mrs Denholm used to tell me, is the greatest form of emphasis.

Another example is Nike's New House of Go pop-up in Chicago in 2018. People signed up to try on these new sneakers and interact by running alongside their own avatar, before moving on to free treadmill classes taught by Nike experts. Both examples show how to stage a learning event to engage, teach something new, develop a community of learners and promise an opportunity for growth and change. Both are designed with the user in mind. I'm not suggesting that teachers need to become Apple or Nike executives and use tools of capitalism to exploit young people! I'm saying that we can learn from how these companies stage events to engage our students in their learning in small, yet significant, ways; Steve Jobs and Mrs Denholm taught me the power of the pause and Nike showed me the power of colour and movement.

Performance is key to successfully persuading an audience to think, do or understand something new. I need to use my voice, body and script (the lesson design) to persuade an audience (the students) to think and/or feel something new. It used to be more common that teachers were seen as the 'sage on the stage', the one who knew everything and taught the audience from a traditional proscenium arch stage (the front of the room), while they sat in the audience soaking it up. Some people teach like this all the time. What I have found more effective is to vary my performance skills, and it's more common that the students and I are involved in immersive learning through explicit teaching, project-based learning activities, experiential learning, design thinking activities, individual activities, group work and/or any number of exploratory activities where everyone in the room is involved in learning together.

Immersive theatre is about the actors and audience interacting with each other and their surroundings, thereby breaking the 'fourth wall' that separated them in more traditional theatre settings. Sometimes, it's necessary that I'm the sage on the stage and I teach explicit skills and content to students, but I use this method carefully and for short periods of time, just like the Queen of Hearts did in a London immersive theatre production of *Alice's Adventures Underground*. On holidays in 2015, in the old London Underground tunnels of Waterloo station, I sat, with my fellow audience members, awestruck as she lectured us. But this was only a small part of the theatrical experience as a whole, and that's one of the factors that made it work so well. What struck me was how the actors worked with us, as individuals and as a collective audience, to create a story world of possibility and excitement in which we were all truly engaged. And as I learn how to teach more sustainably, I can do the same with the young people I teach.

I aim to include one big idea in a lesson or lesson sequence. That idea needs to be clearly communicated to the students, in more than one mode of communication. They have so much information bombarding them on a daily basis that it's easy for them to miss the whole point of what they're doing and instead focus on a minor detail. When they can identify the big idea, they can link it to all the activities within the sequence. One strategy for communicating the big idea is the use of learning intentions and success criteria, as explained by researchers such as Professor Dylan Wiliam. For example, a learning intention might be, 'To create a webpage about a topic', and related success criteria to show that the student has achieved that learning intention may include, 'I understand the features of a webpage', 'I can research facts from a variety of sources' and 'I can use the research I have collected to write clearly about a topic in my own words'.

James and Jill Nottingham's book, *Challenging Learning Through Feedback*, provides worked examples of learning habits and success criteria in a variety of classroom settings. What I've noticed is that sometimes learning intentions and success criteria can be shared in teacher-speak and read like a lesson menu. I like to put myself in the shoes of a student in the class, like a 14-year-old avatar and think about how that version of me would read what teacher me has written. And if it sounds dull, complicated or jargonistic, I change it.

Sometimes, at the beginning of a lesson sequence, I don't use a learning intention at all; instead, I use a question or a goal or even a punctuation mark – all forms of what I refer to as metacognitive glue.

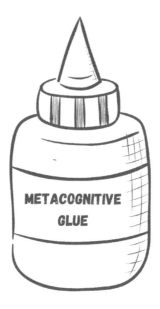

Later, I work with the students to flesh out our learning exploration's goals and how we know we have achieved them.

> **I am cautious of overusing any strategy because I may bore the students (and myself) with the result that we all 'turn off' and lose focus.**

With all due respect to Edward de Bono, I remember being overdosed with 'Six Thinking Hats' at school. I was 10 when he published that book and I remember that in my upper primary and lower secondary years his ideas were very fashionable, but when it seemed like everyone was using them, it became overkill for us.

Whatever metacognitive glue you use, whether it be learning intentions, success criteria, goals and/or inquiry questions, I recommend a varied choice of adhesives. Variety engages interest. In the daily life of your average high school student, they will hear important/key/essential/must-pay-attention information from five to six teachers in four to six different subject areas. I can only imagine how exhausting that may be, and how some of the information that teachers believe is so important gets lost in a sea of words and images.

> It's vital that we work on the assumption that if we have any news to tell, we don't hide it in the body copy, we *promise it in the headline* with a benefit for the students.

Unique selling proposition

Have you ever considered your unique selling proposition (USP)? It's a unique selling point or slogan that differentiates you from your competitors. In a high-school setting, I think it's twofold: your USP as a teacher and the USP of the subject or course. For you as a teacher, what are the qualities that make you unique, engaging and worth paying attention to? Why would a student be bothered to engage with what you're selling in a classroom?

My USP revolves around my enthusiasm, curiosity and love of words. My parents tell me I was an enthusiastic 18-month-old who spoke in full paragraphs. As a five-year-old, I vividly recall my excitement in learning to read, which meant sounding out words everywhere from the back of cereal packets to the newspaper and the toothpaste tube – where I learned the chemical compound sodium monofluorophosphate. In Year 8, I learned the word pulchritudinous (beautiful) and dropped it into every story I could. Including one about my English teacher, Ms Pennay, and her new fictional boyfriend, Miles, I'd decided she met at a party the previous weekend, where he told her she was pulchritudinous!

My Year 9s have complained that my voice is so animated that they can't go to sleep in our class. I'm 175cm tall and I have a big dramatic voice when I need to use it. I find it difficult to keep still and constantly roam a learning space to engage students and ask if they need assistance. A few years ago, my Year 12s jokingly mentioned me in their graduation ceremony speech, referencing my enthusiastic habit of asking, "Are you OK? Really?". These are a few facets of my USP. They all convey authenticity to the students and help them to (I hope) trust me and the learning opportunities that I'm selling.

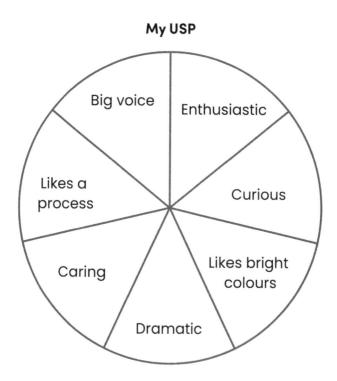

My USP is a way to authentically convey my personality. Young people trust that and are more likely to trust the learning experiences I am selling them. I'm not cool or mysterious. Some teachers are. I'm more of an enthusiastic nerd. A group of Year 11 students once pleaded with me to dress more like one of the Art teachers whose wardrobe is cool and monochromatic, whereas I tend to experiment more with bright colours. Maybe it had something to do with their perceptions of risk. If I wear a pink and navy dress, I tend to stand out more. It could also have been that they just didn't like my clothing choices for that week. I'm like a brightly coloured Swatch watch to the Art teacher's black Rolex. If I tried to muddle or change my USP, I believe students would be less likely to trust in me and the learning experiences I am selling them. I feel it's important that we model for students how to be comfortable in our own skin.

The USP of the course or subject is a way to explain what is important for the students to know, understand and become skilled in. I teach English and it's about concepts like narrative, theme and perspective; communication skills like writing; and thinking skills like distillation and argument. It's a subject that can be tailored to the needs of the young person. I sell it to them as a bento box of communication, conceptual understanding and skills development opportunities. Our activities are varied from exploring how characters are created in novels and films to investigating the nature of bias in a politician's Twitter, Facebook and Instagram posts.

USP for the subject of English

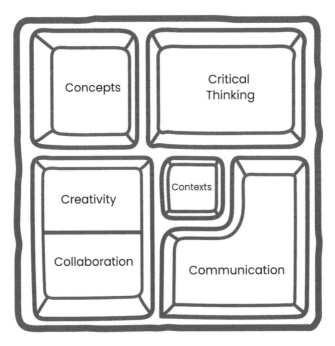

How is English different from other subjects? The government helps me sell that aspect of it because the study of English is compulsory. Sometimes I find myself presenting an argument as to why English is at the foundation of everything we do at school. For example, when a student comments that Maths is easier or more important than English, I jokingly highlight that you can't do Maths without English. English is based on sounds (phonemes), which are represented as a letter/s (graphemes). Maths is basically patterns that are vocalised using phonemes. If I've still got their attention, I'll point out that the cavemen were grunting before they carved number strokes on the walls of their caves. A Mathematics Head Teacher friend and I have a running joke about which subject is the more important. It's important to respect the integrity of each discipline, but it's equally important to show the intersections between them as we show that knowledge is inextricably connected.

Cognitive load theory

Have you ever wondered why you remember advertising slogans so easily? It's because advertising agencies know that there is only so much room in people's heads for new information and that the way they present that information will make it stick with you. One of the techniques they use is slogans or taglines that sum up a product or service and how they believe it will benefit you. Advertising slogans are often in the form of questions, short statements, commands or they feature alliteration. For example, Coca Cola's 'Making life's everyday moments more meaningful' (alliteration); Hungry Jack's 'The burgers are better at Hungry Jack's' (statement); Apple's 'Think different' (command); and Ford's 'Have you driven a Ford lately?' (question). The use of these techniques helps to reduce the cognitive load for the audience.

Cognitive load theory is about how human brains learn and store knowledge.

Advertising people worked it out a long time ago that catchy slogans are a technique through which they could anchor an idea in people's minds so that they would remember it. In education, cognitive load theory was developed from the research of Australian educational psychologist Professor John Sweller and his colleagues. The New South Wales Government's Centre for Education Statistics and Evaluation has a brilliant practical guide called *Cognitive load theory: Research that teachers really need to understand.*

Cognitive overload occurs when I give students too much information without activating any prior knowledge, it's often not well-designed and I've probably asked them to do too many activities simultaneously. That's when I see a look of confusion on their faces and they whisper to each other, asking:

"What does she REALLY want us to do?"

This is when the language processing demands of the activity I've created are beyond the current language processing limits of the students at that particular time, usually some random Thursday afternoon in last period, after I've taught all day and had to attend a meeting at lunch. When this happens, I know I have to pivot quickly to change what I have created to reduce the cognitive load for the students.

Cognitive load theory is about purposeful instructional design. You bring the visual, print, oral and digital together in ways that maximise the chances that your students will learn what they need to know, understand and do, with just the right amount of effort from you and them.

I use cognitive load theory when designing learning materials because it's the best way to optimise the efficiency of students' working memories, which will (hopefully!) maximise their learning experiences. I keep their cognitive load at a minimum so that they are more likely to remember the new concept or idea and link it to their pre-existing knowledge. It's also more sustainable for me as a teacher, because I know the effort I make in designing and curating learning materials for my students is purposeful and the design process backed by research. I'm focused on their engagement in the learning experience using deliberate and explicit techniques such as: designing lessons according to their existing knowledge and skills; using models or examples to teach new content and skills; gradually providing opportunities for independent problem-solving and skills development; removing inessential information; grouping all essential information together; presenting complex information visually and orally; and encouraging them to access their imaginations to visualise concepts that we have just explored.

Something else advertising executives know is that rapport reduces cognitive load. By that I mean if there is a culture of support, mutual respect and fun in a classroom, then it's more likely students will remember what they're learning. And this is where I borrow again from the techniques of advertisers to use slogans, acronyms, questions, jingles, alliteration, metaphors, colour and analogies to create and maintain those connections.

As a professional persuader, I ensure that whatever learning material I create, curate and/or adapt for my students, it's effortlessly readable. I pitch the language choice, the type of text and the layout in a way that minimises cognitive load and maximises learning opportunities. It doesn't mean that I avoid new vocabulary, nor does it mean that I 'dumb down' content and concepts. It means that I focus on ensuring that students have mind space as they read/view/experience a print or digital text to think and make connections about what they're learning. Too often new information is presented in ways that split students' attention, causing frustration and difficulty in understanding. For example, a diagram of the respiratory system, which may label the essentials like lungs, alveoli, trachea, etc, but then have a list of definitions for these parts listed at the bottom of the page. When essential information is grouped together, such as these definitions listed beneath each label, this decreases students' cognitive load and enhances their understanding.

Using the right layout matters – ensure that your message and your visuals match. It's a sad fact, universally acknowledged by every 13-year-old I know, that 'Death by PowerPoint' is real. As is Death by Keynote, SlideShare, Prezi, Google Slides or any other slide presentation application you care to name. When I was in high school, in what I tell Year 7 was the ancient times of the early 1990s, I was taught the '6 × 6 rule'. On a PowerPoint slide, use no more than six lines and no more than six words per line. If you stepped outside those boundaries, well, God would be watching, as would Bill Gates, the Computing teacher and, most scarily, my Year 9 classmates. Me, being the goody two-shoes nerd that I am, stuck to that rule and even went further by not including words on some slides! I felt empowered as they listened to me because what was on the slide complemented my message, it didn't distract from it. The slideshow itself is just one communication mode, there's also your stage presence, gesture, appearance, voice control, printed handouts and the words you speak. All are powerful tools to persuade people to embrace your message.

Teacher tips

- "As hard as it is, never take anything personally. If you do, it will eat away at you. These are kids who have a lot of big feelings from one moment to the next, and they are grappling with a myriad of external and internal pressures. Always bring kindness and compassion to your classroom, especially on the days when you are seething or feeling like a deflated balloon. If you start getting overwhelmed, focus on your breathing and regulate, because you are the teacher in the room modelling the correct behaviour. You've got this!" Belinda R – English teacher

- "Don't create new resources. There's a 99% chance it's been made already. Less is more." Pip M – Primary teacher

- "A catchphrase for practical lessons is key. The one I use is 'Stop, freeze and listen'. I've found it the most effective way to get everyone's attention when there's a lot going on." Nicole W – Science teacher

6

ASSESS

An assessment helps people learn because it gives them information about how they have achieved something and what they can do to improve. Assessment is part of a learning cycle or continuum. It isn't an end point, it's a check-in point. Assessment takes many forms, including a teacher's observation, an essay, a woodwork product, an experiment design, a Kahoot! quiz, a self-evaluation and a peer conference about a short story. The purpose behind an assessment is to evaluate and provide feedback for a student to continue their learning journey, which is cyclical.

Measuring is different. When we measure a student's performance, we give them a result – often a mark or grade – that labels them as achieving at a certain standard according to the criteria used in a particular test, exam or assessment tool. It is an end point and it's used to state where the student is at compared to an agreed set of criteria (standards) and/or other people at a particular time and place in their lives. In Australia the external measuring tools we use include Basic Skills Tests like the National Assessment Program – Literacy and Numeracy (NAPLAN); matriculation exams like the Higher School Certificate (HSC) in New South Wales; the Victorian Certificate of Education (VCE) in Victoria. The purpose behind a measurement is to evaluate, rank and categorise student learning.

Assessment

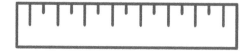

Measurement

Assessing or measuring?

The thing is, we often get mixed up about whether we are assessing or measuring. Students, parents, politicians, the media and the general public can get confused about it, too. Understanding the purpose and context of an assessment and/or measurement tool is vital to using the information provided in a useful way. If we don't, we can unintentionally cause students (and their parents) to become distressed and feel that their performance in an activity, which was used as an assessment tool by the teacher, is actually a measurement of their ability. When they see that number, grade, rank or category, people tend to view it as a label that fixes them to a certain level of intelligence or capability.

An American psychologist, Professor Carol Dweck, calls it 'a fixed mindset', which is when you believe that intelligence is 'static' or 'fixed'. A 'growth mindset', naturally enough, is about the exact opposite. It is when you believe that intelligence can be developed through challenge, feedback, effort and practice. Basically, people with a growth mindset know that they can grow the strength of their qualities through effort, practice, observation and feedback. This is linked to the scientific theory of neuroplasticity, which is all about the brain's ability to change and adapt due to experiences. People I've met with a fixed mindset tend to say things like:

"I'm hopeless at Maths, I always get everything wrong";

"I can't write essays because I just sound dumb"; or

"My Year 3 teacher told me I can't spell".

Assessment record

Assessment is a process through which we improve learning opportunities for students. It happens before we even meet them in person and continues in many different forms throughout the year. Recording the results of assessments – the data – can be a challenging process, as you juggle sector, school, parent, teacher and colleague expectations.

As a teacher, you use data to design the best learning experiences for the needs of each of your students. In education, data can be used in unproductive ways by people with little understanding of the context and purpose for which it was collected. Sometimes data inspires fear as administrators and politicians use it to compare teachers in negative ways that push a narrow agenda. This happens when people, holding certain values or beliefs, link it to data that supports that belief and draw a conclusion that best suits them to lay blame at the feet of others. In my experience, when data is used with this end goal in mind, it creates a culture of fear, blame and accountability rather than a culture of responsibility, growth and action. At the risk of stating the obvious, the ideal is a culture of responsibility in which every teacher is encouraged to understand and tell the story of the data they collect on their students and then make decisions for changes to their practice and turn that into action.

The best method for recording assessment data is the one that matches your student/s and the activity. I record annotations of student writing skills on student work samples, spelling test results as marks, students' understanding of their progress in skill development using exit tickets or Google Forms.

An approach I find most useful is dividing your assessment records into four categories:

1. Basic skills and external tests, for example, NAPLAN, Best Start and HSC
2. School-mandated assessment records, for example, digital markbook on an LMS like Sentral

3. Class records, for example, rubrics, spelling test marks, notations about student progress on paper or digital

4. Student records, for example, self-assessment grids in portfolios, peer feedback on Post-it notes

'Data' is a big thing in education, more so in the past 10 years, as digital storage and collection of information has become more commonplace. As a teacher, the amount of data you are asked to collect, how to store it, strategies for interpreting it and how to communicate it effectively can seem like overwhelming tasks. I know. I've felt it and still do on some days. The trick is to always remember that the data tells a story about a person (student), or a group of people (class, year group) and you know that story better than anyone. You need to trust yourself that you can tell the story behind, say, why Year 7 and 9 NAPLAN Reading results are 'terrible', without becoming defensive or feeling personally responsible, and you can suggest strategies to move forward so that you and your colleagues can help the students in your care to create a new story with the data collected in the next assessment.

You also need to be organised so that you regularly collect data and store it safely in ways that protect student privacy. It's important that you keep backups of all data. I say this because there will be times when a student, parent/carer, Head Teacher, Coordinator, Deputy or Principal will ask you for some assessment data at short notice, and if you don't know where to quickly find it, you will become stressed. And that is stress that you do not need. Organised and efficient planning systems save you valuable time.

Cultivate a growth mindset

A sustainable teacher is someone who can empower young people and their parents to understand and cultivate a growth mindset. It's great for them as people and learners, and the bonus is, it helps you as well! Teaching students with a fixed mindset has the potential to soak up a teacher's time and energy in a big way. These students are, on the whole, anxious and very judgemental of themselves. They are more worried about the destination (the mark, grade or result) than the journey (the experience of creating a project). They get upset if they don't achieve to their (or their parents') expectation and for them, perfection is attainable.

I once had an interesting discussion with a Year 12 English student who was upset that they had not received full marks for an assessment task. We discussed the feedback they'd received and why they hadn't achieved at that level and they said they understood why. But they were still concerned that they hadn't achieved full marks and someone else had. When I asked why, they said that they needed to be perfect. I knew they did higher levels of Mathematics, so I asked them to calculate the probability of being 'perfect' in every assessment in every subject. They couldn't. I asked if it was statistically possible, as a human being, to be perfect. I conceded that you could argue it was possible for androids, but even they fail because they are programmed by humans, after all! They admitted it wasn't. I also commented that I personally would find it boring if I got everything 'right' all the time. They met me halfway in agreeing that it was hard to be perfect, but they were going to keep aiming for it. I admired their chutzpah.

It is times like these when I remember that *Frozen* song, 'Let It Go.' They needed to learn from their own experiences, and they would, when they were ready, no matter what their somewhat annoying English teacher said. On a side note, English was their only Band 5 subject in the HSC, in the rest they achieved a Band 6. When they received their results, they made a point of reassuring me that they still liked me anyway and a year later told me that the skills they'd learned in our class came in very handy at uni, as I'd taught them how to think and trust themselves. Cue: my warm feelings of pride in their developing growth mindset.

Students with a growth mindset are less angsty, less reactive when receiving feedback and they understand that they're on a learning journey with you.

They get that to F.A.I.L. is to make a first attempt in learning and not a cataclysmic doomsday event. They have developed resilience and an understanding that learning is a process. This knowledge is developed through experiences with family, sport, friends and school. They know that delight ("Yay! I got an A") and disappointment ("Oh, I didn't expect that, I got a D") are emotions that they're able to feel and move on from. They have been taught that effort counts more than result and that their value as a human being is not determined by the mark or grade they receive.

You can help students to develop a growth mindset. James Nottingham and his team at Challenging Learning have developed fabulous ideas and resources about how you can do exactly that in a practical way, in any classroom. I highly recommend Nottingham's books, *Challenging Mindset* and *Challenging Learning*. The effort you make in fostering a growth mindset within your classroom is so worthwhile for them and you. When they see you as more of a guide who co-constructs learning experiences with them and less as a judge who imposes a curriculum upon them, they are more open to taking risks in their learning and to trying new things. They are also more likely to take ownership over a learning experience and to ask questions. Students with a fixed mindset tend to be more passive in their learning. They want an HDMI connection between your brain and theirs so you can just pour the information in. But learning is so multidimensional that such an aspiration is narrow and reductive. It doesn't stop some people trying this approach, though.

> Developing and sustaining a growth mindset is hard because it means you have to feel your feelings, and in our world that's tough for so many people.

As a society, we like to protect our young people – and ourselves – from unwelcome feelings. We need to teach them that all emotions are valuable and that they can feel difficult emotions like disappointment, anger and shame and move through an uncomfortable moment where things hurt emotionally and still be OK. They have space in their body and mind for all these emotions and more.

Assessment album

I use a colour metaphor with students to show how we can all learn how to 'be' with our emotions. I've been influenced by the psychological approach called acceptance and commitment therapy (ACT). At the beginning of the year when I chat with a class about an activity or task for which they will receive feedback, I explain the process of assessment using a photography album metaphor.

Assessment is a process, like photography. We take photos using many tools, like DSLR cameras, mobile phones and tablets, and for many different purposes. I use this analogy with pictures on the whiteboard to explain to students how together we build an assessment album, print and digital, of snapshots of what they know, understand and can do. When we compile this assessment album, it tells the story of their learning journey throughout the year. Sometimes the snapshots are taken by surprise like when I write down something I observe about their understanding of a concept. Other times they involve students completing an 'assessment task' that they know they will be assessed according to specific marking criteria. Then there are the occasions where I make notes about their level of achievement in a class activity. And then there are times when we have a snapshot taken by an outside photographer like when they do a NAPLAN Test or sit an external exam, such as the HSC.

I show them that just like photos are representations of them, these assessment snapshots are not them either, rather, they are representations of what they achieved at a particular moment in time, when they were feeling a certain way. We take lots of assessment snapshots to build the most comprehensive assessment album of their achievements. As teachers, we work hard to not judge them on their results in one test on one day. Unfortunately, some people in society can do this and so it is hard for young people, as they may receive conflicting messages.

Assessment photo album

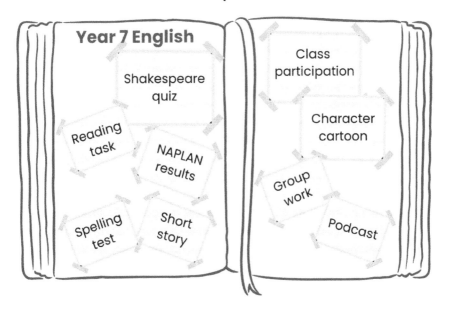

Just before they receive feedback, I ask them about what colour they associate with different emotions and where in the body each emotion and its colour sits for them. For example, my disappointment is a murky grey colour and it sits in my head. When I feel anxious or worried it's bright red and I feel it in my neck and shoulders. When I feel joyful it's a gorgeous green and I see it in my chest. Lots of young people feel disappointment and anxiety in their stomach. Many feel joy or happiness in their arms and hands. I ask them to put their hand on that area and imagine making room for that emotion. Feeling it and knowing that whether it is a welcome or unwelcome emotion, they have space to be with it. I talk about how feelings come and go. I explain that we are not our emotions and emotions are transient. When we feel unwelcome emotions, such as disappointment about our achievement in a task, then we can learn how to feel that emotion, talk about it with our friends, teacher and/or family and develop a plan to accept what happened and set goals for the future. Sometimes, in accepting what happened, letting ourselves feel disappointed, for example, we can turn that murky grey colour into something more welcome like a gorgeous green. After all, wellbeing is not about being happy all the time.

Feedback

Feedback is central to everything you do as a teacher. It comes in many forms and is used for many purposes, but at its heart it involves providing someone with information about how they may improve. It is a part of the assessment process in which you give a student information about how they performed according to a set of criteria (learning intentions) and guidance about how to improve. In a less formal way, we give feedback daily without consciously thinking about it, like when we thank students for lining up outside a classroom or when we comment on a student's active participation in a class discussion or even when we encounter a student in the playground and ask how they are feeling.

> **For feedback to have an impact, it must be given within a productive learning culture where everyone is actively engaged in improvement – including me.**

My aim is to ensure the type of feedback, the amount and the timing is carefully calibrated to the student and class. Nothing matters more than what students do with the feedback they receive. I need to create the conditions that make them curious enough to make a change in what they write, create, think, research and/or do. If they don't have a 'buy-in', then it's a waste of everyone's time.

As part of creating this culture, I have learned to examine my own values about why and how I give feedback:

- Do I give it to justify a grade/mark?
- Do I give it to show that I am right?
- Do I give it because I am scared that someone will judge me and accuse me of being a bad teacher?
- Do I give it to point out all the ways that a student didn't listen in class?
- Do we give each other targeted and timely feedback so that we can all improve our skills, knowledge and understanding and grow as learners?

As teachers, we are naturally helpful, and research shows highly empathetic people. It's kind of built into our teacher DNA. We want the young people we teach to 'get it right'. We want them to improve, grow and to develop into well-educated and engaged humans who will make a difference in society. BUT there is a power imbalance built into teaching, which affects how students receive and act upon feedback.

Yes, I am the adult in the class who has the job of teaching a group of young people skills, knowledge and understanding in a subject area.

I could choose to take the attitude that any feedback I give them must be acted upon because I am the teacher and I know more and therefore I am right. In this scenario I am valuing 'being right' over a student taking ownership over their learning and taking action to improve. The feedback given has no stickability. The compliant students will do exactly what I say, the apathetic students will claim that they get it and ignore me, the struggling students will stay confused and the sparky assertive students will basically tell me to get f#$@*d; hopefully not in those exact words, but it has happened to me.

Overall, it won't make any student curious enough to make a change that 'sticks'. They likely will continue to make the same mistake because they haven't been given a chance to own the feedback and move forward. They just feel that I have used my authority as a teacher to judge and label them. Kind of like putting a fruit sticker on them, I mean well, but it feels like I've labelled them for all to see. I haven't shared status with them to work on a learning challenge.

> **A more effective alternative is to work with the students in creating a productive feedback culture in which they know what skills and understanding they need to show to achieve a task or activity and they take ownership to make a change.**

Social media has affected the way students receive feedback from their teachers. The majority of high school students have a social media presence, be it on Instagram, Snapchat, TikTok or other platforms. They live in a culture of social media feedback during the time of adolescence in which they are hormonally primed to want acceptance, be part of the group and be acutely sensitive to a whiff of judgement from others.

Enter into the mix your average teacher who is striving to help them improve and you have the conditions for tumultuous emotional weather. If a teacher, like me, gives feedback on a short story or essay and the student doesn't like the feedback they receive, they may think I'm wrong, too hard, too picky, unfair or too critical for their liking. And then they could become emotional and start to blame people. Some even text their parents, at the earliest available opportunity, to share the gross injustice that has befallen them at the hands of their utterly incompetent excuse for a teacher. They do this because that is what they see modelled in society through social media and, in fact, the media as a whole on a daily basis. They do this because they feel the feedback that you have provided is PERSONAL: neon lights, all-caps kind of personal. And it hurts. They can't yet see the intention behind the feedback, and this is when a culture of strong supportive relationships within the classroom helps students to overcome this fear of feedback, take ownership of it and make judgements about how they can set a goal (or two) to move forward.

I used to be a little confused as to why it felt like, all of a sudden, so many students were so anxious and sometimes combative about the feedback they received in class. What had changed? I'd been teaching for more than 15 years when I noticed this pattern. I started to think about social media and how it's a form of 24/7 feedback. I considered how my perspective about feedback (of any kind) would change if I was given feedback in the form of likes and/or comments on photos of me and comments I made or that were made about me. It's heady stuff for influencing an individual's perception about themselves and for inducing anxiety. I'd even started to notice how anxious I can feel if I don't receive a reply to a text message for a few hours or even days, and the sight of an ellipsis that appears and then disappears in digital communication can make me overthink. So, if this was happening to me, an adult who didn't grow up with social media, how would it feel for a teenager?

Years ago, I was called to the front office at the end of the day to chat with a parent. I was confused as to why. I'd just received a message to go to the office when the last bell of the day went. Before going, I stopped by the staffroom to ask my colleagues if anyone knew what it was about. This student's teacher told me how, in the last period of the day, she'd become upset about feedback on an assessment task and she'd asked to go to the bathroom. The teacher had already clarified the written feedback for her and provided support but reasoning that she needed some time out, the teacher gave her a bathroom pass and let her go. She never returned. Instead, she called her mother from a toilet cubicle and complained about the mark and feedback. The mother immediately came to school to talk to me, the Head Teacher. They were both now sitting in the front office, waiting. The teacher had done everything possible to help and support the student and was understandably concerned about her. I reassured the teacher and thanked her for all she had done and was doing.

I introduced myself, sat down with the student and her mother, and listened. This young woman was anxious and disappointed. I tried to validate her emotions, ask questions so she could start to see a different perspective about the situation, and I offered to also chat with her tomorrow about her assessment task and the feedback she received. I wasn't going to change it. I was going to spend extra time with her to explain why she had received this result and how she could set goals for the next step. The teacher had already done this within the classroom, but the student wasn't yet able to see the support and kindness she was offering. We were both working together to support the student. Prioritising helping young people understand their emotions is key to sustainable teaching.

Teacher tips

- "It's all about collecting data and triangulating the results to navigate to what your next steps should be." Pip M – Primary teacher

- "I have all students mark their own work first, streamlining the feedback process. Instead of two separate conversations, I can feed back in the first instance on two data sets: their responses and their assessment of those responses. This opens up time to work collaboratively on additional tasks and apply feedback immediately." Matt K – Secondary teacher

- "On non-term time or holidays, I block out a day or two (or three or four, depending on what needs to be achieved) for schoolwork and I work really purposefully during that time. I get marking done first and get into the more fun planning after that!" Christine M – English teacher

PART 3

SHARE

Sharing is about giving and receiving. To share is to dare to be vulnerable – to risk trusting another and to open yourself to feedback that may be surprising or confronting in some way. The social researcher Brené Brown speaks of the power of vulnerability to allow us to make authentic connections with each other and to get stuff done. Sharing is at the heart of all her books, including her focus on teachers as leaders and her TED talks such as 'The Power of Vulnerability'. You may not think of yourself as a leader, but I do, and Brown most definitely does; she states that:

> "I define a leader as anyone who holds themselves accountable for finding the potential in people and processes, and who has the courage to develop that potential. And that means that educators, teachers specifically, are the most important leaders we have in the world today."

We may feel we have a small circle of influence, but like throwing a rock into a lake, our ripple effect is great.

It's easy to share an idea with someone you like and trust. It's harder to share with people you may not feel a connection with, or you may find hard to like – that takes courage, practice and support. Developing a sharing habit is one of the most effective ways I know to be a sustainable teacher. You cannot do it alone, without it affecting your health, happiness and ability to find the fun and joy in teaching. Collaboration and a default positive setting will keep you going when times are feeling tough.

A sustainable teacher shares an attitude of realistic optimism.

Not that over-the-top brand of optimism that ignores all the evidence that sometimes things are just plain hard. No, I mean the kind of optimism that acknowledges the tough aspects of life, processes them, and moves through to create a realistic perspective that places more emphasis on what's possible rather than what's not. When you cultivate this perspective, you will conserve energy for what matters. You'll feel the hard stuff, but it won't drag you down to the depths of despair as easily as it might others. There is a concept called 'negativity bias', which means that, as human beings, we tend to place more importance on negative experiences than positive or neutral ones – unless we try to short-circuit such thinking by actively using techniques to shift this perspective to one of more realistic optimism.

Negativity bias was identified by two American academics: Paul Rozin and Edward B Royzman. They outlined their findings in an article, 'Negativity Bias, Negativity Dominance, and Contagion', published in the *Personality and Social Psychology Review* journal (2001). Negativity was found to be more contagious than positivity, and it just has more stickability in your mind, especially when under pressure.

When you develop a daily habit of realistic optimism, it helps you to manage the day-to-day pressures of teaching and avoid being sucked into a black hole of negativity. It's normal to have bad days, tough moments and feel doubt.

Doubt is a superpower that often receives a bad rap. It's useful because it helps you to reflect, analyse and work towards a better way of doing things. The trick is to control it wisely.

Too much doubt and you'll be paralysed. Just the right amount and it gives you a performance edge – enabling you to strive to improve your skills and understanding. If you're too comfortable, confident or complacent, you're more likely to lose focus and become detached from the young people in your care. What's not normal or healthy is to become negative, disenchanted and resentful for an extended period. Negativity is easy to catch and sometimes you will encounter someone in the staffroom or a group of people who are feeling negative and venting their grievances. You may share in their dissatisfaction. You may empathise with them. You may find yourself sucked into a form of negative groupthink.

To be a sustainable teacher, I suggest you don't spend too long in that space, or you'll find you're drained of energy, your enthusiasm has flown to Antarctica and you hate your job. Instead, shift your perspective to one of realistic optimism. Remember, there is always hope and a chance to move forward in some way. Use one of the many psychological techniques to pivot your perspective, for example, reframe the situation, dump the negative self-talk in the trash, focus on one positive (however small) from your day or create a new pattern of behaviour. One word of caution: try not to be judgy of others who are in that fixed, somewhat negative mindset. They're likely to shoot the messenger and accuse you of toxic positivity. Hear and empathise with their pain and grievances, visit with them in that state, but hold on to your own realistic optimism.

TEAM

There is a popular movie myth of the crusading teacher who single-handedly turns kids' lives around, fighting against the old-fashioned beliefs of the other teachers, the school leadership and the system. Think Robin Williams in *Dead Poets Society*, Michelle Pfeiffer in *Dangerous Minds* or Jack Black in *School of Rock*. They're fun to watch, but it's a dangerous myth because it romanticises education and it simplifies the complexity of teaching and learning. It suggests that to make an impact you need to be the lone wolf who sacrifices everything for the students you teach. It ignores the reality that change is complex, incremental and everyone, including these amazing teacher characters, made a difference by working together with students, colleagues, parents and carers.

These stories often ignore the fact that teachers and students *share* the process of change and development together; they are not 'saved' by a charismatic teacher leader. Students are not blank social media feeds – they have a history, relationships, opinions, values and choices that all impact on their learning. They can, will and should challenge, in an appropriate way, the adults who teach them, for in doing so they are learning valuable skills.

Wherever you work, there will be a team of colleagues with whom you collaborate and share the load. That load may be writing units of work, creating resources, researching new ideas, running excursions, making presentations, taking detentions, workshopping classroom management strategies and/or listening to worries.

In the words of a great Principal I know:

"It's about evolution, not revolution."

This collaborative approach makes for strong and effective schools, but it's less entertaining in a Hollywood drama.

Staffroom life

A staffroom is a great place to connect with colleagues, vent about your day and feel supported. Most staffrooms I've worked in are either large open spaces in which the whole school staff is based or small faculty-based staffrooms where six to 15 people have a desk as their home base and access to a kitchenette. Whatever the type of staffroom you're in, there are a few things that will help to sustain you and keep your energy levels and enthusiasm high.

Firstly, headphones are handy to avoid distractions from people catching up on things, marking together or wanting to ask you a question. Over-ear headphones are the best because they're like a 'Please Do Not Disturb' sign. Staffrooms are busy places and lots of time can be unexpectedly swallowed by these interactions. If during your preparation periods you use your headphones, it's a signal to everyone else that you're in the work zone.

Headphones = work zone

Try to use your preparation periods to focus on completing specific work activities. I like to jot down on a Post-it note two to three things I need to achieve in those 45–60 minutes, so I get it done. If I don't, I'm tempted to chat with a colleague about a student's progress or workshop a new lesson idea, and although these are all work-related activities, they are not as important as completing my Year 7 marking, writing reports or creating a hook activity for my Year 10 class. I try to be disciplined by using these tricks to focus my attention. If I don't, what ends up happening is that I do far more of the high-priority tasks after school or on weekends, and that isn't sustainable. I try to use recess, lunch, before/after school for chatting with colleagues. There are times when I will chat with a colleague during a preparation period because it is a high priority and/or that's the only time we have to talk. If so, I try do it as quietly as possible or out in the hallway, to avoid disturbing colleagues who are focused on their high-priority tasks. Sometimes I stuff up and I am that annoyingly loud person, so now it's on the public record, please feel free to (politely) remind me to put a sock in it!

We all talk about other people. Be aware there are politics in a school, just like any other organisation and that it will take you years to know who is connected to whom and how. Gossip is common in any workplace because we're all human. It can get very tricky if you enter the gossip cycle because you never really know everything that's happening. We've all done it at some stage, to a lesser or greater extent. Remember that if someone is telling you something about someone else, what's to stop them talking about you, too? There is a great approach called the 'no triangles' way of being. Talk directly to each other when there is an issue.

If you make it a habit to be kind, fair and positive, you put yourself in the best position to get on with everyone.

The social researcher Brené Brown summarises this approach as: "Clear is kind. Unclear is unkind." If you're honest and transparent and try to find something good in everyone you meet, you will make your life much easier. If you remember that people are generally motivated by either love or fear, it will help you to understand the motivations behind their words and actions and lead you to a more compassionate response. It's that philosophy of focusing on what you have in common rather than your differences, which will provide you with the best chance to feel energised, working happily in a staffroom of diverse individuals.

Sharing with other teachers can be scary because they're our colleagues we see every day and what happens if they think what we have created isn't good or, even worse, they think it's stupid and comment about it to other people, behind our back? Some teachers are reluctant to share a resource until they know it's 'perfect.' You and whatever you have created is a work in progress – there will be mistakes and room for improvement in whatever you create and that's OK. You don't have time for perfect because you live in the messy reality of now. Besides, perfect is impossible by definition, according to experts like Brené Brown, Oprah and my mum.

What (I hope) is far more likely is that your colleagues will wholeheartedly embrace what you have created, thank you for it, use it in their classes and make great suggestions for how it can be adapted and changed to benefit even more students and teachers. Then they will share things they have created with you, too. In doing so, you save time and energy and learn from others new ways to help your students learn and grow. That's a sustainable way of doing things.

Sometimes teachers don't share resources, because they see that another person has already done the work, so they think why bother 'reinventing the wheel'? Other times they do it because they are overwhelmed and looking for any way they can save time, and then there are those who are feeling insecure about creating resources because they're new to teaching or feel nervous, so rely on others. At times, people don't share resources they create because, in the past, they discovered that their sharing wasn't reciprocated and they were doing more work than others. They feel that other people have taken advantage of them and unfairly benefitted from their hard work. Early in my teaching life, I was puzzled by an original copy of a comprehension I created disappearing from the photocopier before I had a chance to put a copy in the faculty files. And then it mysteriously reappeared the next day. On other occasions I've seen a colleague's frustration as they realised that they have done most of the work of creating resources for a course, but some of the other teachers hadn't reciprocated.

Years ago, I created an activity using a Google Doc for a Year 10 class and posted it to our Google Classroom. I'd invited all the teachers in our team to the Google Classroom. In class I was reading through it with my students and explaining the activity, but it kept moving without any of us touching a keyboard or screen. It felt like we were in the middle of a digital seance. My students thought it was hilarious. Another teacher's initials were on the screen and it was soon clear none of us were making the changes when I called "HOK" (hands-off keyboards) to check what was going on. The teacher was using the Google Doc with their class at the same time my class was using it. They'd forgotten to copy it and post it to their own Year 10 Google Classroom. I wasn't upset – after all, I'd freely shared it – I just felt awkward about the situation and I'd wished they had taken the time to adapt the activity for their class. I sent a student to let them know what was happening so we could end the digital seance.

In this climate of data-driven decision-making, politicians lecturing about accountability, social media-induced anxiety, funding inequities, government targets, basic skills testing mania and COVID-19 pandemic-induced panic about students being 'left behind', teachers are under pressure. I feel it's clichéd to say more pressure than ever before, but this belief is supported by people I know who have been teaching for more than 30 years.

> We have the power to face that pressure together by sharing as much as possible in every aspect of what we do. I like to think of it as the 'hive mind' – the collective ideas and opinions of a group of people working together to achieve a shared purpose.

Hive mind

For example, let's say you teach in a high school English faculty like ours. If we need to create new programs that we will all teach from and adapt for the needs of the students within our classes, we will decide on the scope and sequence together, create a broad outline of what will be in each unit of work and then divide the writing between us. This is usually done working in pairs to write a program designed with differentiated activities that individual teachers can use and/or modify for the students in their classrooms. In sharing like this, we learn from each other about different ways to teach the concepts, skills and contexts in our syllabus and we save duplication of effort. Why would five to six people write individual programs for the one course? Why not create an outline of a core program together, then one to two people write it and we all share the result? This requires a clear purpose, equitable distribution of the workload and regular check-ins at faculty or stage meetings.

It's key that everyone is open and fair about sharing and that we build upon what we make from class to class and year to year. We're not just creating resources, we're also professionally developing each other and strengthening our teaching skills as individuals and as a team. Whenever I create a resource, write a program or develop anything really, I build into its design some longevity. By that I mean that I design and store it in such a way that it will be used by more than me and my students in this class in this calendar year. That saves energy and time and avoids duplication of effort.

> We're creating a foundation, a resource legacy for all who work and learn alongside us and all who will follow us. That's sustainable teaching in action.

Sick day/s

Calling into work to say you're sick and taking a few days off to recuperate before returning with a doctor's certificate sounds simple enough. But it's a little more complex for a teacher. Being sick involves more work for you, your colleagues and, potentially, your students. You have responsibilities and, unfortunately in the current education climate, they don't stop while you're sick.

A teacher who is calling in sick will prepare a lesson plan and resources for their students. For a high school teacher that's potentially five or six classes in a day. We all use teaching programs, but we're not all necessarily at the same spot of the program on the same day, and we differentiate the activities for the needs of the students in our class. It's not like a training manual where you deliver the same content to each group of people. So, because we don't want our students to fall behind, we create a lesson plan or, at the very least, advice about what the focus is for the lesson and often resources, all while coughing up a lung or feeling all snotty and gross.

We want the casual teacher assigned to our classes to have a productive day. We don't want our students to be bored, nor do we want classroom management problems to arise because some students have decided to take advantage of our absence. The lessons may be prepared the night before or early in the morning of the day we call in sick. Sometimes these lesson ideas can be in print or a digital folder and when you email your colleagues, they help to organise any printing or resources for you. Ideally, we would all have time to be able to prepare these lessons for our colleagues, but the fact is we don't, and we also teach our own classes, so we aren't necessarily up to date with where everyone else is in their classes.

> **Over the past few years casual teachers have become an increasingly rare species – it's like trying to find a rainbow-coloured unicorn.**

Through a series of unfortunate circumstances, including state and federal government policy decisions, issues with registration and accreditation, recruitment challenges, teacher attrition, retirements and COVID-19, what used to be a challenge for some rural and regional schools is now felt nationwide. All too frequently, in a public high school, if you call in sick, all your classes may not be covered. Instead, the Head Teacher will let your class know that the class has been cancelled because you're sick and they couldn't find enough casual teachers today, and they will be directed to sit in a central area in the playground for the period. There is money to pay casual teachers, but often there is just no one available. This means that the students have a 'free period.' That loss of learning time comes at a cost to them, to you and to our society.

When I took 11 days' sick leave because I had an operation, my Year 12 class was only covered for two of their eight periods. I was preparing all lessons from home because I wanted to ensure the students were engaged and learning, and I didn't want to put pressure on my already overworked colleagues. I had sick leave and there was money to pay a casual teacher, but there was no casual teacher available. For safety reasons, the Senior Executive had decided that the younger classes took priority when assigning casual teachers. It is frustrating for all involved. In business, I believe they call it a supply chain issue.

When I returned, I had to work with the students to 'catch up' on eight hours of missed learning. Some of the students had worked independently in the library, but many had not. I expected this to happen, so I built into my lesson design activities that could be done independently and supported the students' progress via email and Google messages from home. This supply chain issue must be resolved by governments, education sectors and unions so that teachers never have to work like this while they're on sick leave.

Since the COVID-19 pandemic, everyone is more aware of infection control, so if they have cold or flu symptoms they stay home, get a COVID test, see a doctor and do all they can to get well before returning. Prior to the pandemic, that wasn't always the case because being away from school caused you and your colleagues more work than soldiering on. I know I've kept going to school when I felt sick because I felt that I was letting everyone down if I stayed home and I just couldn't face the hassle of organising things for a casual teacher. If you take this approach, what happens is that whatever virus or infection you had would do the rounds of the staffroom and more people would get sick. In trying to avoid putting pressure on colleagues, a teacher that soldiers on often causes them more trouble than if they'd just stayed at home. One year, I was at home sick on my birthday because I'd caught the virus that another colleague had spread around the staffroom. Over a two-week period, we all went down like flies. It took me a few days to forgive her!

The pandemic changed all that, which is better for everyone's health in the long run, but what hasn't changed is the lack of casual teachers and the pressure teachers feel to not let people down. I've learned to channel Elsa (from *Frozen*) at times like these and just 'let it go'. If you're sick, you're sick. So, do what you must do to get better. And always, get a doctor's certificate if you're away for more than a day. In terms of work, you need to plan and have contingencies for when you will be sick. And it will happen, especially in your first few years of teaching. In our faculty a group of very smart teachers collated emergency folders of lesson resources matched to our units of work. They started these in print and are migrating them to digital versions as well.

A long time ago, when I was a casual teacher, I came prepared with class sets of photocopied activities relevant to different subject areas. These days, you can be lucky and hit the jackpot with an effective and experienced casual teacher who is able to create a relevant and engaging lesson at short notice. But mostly casual teachers are new to teaching and it's always better that the class teacher and their colleagues can give them as much information as possible for an effective lesson.

In high school, when the teacher is away there's a good chance the students will use your absence to test out the casual teacher and cause some classroom management issues. They play up because they think they'll get away with it. Here's where it's a good idea to be a step ahead of them. The more engaging and relevant the lesson design, the less likely it is that this will occur. The trick is to include more rather than less for them to do and minimise the amount of interaction in the lesson. Give the casual teacher five to 10 minutes of explanation time and then most of the lesson keep students working to achieve something and ensure they must hand it in. It's strange how powerful a motivator it is for them to either physically or digitally submit something they have created. This will (hopefully) minimise any 'mopping up' you need to do upon your return.

When students see an opportunity to slacken off or have some fun with a casual teacher, they will most definitely take it. And the clean-up for you, as their classroom teacher, can be extensive. A long time ago one class knew the casual teacher was an older gentleman who used a hearing aid. A few students decided that they would mess with him by making everyone mime the whole lesson so he would think there was something wrong with his hearing aid. Not one person broke. Impressive commitment from them! The poor teacher was rightly baffled and figured it out when in his next class he could hear perfectly. The whole class sat through a detention the next day.

As a casual teacher in London, I once took a Drama class where some bright spark decided to turn off the lights in the Drama room when I was furthest from the light switch, then other students thought it would be fun to start throwing chairs across the room. You can imagine how delighted 22-year-old me was at this turn of events! Feeling somewhat panicked but knowing yelling at them was useless, I backed up against a wall, inching along until I reached the light switch at the door to the Drama studio and dramatically turned the lights on. I yelled into the hallway for help and a Deputy came running to assist. After that lesson, there were a lot of detentions the next day and at least one suspension for dangerous behaviour.

Sometimes, no matter how hard you work to create a structured lesson for the casual teacher, things happen and that's when it's important to have a team approach and to follow up so the students understand that they need to respect the casual teacher as they would any member of staff. We all understand how vital casual teachers are in a school and so we work hard to support and nurture them as we would any member of our teaching team.

At one London school, I remember two 15-year-old boys who got into a fistfight in class. I learned later they had an ongoing feud that they brought from the playground into the classroom. Thinking quickly, I instructed one student to run to get a Deputy and, thankfully, four other boys – two for each of the wannabe boxers – helped by pulling them away from each other. I was at a safe distance and gave instructions to the boys to separate them on the other side of the room, while trying to encourage everyone else to calm down and not get involved. It was frightening how quickly things can escalate. All was resolved with the support of the Deputy, the Principal and the students' parents.

> It's inevitable that conflict arises in a classroom, but you can minimise the risks of an incident escalating when you have a lesson plan and a supportive network of people to share the load with the casual teacher.

Students

Teenagers tend to take things personally and, paradoxically, they can also be the most compassionate and forgiving people on the planet. Maybe it's the hormones. I've experienced a student holding a grudge against me for weeks because they received a lunch detention. Another student burst into tears because they thought I was disappointed in them personally, when in fact I'd been referring to other students within the class.

Clear communication is essential when sharing learning time with young people. On the whole, most are still developing the social cues and filters that many adults take for granted. Many don't read your tone of voice easily. Most will take it personally if you come into a learning space looking and sounding like you're in a bad mood. You may think your words are polite, kind and calm, but your facial and body expressions may not match, and that can be incredibly confusing for a young person. It may be the case that you've just received bad news, you had an argument with someone just before coming into class or you feel sick. If you don't let them know what's going on they will revert to teenager default setting, which is to think they've done something wrong and you are unfair, a beatch, a bastard, a cow, mean, horrible, just don't get it or any combination of the above.

Appropriately sharing with students selected details of your own life helps them to see that you are:

- Human and not a cardboard cut-out stereotype
- Interested in them as people
- Want to help them with their learning

At the risk of stating the obvious, what you share must be appropriate for a teenage audience in your care, in a professional setting. Appropriate may include:

- Family members and their interests
- Hobbies
- Holidays
- Favourite sport/s
- Likes/dislikes

It does not include:

- Details about romantic relationships
- Experiences with domestic violence
- Mental health status of family members
- Drinking and/or drug-taking activities
- Illegal activity
- Advocating for a political party, a faith-based organisation or a protest group

It may seem obvious what is appropriate (or not) to share with young people, but that's not always the case. Sometimes teachers may share a meme or a social media post with a group of students that they later realise was more appropriate to share with their friends. Other teachers may speak enthusiastically about a political or social cause they are passionate about and not realise that students in their class have gone home to share those views and claim this is what they are being taught at school. Parents may interpret this as you 'pushing' your personal political or social views on vulnerable students and abusing your position, they may complain to the Principal and then you're in the middle of a complaints process. You'll then find yourself feeling stressed and overwhelmed – the opposite of sustainable teaching.

The trick to avoiding such a situation and staying on the sustainable side of the teaching equation is to realise that schools are diverse communities, and you are an objective voice working within them. No matter whether you work in a public or independent school, the community is made up of people with a variety of opinions, faiths, experiences, traditions, cultural backgrounds and ways of life.

At work, it's the values of the school and education sector that you need to follow before your personal values.

One example of this is the screening of films classified as M in a high school setting. Some families allow their 11- to 14-year-olds to view M films or TV shows. Some teachers let their own children view audiovisual material with this classification, according to their own values. But, in a school setting in their professional role as a classroom teacher, this is not permitted. Within the New South Wales Department of Education, you must abide by the school sector's values in which the viewing of M classified material must be approved by the Principal, according to guidelines outlined in the 'Audiovisual materials in schools – procedures for use' document.

As clichéd as it sounds, teaching is a privilege and with it comes responsibility. A lot of responsibility. Schools have a code of conduct, which sets out the way teachers behave responsibly in a professional setting. Reading and understanding your school's code of conduct can help you to navigate your work life and make sustainable choices. For example, in New South Wales, the Department of Education also has a Controversial Issues in Schools Policy, which explains that:

"Schools are neutral places for rational discourse and objective study."

And that teachers need to:

"...maintain objectivity, avoiding distortion of discussion and acknowledge the rights of students, parents and carers to hold different viewpoints."

Students love to help and advise you. Once, I was advised by a part-time Sportsgirl model, a 15-year-old in Year 9 English, that I really needed to do something with my hair. My hair is incredibly curly, somewhat unruly and definitely not used to behaving with any manners. Our lesson didn't feature anything about the properties of curly hair – her advice came out of the blue and she had yet to apply herself to the day's learning activity, as she wasn't a keen student. I thought maybe if I'm open to learning from an expert like herself, she might be more willing to apply herself in class. So, I promptly replied, "I know! What should I do?" And that was all she needed to launch into a full verbal essay on the merits of silicone versus non-silicone curly hair-styling products, what stylists on a photo shoot use on her hair, whether I'd really seriously considered straightening my hair ("GHDs are expensive, but the best, you know, Miss"), the fact her cousin's friend has hair kind of sort of like mine and... did I know that the cheapest and best product to avoid frizz and control curls ("...but not too much cause then you look greasy") is Sorbolene cream.

This one small act of vulnerability, on my part, opened a window for this student to feel a sense of her own expertise and power in learning. It also allowed me to learn more about how I could help her using metaphors and analogies linked to her own life experiences as a part-time model. My metaphor bank had largely revolved around football, running, surfing or farming to that point. It was good to diversify.

One day, I realised how my experiences as a (very average) runner were a great metaphor for learning. I vividly remember one student, training for a national swimming competition, with an eye for Olympic selection in a few years, telling me as kindly as she could to stop complaining about the first 1–2km that I ran. She asked me:

"Why do you expect it will be easy?"

She told me I needed to stop fighting the uncomfortable feelings and work with them to break through that barrier and settle into a rhythm. When I was in a rhythm, she said, then it would feel right. Not good necessarily, but right because I'd be getting somewhere both distance-wise and improving my fitness. I was impressed. A 13-year-old had mentored me with a sharp lesson in resilience. And she'd summarised James Nottingham's theory of 'the learning pit', quite a few years before he published it. What I'd done as a teacher, unintentionally, mind you, was to be open to the possibility that I could learn something of value from someone a third of my age.

> **This kind of sharing builds strong student-teacher relationships and is a great way to create more sustainable teaching practices because it builds trust and shared understanding.**

I wish I could tell you I had known exactly what I was doing in this interaction, but I didn't. It was only later that I realised I could have taken another approach, which wouldn't have had such positive results. I could have told the student to stop calling out or to stop asking unnecessary questions. Such a decision would have been taken, consciously or not, from a place of fear on my part. A place of wanting to control the environment and be the 'authority' in the room. Instead, I chose to be open to accept the offer of connection that she was offering.

Appropriately sharing with students can give them an opportunity to show how much they care about you and each other. I had another melanoma operation called a wide excision left flap repair in 2021. I look like I have an isosceles triangle scar on my lower left leg. Cue the bad geometry jokes from me and groans from the students. I was off work to elevate my leg for just over two weeks. My step count went down to 2–4% of my regular daily percentage. When I returned to school, I had to be super-careful that my wound didn't get bumped accidentally, I didn't walk much, I elevated my leg when possible and I didn't stand up for long. The students were so supportive. They policed each other around me, reminding everybody to be careful and exclaiming:

"Don't bump Miss's leg!"

They were also sweetly bossy in ensuring that I didn't stand for too long in a class. The Year 12s regularly reminded me that I really did need to sit down:

"Sit down, Miss! It'll swell up if you don't sit down, Miss! Just sit."

I'm sure a few of them were relieved I wasn't roaming the room, ensuring nobody was playing a computer game or searching for new sneakers at the Platypus Shoes sale. But I could keep an eye on them sitting down and I was able to move my chair around the room when needed.

> **Community building within a class involves trust and reciprocal opportunities for caring.**

As a sustainable teacher, it's important to give students day-to-day opportunities to share status with you, in appropriate ways at the right time. It creates relationship glue that enables them to trust you, be vulnerable and be more open to taking risks with their learning.

Failures and successes

When you share your failures, you're sharing your first attempts in learning something. You are sharing the idea that you took a risk and it didn't work out, but that's OK. You're normalising taking chances. You're normalising experiencing disappointment and moving through it. It makes your teaching life more sustainable because in modelling the behaviour you want the students to practise, you're creating a culture that they can emulate and reducing the time you will spend teaching them why failures are an integral part of learning something new. As a society we tend to value the success, the end product, more than the journey we took to achieve it, the ups and downs of the process. For young people, swimming in social media messages about what it means to achieve, they can often find it difficult to see the two steps forward, 10 steps backward, three steps forward, face-plant spectacularly nature of the journey towards a goal.

Comparison is a natural human habit and when you're fed these ideas about what success means, you can become more self-conscious and less likely to take a risk.

> **Mobile phones and social media have been a game-changer because everything you do now carries a much higher risk of being exposed and shared than ever before. It's basic self-preservation for any teenager to minimise taking risks.**

You don't want to go viral on TikTok or any other social media platform for the wrong reason. In my experience, it seems the more often students are encouraged to take risks in low stakes learning activities and the more often teachers encourage the sharing of failures within a supportive culture, the more resilient students become. I like to call that skill 'creative bounce'.

When you celebrate and share success, you create a self-sustaining culture of encouragement. People thrive on praise that's specific and well-timed. Nobody believes you are sincere if you deliver your praise a week after they do whatever it is you're praising them for. As the leader in the classroom, when you create a culture of praise that acknowledges the effort students put in to achieving success, they're more likely to feel comfortable to claim their own achievements and to celebrate those of their classmates.

Success comes in many forms. It's the acknowledgement of the effort, commitment and hard work that contributed to achieving that success, which people need to hear. You may be praising the fact that they volunteered to contribute to a class discussion, remembered to use a capital letter to begin a proper noun, won a tennis game or came first in a class quiz. Success is on a continuum and praise is the slider which will help to move it forward for any individual person. The extent of an individual's achievement is relative to their context, skills, knowledge, understanding and personality. What's common to everyone is that when people share in our success, it motivates us to grow.

> As a sustainable teacher, tapping into that intrinsic motivation and cultivating gives you joy, pride, job satisfaction and conserves your time and energy.

Kindred spirits

Kindred spirits are people with whom you share similar interests. In teaching, it's important to foster a circle of teacher friends and acquaintances who support and energise you. They understand you and your teaching life. They actively listen, ask questions, offer useful advice and tell you you're being an idiot if you need a reality check. They're real with you. What's key is to try to create connections, at work and more widely. Sometimes you will feel like you're in the depths of despair and nothing is working. When you have a network of supportive people, you can share, workshop a solution for whatever is causing you angst and you can also support them. These people are your trampoline, bouncing you high when all is going well and catching you when you need it.

When things happen, like a lesson just doesn't work the way you thought it would, a colleague challenges you about an issue, a student persistently refuses to follow your instructions, you're sworn at or maybe there's a fight in class, you will need support. Most of us are lucky to have the support of family and/or friends, but there's something about the support of another teacher that is worth its weight in gold. It feels like you have a shorthand with them, a shared language of words, phrases and gestures that they just get. I call it your teaching mafia.

Developing a teacher network involves being open and approachable to others, sharing ideas and resources, offering to help out and pulling your weight as part of a team, participating in school activities and attending social events. Such support is really important when you move to a new town or area for a teaching job. What gradually happens is you start to discover a close circle of friends – often those from your teaching team or faculty and a wider group of friends and acquaintances within your school, local area and social media networks.

Your teacher friends help you in so many ways. When we returned to school after one of the COVID-19 lockdowns, we had different breaktimes for Junior and Senior students, which meant that I, on my allocated day, had longer time on duty and there was a scheduling conflict with the first 20 minutes of my Year 8 class, once a fortnight. Two of my teacher friends, from different faculties, offered to help me out and look after my Year 8 class until I arrived. They were under no obligation to help me at all. They just offered because that's what you do. At other times, I've been distressed by a student's words or actions and a teacher friend has taken the time to listen, without judgement, and workshop ideas for moving forward. And you will be there for them, too, to share in exciting news or help them with an issue.

When I first started teaching, I was perplexed by an invite from an older teacher to Friday afternoon 'benediction'. I knew the meaning of the word as a short blessing of people or objects, performed by a priest or minister, but I wasn't teaching in a Catholic school and, seriously, did this man in his 50s just invite me and others in the staffroom to church on a Friday afternoon after school? Of course he didn't. He was just winding me up. It was an invite to the pub for afternoon drinks. I'm sure he had a good laugh about the naive, young English teacher who had no idea what he meant by 'benediction'. I remember it as a great afternoon in which we all got to know each other and shared stories about teaching, life and random stuff that cropped up.

Teacher tips

- "Find one or two trusted colleagues. This will take time. There will be days when you want to celebrate the wins with everybody, but there will be other days when you challenge your effectiveness, and even ask yourself if it is the future path that you want to continue on. Feeling this way is absolutely normal. Talk to your inner trusted circle. Listen to them. Heal with them." Frank G – Mathematics Head Teacher

- "Your Head Teacher or Subject Coordinator is a good person to start a conversation with when developing positive relationships with students, classes and colleagues." Jenny W – Technology and Applied Studies Coordinator

- "Know/identify the beverage of choice of your colleagues and keep this on a handy list (for birthdays, hard days, random acts of kindness, etc)." Alex W – English teacher

COMMUNITY

A more experienced teacher once told me that parents gift their children to us for the year, and our job is to ensure that we treat them as if they were our own. Another educator once told me that his favourite rowing team would consist of orphans! Both points of view are different ways to think of parents and their impacts on teachers. Sharing with parents/carers regularly, constructively and positively makes a massive difference to your workload as a teacher and to the success of the young people you teach. When you communicate regularly with parents/carers, you learn more about their child's context and that helps you to know which strategies will help them to achieve success in whatever learning experience you are designing for them.

Sharing with parents/carers is about communicating information from the school context with the home context. The common factor in both contexts is their child. The tricky factors include hormones, cognitive growth rates, social issues, economic challenges, learning differences and emotions. Understanding each other's context and the way their child operates within both can be complex. I like to think of it as us working as a team on a group project, which is the success of their child's learning: social, emotional, physical and intellectual within both our contexts.

Social media

Social media has changed the way schools communicate with parents/carers. There are Facebook and Instagram posts, text alerts, parent apps, LMS messages, websites, digital newsletters and emails. The school communicates more often than ever before, but individual teachers – especially those in high school – still have the four main ways we communicate with parents: phone calls, emails, parent-teacher interviews and school reports. The reality is that we just don't have time to do more than this on a consistent basis. To be a sustainable teacher, it's important to focus on these four basic modes of communication first as essential services. Sure, if you can write a Facebook post about a school activity, include an appropriate photo after checking that no student in it is on the 'Do Not Publish' list, check that your post has been edited, email it to whomever is your school's volunteer Facebook moderator and you don't feel rushed or overwhelmed, then please go ahead.

But, if you're struggling to meet your school report deadlines and you're yet to return a phone call from Mrs Zhu whose son Li is in your Year 8 Maths class, then I want you to stop, re-evaluate and listen to your teacher gut. Why are you spending time on this Facebook post? It's a lovely added extra but it's not essential, especially when yo're feeling like everything is about to collapse on top of you. You need to train yourself to share what is essential with parents, what is at the core of your role, what the teaching standards state is essential and then, if you have time and feel the need to, do more via social media, school websites and the like.

Phone calls

Calling a parent/carer can be a scary business for a new teacher. I remember the first time I had to do it, years ago. I was so nervous that I wrote down a script of what I would say before I started. I still recommend this tip to early career teachers. It was something about homework that I needed to talk to this parent about. I don't think the student, in Year 10, had been submitting any homework tasks. It was the middle of the day and her father answered during his lunch break at home. It turned out that they were short-handed on the farm and she hadn't been doing her homework because she was helping with harvest and all the other jobs that had to be done during this time. I felt terrible that I'd put pressure on her and the whole family, because what's homework when you must get a crop in?

It was understandably a low priority in their lives at that moment, but in the long term the student needed to be consolidating her skills, knowledge and understanding in some way so she had options for future study. I recall cautiously feeling out the dad's position on this issue, asking intelligent questions about the harvest (it pays to have a few farmers in my extended family) and gently suggesting that his daughter did need to submit at least some of the tasks. He was receptive, chatted to me freely and we agreed that I'd modify the tasks and expectations while harvest was on and he would ensure she had some time at home to do some homework. I was relieved. I think I was expecting more resistance.

I didn't know it at the time, but I'd used some of the core negotiation skills they teach people in business schools. I'd built rapport, actively listened, solved problems we both had in our contexts, collaboratively planned a way forward that benefitted his daughter's educational progress and allowed her to maintain her family commitments on the farm. When I work with people studying teaching at university (PEX students) and early career teachers, I coach them through using these core negotiation skills with parents, which supports two of the key Principles of Sustainable Teaching: clear communication and saving time.

It doesn't always work out the way it did with the farmer dad. Sometimes, a parent can react to whatever you have to say about their child in a rude, angry or intimidating way. That's hard. It can feel intimidating, confronting and potentially upsetting. You may feel like it's personal. I have, plenty of times. You may find yourself feeling defensive and wanting to say:

"But, but, but don't you realise I'm just trying to help?"

Here is where you need to stop yourself, take a deep breath and remember that the parent/carer is processing whatever news you are imparting to them and for some people their reactions may not be positive. And it isn't personal. It may be that their child is falling behind in their classwork, hasn't submitted an assessment task, has sworn in class, has made inappropriate remarks or behaved in a way that doesn't support the school values. They may be surprised, shocked, confronted, disappointed and/or defensive and often that will result in them 'shooting the messenger'.

Here is where you need to don your Teflon suit and patiently follow the school's process for managing parent interactions. Have a trusted colleague, your Head Teacher or team leader nearby for support and, if possible, choose a time when you won't be too rushed. It is totally awkward if you're in the middle of a conversation with a parent, the bell goes and you need to rush off to teach your Year 10 class so you must end the call. It helps to write a script with sentence starters to guide you through the conversation. Know what the aim of your call is, such as:

- Are you phoning to give the parent/carer information?
- Do you want them to reinforce the school's expectations at home?
- Are you asking them for context so together you can help their child make more appropriate choices?

Be aware of your tone of voice from the start. A radio announcer boyfriend once gave me excellent tips about preparing to talk over the phone, especially with someone you don't know. To sound open and relaxed you should yawn and then smile – even a fake smile is better than none – this will help you to convey a warm and supportive tone of voice. Say good morning or afternoon, introduce yourself and politely ask whether they have a moment to chat about <insert name of child> because <insert summary of reason for call>.

Smile before phoning home

I always find it better to give parents/carers a 'heads-up' about why you are calling. Some people, with high school-aged children, may receive numerous calls a week from school and, as a result, they may feel anxious and defensive as soon as they see the school's number pop up on their phone. It's a sad reality that usually we're so busy that we only have time to call when something isn't going well, rather than if it is. If you foreshadow what you want to talk about, it gives them a chance to be prepared. Nobody likes to be surprised in these instances. Your summary reason for calling them may be something like:

> *"Omar is having challenges following instructions in class. I was wondering if we could have a chat about strategies that may help him?"*

> *"Jack made an inappropriate choice in class today and I am phoning to let you know what happened."*

> *"Catriona swore at me when I asked her to follow our class seating plan. She later told me it was because she felt frustrated. I wanted to let you know alternative strategies we discussed for managing feelings of frustration and to let you know that the Deputy will be in touch about consequences for Catriona's inappropriate choice."*

> *"In class today, Belinda was on Snapchat and wasn't following our school's mobile phone and digital device policy. I just wanted to outline what happened and explain why Belinda's phone was confiscated for the day."*

> *"Amira unexpectedly ran out of class last period. We've since chatted and she tells me she feels anxious. I was wondering if she has been having these challenges at home?"*

If they're free to chat, you can then give them an outline of what happened and what the next step/s are, within your school context, to manage their child's behaviour/s. Always have evidence about a student's words or actions so you can be factual when speaking with a parent/carer. Every person makes mistakes and every person deserves to be treated fairly. Try to remember that you are working in a team with the parent/carer to help their child. Listen carefully to both what they say and how they say it. You can learn a lot from the difference between a person's words and their tone of voice. Use the tools of negotiation I mentioned earlier. Try to be brief.

Sometimes parents are struggling with the hard things that being a parent involves and it can feel like they are hostile towards you. Most frequently this is because they are overwhelmed and need help in moving forward.

You want to help them, but you are not a psychologist nor a doctor, so you need to be aware of when and how to offer them ideas for where to go for specialised help. It's all about boundaries: yours and theirs. Depending on your school sector and the individual context of your school, there is specialised help available within school – that may be a referral to the school counsellor, the Learning Support team, the school youth worker or a chat with the Deputy Principal. There are also lots of resources available that parents/carers can access within the community. This may include a mental health treatment plan from the GP, a referral to Headspace, Smith Family education support programs and online services such as Parent Line, ReachOut Australia, Service NSW and Lifeline.

Your role is to educate their child and, in these situations, refer them on to the people who have the expertise and time to help them. The challenge is that if you don't keep the conversation focused on the issue you called them about and you don't calmly and firmly reinforce boundaries, you can find yourself spending more time than you have available listening to them talk about things that you can't help them with. This has a flow-on effect for you because it compresses all your other tasks into a shorter amount of time and causes you to feel overwhelmed. Never be afraid to say:

> *"Let's find someone together who can help."*

Just occasionally you will discover you're talking to a parent/carer who says they're not happy with you and it feels like they're blaming you for whatever situation has arisen. Their tone may be aggressive and their words may match it. You may find yourself feeling anxious and/or defensive. Never be afraid to politely say:

> *"I'm sorry that you feel that way. I will ask my <insert name of Stage Coordinator, Head Teacher, Assistant Principal, Deputy or Principal> to get back to you to discuss your concerns. Thank you for your time."*

When people are in a heightened state of emotion, it is very difficult to discuss an issue with them in a calm and measured way. You need to step away from the situation. People are human and sometimes they will blame you, sound cross with you and/or be aggressive towards you. That is not your fault and you don't deserve to be spoken to in any way that is not polite and respectful. However, it happens because people, families and schools are complex. The way to manage it is to follow the school processes, be polite and respectful, and calmly reinforce your boundaries.

Stage Coordinators, Head Teachers, Assistant Principals, Deputies and Principals can be fabulously supportive in these situations. They can help you to work out a strategy to move forward in resolving whatever issue has arisen. Often, they have a deeper understanding of the dynamic in a particular family and can assist in working out a way to have more productive conversations with the parent/carer. Usually, it's the Deputy or the Principal that manages the super-challenging parental conversations involving high-level inappropriate behaviour at school. It differs a little from school to school, but those high-level inappropriate behaviours involve things like violence, intentionally swearing at a teacher or student, high-level defiance, dangerous behaviour, smoking/vaping and possession of banned items such as weapons.

Email

Email can't handle the complexities of human interactions that phone calls and face-to-face meetings can. When I write to parents or reply to emails from them, I try to be brief, clear about why I'm writing and I offer an opportunity to chat via phone or face to face. If I need to share any detailed information with them, I do so via a Word attachment or a link to a webpage. At the risk of stating the obvious, parents are super-busy and don't have time to read long emails from teachers. They, like most of us, are also often reading personal emails on mobile phones, iPads, watches and tablets. If I accidentally find myself in an email conversation with a parent, I will try to phone them instead as it's a more efficient way of discussing and resolving an issue.

A long time ago, I received an email from a parent who wasn't happy about something that happened in class. I could sense he was cranky. I realised he didn't have the whole context. He had just heard his child's point of view, which was a narrower picture of what had happened. So, I decided to call him, to say I was sorry that he was upset and to ask if he would mind me explaining what had happened. Just after I'd greeted him, he interrupted me to apologise profusely for his email, explaining that he'd been having a bad day and he had arrived home to his son complaining that I was sexist as I'd given two boys in the class, including his son, a detention but I hadn't given a detention to a girl in the class who had done the same thing. He then said his son had later confessed that he'd lied to him about being 20 minutes late to class. He hadn't been helping a friend who was upset; he had in fact been playing basketball and was truanting. The girl in question had arrived at the door 25 minutes late with a reason and a note from a teacher. The father apologised for his email and his son apologised to me the next day. The whole thing was cleared up much faster via a phone call than could ever have been accomplished via email. It saved all of us a lot of time and energy.

Parent meetings

When I first started teaching, I was scared of parents. I feared they would judge me. This could possibly be because I was – and likely still am – an earnest person. I wanted parents to like and approve of how hard I was working to design and teach interesting lessons for their child. Then I worked out that parents are people, too, who are just trying to do their best for their child. I also learned that many parents were a little scared of teachers. They fear that we are judging them. So, I learned the negotiation and team-building skills I've mentioned through practice and reflection.

Parent meetings fall into two categories:

1. Meetings to discuss specific issues
2. Parent-teacher interviews

The parent meetings I've been involved in most frequently are to do with student academic progress and issues like anxiety or wanting to change classes. Year Advisers, Deputies and Principals are usually the ones who take more parent meetings than teachers. Depending on the reason for the meeting, it's often a good idea for a teacher – especially an early career teacher – to go to the meeting with a Head Teacher or Deputy. It helps to have someone there as a support and guide.

> The key is to be clear on the purpose of the meeting, actively listen, discuss ideas and work together to come to a solution that best meets the student's needs, within the school's policies and procedures.

Sometimes parents want something to happen which isn't possible because of school policies, resource limitations or the need to ensure equity for all. If your body language is open and you are relaxed, this helps the parent to feel relaxed and receptive to what you have to say. Write notes about any key points so you keep a record of what was said by whom and what decisions were made. A follow-up parent call or email, as appropriate, is always useful as it gives them information about how the plan is working as well as confidence that their child's needs are being met. It might be a quick email to say, "Sara has settled in well to her new class", or a phone call in which you reveal that Jack is using the strategies we discussed to manage his anxiety and he is feeling good about participating in class discussions.

In this post-COVID-19 pandemic era, parent-teacher interviews can look a lot different. In recent years I've held Zoom interviews, which could be more aptly named parent, teacher, student, little sister and cat interviews. Despite the challenges of Zoom, Microsoft Teams or any other videoconferencing tool, these interviews are an important chance to give and receive feedback on a student's learning progress to that point in time.

Parent-teacher interviews

As a teacher, parent-teacher interviews are the most common parent meetings you have; some schools hold them face to face and others also offer an online option. In some schools they are held twice a year, others once per year. Whatever the frequency, it pays to be prepared. For me, being a sustainable teacher involves preparing for each interview by doing a few things beforehand. Firstly, know who is coming. These days, most schools do interview bookings online. Many moons ago you had a booking sheet, the students had one, too, and you booked in with them. Knowing which parents/carers are attending the interview is important information. It can help you to establish rapport and avoid awkward situations.

More than 20 years ago, I was in a parent-teacher interview with two women who I quickly realised were a couple parenting the student in question; one seemed to be taking the lead more often than the other and she also referred to a 'he' who she would have to 'run things by'. I quickly figured out that she was the student's biological mother and that 'he' was the student's biological father and that the other woman sitting in front of me was also an active parent who had started a relationship with the student's biological mum when the student was in primary school. I worked all this out within the first five minutes of a 10-minute parent-teacher interview. It was clear that this young person had three very loving and involved parents. It would have helped me immensely to know more about the student's parents before the interview began because I would have felt more relaxed knowing who was who and not wanting to inadvertently offend anyone. I was 23 years old at the time.

Sometimes I discover that a student's parents had a tough divorce and I can sense the tension, but don't know what's going on. I have made it a habit to ask students who will be attending the parent-teacher interview. Information is power and the more information you have, the more easily you can manage situations that may arise to maximise the chances of a successful interview. Students reveal so much when you ask simple questions like:

"Who is coming to the interview?" and

"What do they like to be called?"

I'm so grateful I developed this habit because it has helped me on numerous occasions.

Sometimes parents come to parent-teacher interviews with something they want to tell you which is not so positive. You try hard to use your active listening skills. You are calm, reasonable and professional, and still they want to blame you, tell you that you are wrong or complain about something. In these cases, I recommend using the following script – or a variation of it:

> *"I understand and I am so sorry you feel that way. I will ask my Assistant Principal or Head Teacher to contact you as soon as possible to discuss this issue with you. I have another interview now, so I must move on. My apologies."*

Most people accept that and let you welcome your next interview without any hassles. On rare occasions, there are parents who want to keep talking. In this instance, I always find it useful to have another teacher nearby who can help me to encourage the parent to move on. Sticking to the time limit is vital in parent-teacher interviews. I find it helpful to use body language to emphasise that the interview is at an end. If I politely thank them for their time and stand up as I am doing this, people are more likely to realise that they need to move on. In pre-COVID-19 times, I used to shake hands. Attempting to shake someone's hand seems rude now! If the interview is being conducted online, this strategy still works, just add:

> *"My next interview is in the waiting room so I must let them in."*

I ask students to tell their parents that 'Ms' sticks to the time limits so she can be fair to everyone; I also reinforce that with parents, whether they be in IRL or online interviews. If you don't do this, it becomes very difficult for you as the row of dominoes fall and you find parents becoming resentful that their interview was pushed back because the person before them was late. You may find yourself apologising to 15–20 parents/carers for running late, and later to 15–20 colleagues whose interview schedule was also affected, whereas if you had stuck to the time limit with the first parent, then there would be only one person feeling put out because they wanted to talk for longer than the time they were allocated.

I think of parent-teacher interviews as Student Performance Evaluations. That's what I tell students when I ask them to complete an evaluation of their performance in the semester. I often make a questionnaire, print it on coloured paper (different colour for each class) and ask them to fill it out in the week leading up to the interviews. I try to make it easy to answer and as fun as possible. Sometimes we set goals using colourful Post-it notes. It's hard to be reflective and if we don't design regular low-stakes tasks for students to practise being reflective from an early age, by the time they get to the Senior years of schooling, they can just clam up and be resistant to taking ownership of their learning.

Before completing the questionnaire, we discuss what they learned, how best they learned and what goals they set for themselves in the next semester. During the semester we try to collect print and digital portfolio work samples to show parents. I give students time to organise their print work samples and digital work samples in a way that suits them and best reflects their achievements. Lastly, I write and print a list of 'Things we can do at home to help our learning...' for each year group/class. I've built these generic lists of advice over the years and I alter them each year, as needed.

Parent-teacher interviews potentially involve three and a half to four hours of talking, which can be hard on your voice and your brain. The more sustainable teaching approach is to arrange each interview in such a way that you target your talking time to the essentials. All parents who attend interviews ask how they can help their child at home, so why should I repeat the same advice each time when I can give it to them on a lovely, coloured slip of paper? That then gives me time and energy to give what I call 'highlighted advice'. It's kind of like the number one piece of advice for this student. I print my interview schedule and then organise all these materials in order of interview time. I place them next to me, with my laptop. I also have spare pens and Post-it notes for parents to write down anything they want to note down.

I think it's really helpful – for them and for me – when students join their parents in the interview. It saves so much time and helps everyone to be on the same page. I think they should be called Learning Conversations. It's wonderful to see the smile of pride on a student's face when you praise them in front of their parents and the acknowledgment that you may be right when you suggest strategies for improving an area of weakness. You can really bridge the gaps between the learning from home context and the learning at school context when you are all sitting down IRL or virtually together. Also, when you share the student's own reflection and compare/contrast it to your evaluation of their progress, it opens opportunities to discuss their strengths and areas for improvement.

If the student is present in the interview, I always open by asking what they are most proud of achieving during the term or semester and then, based on their responses, I coach them through reflecting on their strengths and weaknesses. We share work samples with their parents/carers and work on strategies for them to improve in the next six months. If a student or parent asks me to follow up something like a referral to the Learning Support team, email to the Deputy asking for advice or even a list of recommended reading, then I write it in a new entry on the Notes app on my iPhone and email it to myself at the end of the interviews that night. That way, I have my 'To-do' list to follow up straight away the next day and I'm not struggling to remember whether it was Parent G or Parent W who wanted that Learning Support referral. If the student is present in the interview, I try to encourage them to open up and take ownership of their learning to the extent that is appropriate for their age and individual circumstances. I might start with:

"How do you feel you are doing in class, <insert student's name>?"

I find this a super-helpful approach to take because it puts the onus on them to take responsibility, within the structures of school and home environment. No student will ever improve because I tell them to. No student will ever improve because their parent/carer tells them to. A student will improve when they are interested enough to find out how they can make a change in what they think, say or do and then curious enough to try. They will also improve when they can see how it will benefit them in practical ways – when they can see the connection between what they do in lessons and the bigger world in which they live. This creates a culture of responsibility and ownership in the classes I teach. Change doesn't happen without ownership and enough curiosity to take risks.

Most parent-teacher interviews are a wonderful opportunity to get to know more about the student you teach and how to help them with their learning. At the time they may not feel like it because they can be intense but, in retrospect, they're an efficient way to meet lots of families in a short amount of time and find out information about a student's home context that would be more difficult to discover otherwise.

Sometimes parent-teacher interviews can be unexpected, like the time a father brought along his new, much younger partner, and spent the whole interview enthusiastically stroking her thigh and she kept trying to fend him off. It was obvious. She and I were both so embarrassed. I tried to keep a straight face and continue talking. Thankfully, the student wasn't present to witness his dad's public display of affection.

Sometimes parents will disclose personal information in a parent-teacher interview. This may include issues of depression, anxiety, self-harm, suicidal ideation and domestic violence. It can be confronting for you, as the teacher. On the one hand, you're happy that they see you as empathetic and supportive and trust you enough to share with you. But you aren't their doctor or psychologist – you have mandatory reporting obligations through child-protection protocols, and you want to keep to your interview schedule so that you respect everyone's time. In situations like these, I gently ask if myself, a Deputy or someone else at the school can call them tomorrow to follow up on ways we can help. If the need is more urgent and the parent needs to continue the conversation now, I ask them whether I can outline their concern to the Deputy or Principal and they can have a quick chat with them because, unfortunately, I've run out of time and have other parents scheduled for interviews.

Just like I do with parent phone calls, I've referred them to someone who has the expertise and time to help them with their concern. I have respected my boundaries and behaved in a more sustainable way for me.

> **It can feel good to unburden yourself to a sympathetic listening ear but, equally, it can be traumatic for people to continually tell their story to others, so finding them the right person at the right time is vital.**

If the parent says they don't want me to refer them to anyone, but the issue is one that is mandatory to report, I follow it up by confidentially talking to the Principal and following the protocols.

Reports

Reporting can be a stressful time sucker if you aren't prepared. We have a legal obligation to formally report to parents twice per year. What saves me time and energy is:

- Keeping regular assessment records – grade/mark book, written observations on student progress, etc
- Collating student work samples in print and/or digital folders

- Starting the process as early as possible
- Following the school's report-writing style guide or, if there isn't one, knowing what my Head Teacher or report-editing buddy expects
- Using an online reporting system's comment banks
- Keeping a backup copy

I then organise this information in alphabetical order so I can refer to this data as I write. I know it may sound over-organised, but it's super-efficient when I start clicking boxes and typing comments into our online reporting software. I don't have to search for any information and, most importantly, I can avoid the temptation to be distracted by anyone or anything. It's always easier to write reports at school, but there are times when I need to write them at home, and there are lots of distractions like family, friends and social media. Scrolling Instagram, TikTok, Facebook or whatever can see you hurtling through a time-sucking black hole, which sees you three coffees down and the clock saying 1am. I turn my phone off or, at the very least, put it on airplane mode. I feel boring saying it, but in my experience, it's essential: forward-thinking and organisation will save you time and energy.

Report comments are a unique writing form. In high school you usually have approximately 600–800 characters to 'sum up' a student's progress in a subject in a semester. In some education sectors report comments are an official, written record of a student's progress. In other education contexts they no longer include personalised subject-based comments on the report at all, just grades and/or marks.

If you are required to write personalised report comments, basic principles include report on what students have achieved, write clearly and concisely and phrase comments constructively. Avoid dropping bombshells on parents without warning. It shouldn't be the first time a parent hears that their child hasn't been handing in homework tasks or that they are rarely cooperative in class. There needs to be phone calls or emails home about these behaviours before the report is written. A report isn't the right forum for you to air your frustration at a student's uncooperative actions or behaviour. Try to be objective and use neutral language, avoiding any emotional phrases. There is a fine art to assessing a student's progress in a way that will positively motivate them to make a change. If you tip too far one way, they may just believe it's pointless to try, attempt to reinforce your opinion of them or take whatever badge they believe you've branded them with and live up to it.

> **Being a sustainable teacher involves thinking ahead to avoid potholes.**

A giant pothole that's to be avoided at all costs is either not knowing or ignoring your school's report-writing style guide. Usually, there is a style guide that a Curriculum Coordinator or Deputy makes available, so teachers know the Senior Executive's expectations about how reports are meant to be written. It's the little things that can be so incredibly time-consuming to correct after you have written the reports. Things like 'year 10' or 'Year 10'; 'Trial HSC', 'Trial H.S.C.' or 'Trial Higher School Certificate'; another is 'exams' or 'examinations'. I'm warning you now because I've been caught out before and had to spend ages making corrections. One way to learn about a school's report-writing style is to ask colleagues for a copy of report comments they wrote the previous year. You can then use these models to shape your own reports.

Teacher tips

- "When I start at a new school, I always take a drive around the area to become familiar with the local attractions, shops and demographic of the community. Being able to reference locality with my students helps to enhance my credibility with them and also to build stronger connections." Marnie T – English teacher

- "Calling parents about behaviour helps nine out of 10 times. It allows you to forge a relationship with the parent, hopefully see a change in the behaviour and get to know the why behind some problematic issues. I've called up a parent before after being sworn at by a student, and they let me know about family issues that were going on and making the student act out of sorts. Making the time to contact home can pay dividends. Just make sure you approach it with compassion, even if you feel rage surging inside you; understanding the why of the behaviour doesn't excuse it, but it can really help you process it." Belinda R – English teacher

- "Switch up your skills – look for a niche and fill it! When I was at a boys' school I hated supervising sport, so I took a course and introduced theatre sports!" Bernardine B – Senior Education Officer

ENERGY

Google says 'to energise' is to share your vitality and enthusiasm with something or someone. The challenge is that you can't do that without regularly replenishing your own energy sources. There is no national database that records how many teachers leave the profession, but it's estimated 30–50% of teachers leave the profession within the first five years, according to University of Melbourne academics Dr Dadvand and Dr Dawborn-Gundlach (2020). The reasons why people feel they have no choice but to leave teaching are complex and personal. Of those I know who have left, none said it was because they didn't enjoy teaching young people. The pressures that led to them making this decision were multifaceted, involving issues such as excessive workload, student welfare issues, challenging student behaviours and the burden of overwhelming administration. They tried to put on their own oxygen mask first and replenish their energy sources, but it just didn't work out for them.

I have the greatest respect for anyone who makes such a tough decision. I don't want to suggest that I have all the answers. Life isn't a recipe and that's never truer of the life of a teacher. It's messy and everyone has their own brand of messy to manage. What I do know, for sure, is that if you can weave some of these energy-conservation strategies into your daily life, you have a greater chance of becoming a sustainable teacher who thrives in this profession.

Food and water

Teaching is a physical and emotional job. If you aren't working towards being your healthiest self, then things will start to hurt. One of the best pieces of advice I ever received was, "Drink regularly!". It was a Friday afternoon at the pub in my first year of teaching (pre-2000s), so I thought they meant wine or beer, but no, I got a long lecture on the benefits of water! In an average high school, you may spend two to three hours teaching in a classroom of 30 students and you're nowhere near a water source.

Moving around and talking regularly, chances are you'll get dehydrated very quickly. Dehydration causes headaches, then you lose patience more easily and then come the guilts because you're wondering what's wrong with you. When I taught in Singapore the importance of drinking water and electrolyte solutions was covered in our formal induction program. Turns out it's invaluable advice for teaching in Singapore's high humidity – my patience meter wore out more quickly than expected in such conditions, so I carried my own water bottle, long before it was fashionable. A 1L reusable water bottle is your best friend and some, like content creator Tinx (Christina Najjar), have gone further to call it an #emotionalsupportwaterbottle on TikTok. Maybe I should start a trend for #teachersupportwaterbottle!

#teachersupportwaterbottle

During summer I pop a Hydralyte tablet in because it's even easier to become dehydrated when classrooms have no air conditioning and the temperature reaches 38ºC plus inside. On days like these I buy Hydralyte ice blocks for teachers and Zooper Doopers for the students. Sometimes you're lucky to work in a school with air conditioning, but that's not guaranteed – not until politicians have to spend days in hot classrooms like teachers and students do.

> **Drinking water regularly ensures you feel better and you're more productive. No one ever told me this simple truth before I started teaching.**

If you're drinking water regularly, then you will face the toilet problem. To go or not to go is the question. If you get a chance, just go, because you don't know the next time you'll be free to do so. I think surgery is the only other time you can't go to the toilet whenever you need to. Doctors and nurses just can't take a toilet break in the middle of a three-hour surgery. In teaching you can't leave a class unsupervised to go to the toilet because you'll be breaching your duty of care. So, you need to make it a habit to go at recess, lunch and/or during a planning period.

Eat, please don't forget to eat. Hanger is real. Those Snickers TV ads with the tagline 'You're not you, when you're hungry' are spot-on.

> **In teaching you're busy, I get it, but I don't believe in being too busy to eat. It's a false economy.**

Eating regularly keeps your sugar levels and hormones on an even keel and ensures you're at your best to manage whatever comes your way that day. Feeling hungry can make you snappier than normal and teenagers aren't going to be that understanding if they feel you're being a beatch. They're more likely to react and then the situation escalates. This isn't a sustainable way to operate. Emotions are heightened, people lose perspective and time is wasted on something that could have been avoided. If you fuel yourself wisely during the day, you can make the best choices possible, in whatever circumstances you find yourself.

Packing your own lunch saves money and calories. I tend to pack a sandwich or salad and a range of high-protein snacks like a boiled egg, protein bar or nuts. Just remember who the students are with anaphylaxis and wash your hands carefully after eating your packet of cashews or almonds. Other people bring fabulous salads, rice paper rolls, wraps or even muesli and yoghurt in a trusty Tupperware container. Most schools also have good canteens that have lots of fabulous options.

Whatever works for you is best, but the more portable your lunch is, the easier it will be for you to eat it on playground duty, in a classroom while supervising a detention, in the staffroom or at a meeting in the staff common room. Teenagers are forensic scientists of personality and appearance. I learned this the hard way teaching in London when I ate a tub of yoghurt while supervising a lunch detention. A young man, somewhat of a comic genius, developed a whole routine mimicking me eating yoghurt. I was mortified to recognise myself when I accidentally saw the act in progress as I walked past. I wanted to hide. Instead, I clapped and congratulated him on his brilliant comic timing. Like all good comedians he had captured the truth.

More recently, I was working with a group of Year 9s and I ate some coconut chips. One of them piped up to ask me why I was eating pencil shavings. I tried to explain but I could see the ripple of laughter circle around the room and I knew it was a lost cause. A week or so later I ate some fruit jellies in the presence of the same group of students. One of the students started having a go, accusing me of eating erasers and then they all joined in. I showed them the packet and attempted to explain, but there really wasn't much point because they were having too much fun teasing me about the fact that I had eaten pencil shavings and now erasers! I just had to laugh and own it. Keep in mind that whenever you eat in their presence they will be looking and taking notes. Just always check your teeth and breath before going to class (mints are a lifesaver), because bad breath is a difficult one to bounce back from and it's best avoided. I have a Tic Tac addiction for this reason.

Avoid smelly fish – please, please, please don't pack it for lunch! Like a lunch space in any organisation, staffrooms are places where people let off steam and are sensitive about noise and smell. Most people aren't concerned about what other people are eating, but there is something about fish, especially tinned tuna, anchovies or salmon, that gets up people's noses. Literally. For your own sake I'd avoid bringing in tuna unless you want to be teased for what feels like an eternity. The fish thing is a common complaint because it leaves a lingering smell in the air. Most school staffrooms have a small kitchenette, but you're basically eating lunch where people are preparing lessons, marking and giving feedback.

You will discover other dos and don'ts unique to eating in your staffroom. Once I learned of a teacher's sensitivity to the 'pop' that occurs when someone eats a blueberry. I suspected I was the someone to whom she was referring. It blew my mind that someone's hearing was that sensitive. I wasn't eating with my mouth open and I'd never heard of such a thing. But I was new, so I read the room and I made sure I didn't eat blueberries anywhere near her again.

Sometimes, a staffroom has a kitchenette roster and everyone takes turns to ensure the washing up is done and the fridge is cleared of any potential Science experiments. In other staffrooms, it's more a case of everyone cleaning up after themselves. You will save yourself time, hassle and embarrassment if you work out what the culture is as soon as you can and just do your best to roll with it. If you make a mistake or unintentionally offend someone, I've learned that it's best to just apologise and do an Elsa and 'let it go'.

Exercise

I think exercise is personal, especially if you want to make it a habit. My sister is a fan of long walks before and after work with her dogs, Smoky and Indy. I prefer running, cycling, Pilates and yoga. Some people warn you that your brain will feel exhausted by the end of a teaching week and others how tiring it can be emotionally. But no one ever told me how physically exhausting it can be. You can regularly clock 7,000-plus steps a day at work. If I'm the fittest version of myself, then I can do all these things more easily and I'm far less likely to be braindead and exhausted by the end of the week.

There's an old saying that if you don't feed the teachers, they eat the students – metaphorically, of course. I think it means that if we don't help teachers to look after their mental health, they will become cranky with their students because of all the demands of their job. People who are in the caring professions like teaching, nursing and the emergency services often leave caring for themselves until last because that's who they are, and the demands of the job can leave little room for them as individuals.

We must put our own oxygen mask on first because if we don't, we will be reactive rather than proactive, say or do something that we regret and maybe even burn out.

What's key is to recognise when you need help and to get it sooner rather than later. There is a growing awareness of the mental health stresses that teachers face, especially since the COVID-19 pandemic, and there is a lot of information out there that can be hard to sift through.

Sometimes we think we need to be tough for the sake of the students, for our colleagues or for a million other reasons.

Taking a risk to be vulnerable and to get help when we need it is a sustainable teaching move.

There are lots of ways to get mental health help at school and in the community. You may like to ask a senior teacher at your school or the counsellor for some advice. In many schools there is a confidential counselling service like the New South Wales Department of Education's Employee Assistance Program Service, which is a free counselling service. It is independent and run by an organisation called Converge International (convergeinternational.com.au). I've used it before, and I can vouch for the fact that your information is kept totally private. There are similar employee assistance programs in each state and territory. You can also see a GP for a mental health care plan referral to a local psychologist and receive Medicare-subsidised sessions. The reality is that it can be hard to find a psychologist, so online services provide a useful source of help. There are so many available, but I would start with the ones that are closest to your school sector and geographical area.

Support services	Contact details
Beyond Blue	Phone: 1300 22 4636 (24 hours a day) Chat online at BeyondBlue.org.au (3pm–12am)
Lifeline	Phone: 13 11 14 (Available 24 hours a day) Chat online at lifeline.org.au (7pm–12am AEST)
Employee Assistance Program (EAP)	Call them anytime on 1800 060 650.
Kids Helpline	Phone: 1800 55 1800 (24 hours a day) Chat online at kidshelpline.com.au (24 hours a day)
1800 Respect	Phone: 1800 737 732 (Available 24 hours a day) Chat online at 1800respect.org.au (24 hours a day)

Sleep

Sleep is massively underrated. In my first 10 years of teaching, I was quite blasé about it. During the week I'd go out after work to social events, I'd work late preparing lessons, watch a movie or read a book until after midnight. For a while I ran on adrenaline and it was fun. I thrived on being busy and the excitement in trying to see whether I could get things done by a deadline. I thought I was like my friends who worked in non-teaching jobs, such as business, law or marketing. They seemed to be able to function on little sleep and power through their days and weeks with no problem. I was wrong. I was more like my friends who worked as nurses, GPs and police officers.

We all had jobs which involved interacting with lots of people in often emotional and/or high-pressure situations. We couldn't spend the morning getting paperwork done in our office if we were feeling tired. We couldn't unexpectedly take a day off work to 'catch up on sleep'. My 'office' has 24–30 young people in it and the staffroom at least 10 people. If I was to take a day off unexpectedly, I was still expected to prepare lessons in my absence and email them in. If I didn't, I would be giving my already overworked colleagues more work to do. This meant that we had to be 'on' at work – always. If we weren't, we gave ourselves and/or other people more work, and who wanted that? I began to realise that being 'on' all the time, at that high level, wasn't sustainable.

I've learned to prioritise sleep. And that means at least six to seven straight hours. Apparently, adults are supposed to aim for eight hours, but I like to be realistic about these things. If you have young kids, then trying to get six to seven hours will be a luxury, but for the rest of us, it's more doable on most weeknights.

Sleep is magic for any teacher. It gives you energy, patience, perspective and a calm presence.

Coffee, I'm afraid, is a poor substitute. For years I tried to energise myself through coffee and, as much as I love it, sleep trumps it every time. And so, I started to listen to all those people who had been talking about the virtues of sleep, such as Arianna Huffington in her book *The Sleep Revolution*. Most importantly, I started to listen to myself. More sleep meant I was less likely to fall into a heap at the end of the term.

One of the things I'm still learning how to do (I'm a work in progress) is to turn off all notifications and break up with my phone each night. Over the years I've gone through cycles of having fabulously healthy phone habits, and then not so much. I've made myself a digital detox routine. I turn off the Google Classroom notifications after 5.30pm. I've removed the Outlook app on my phone, so I don't get notifications and I must physically type in the URL to access my work email. That's a lot more hassle and so I'm less likely to bother checking it. Instead, I am training myself to stop answering emails after 5.30pm.

I got out my old alarm clock, which helped me to avoid the temptation of randomly scrolling through Instagram to view someone else's highlights reel because I was bored and/or procrastinating. I now deliberately charge my phone in the living room. I have a reminder set at 9.15pm to 'wind down' and begin a digital detox routine, which involves avoiding screens after 9.30pm, unless it's curling up with a loved one to watch a good movie. Mostly, this digital detox thing is working. I occasionally slip up, but surprisingly I'm getting better at this sleep thing and the payoff is that I'm more energised and able to be a better teacher and healthier person.

One thing that does help to keep me accountable is being open with students about my phone habits. If you have an iPhone, the 'Screen Time' data is so revealing about your unconscious habits. I stumbled upon Screen Time data when teaching Year 9 about social media use. I had no idea how much time I'd spent unconsciously perusing Instagram, Facebook or reading media articles online, in the evening, until the numbers were glaring back at me. It was hypocritical of me to be telling students that they needed a social media detox if I wasn't willing to do the same.

Weekends and holidays

Teachers carry a mental or emotional load that is invisible to everyone who isn't a teacher. It's the work involved in the planning, caring, teaching and following up for a group of diverse young people who are learning to navigate the complexities of life. In addition, they work in close proximity with a team of adults, also juggling the needs of their own classes, under the tight deadlines of a school day.

In an average high school, an English, Maths or Science teacher may have four Junior classes (Years 7–10) of up to 30 students and one Senior class (11–12) of up to 24 students and work in a teaching team of up to 10 adults. That translates to building relationships with a minimum of 154 individuals. That's before you add the Principal, Deputies, the office staff, maintenance team, the teachers and students you go to Sport with, the library staff and the teachers you're on playground duty with three to four times a fortnight. But those are small numbers compared to those of a PDHPE, Art, Music or TAS teacher, who usually has more classes because they are timetabled for fewer periods a cycle. So, on average, a teacher will need to build relationships with 160 people and be acquainted with, at the very least, 20–25 more people.

In the case of your students, it takes mental and emotional capacity to remember names, personal contexts, health histories, skills/talents, likes/dislikes and their interactions with other students and teachers. This all happens under pressure – both time pressure and the weight of student expectations.

As a teacher, you are constantly making decisions under pressure.

You need to be prepared, alert and effective in triaging any issues that may arise so that students can receive the help and care that they need. This takes preparation, concentration and energy – a mental and emotional load.

Student teachers, during their professional experience placements, and teachers in their first year of teaching are often surprised by how exhausted they feel at the end of a day. You learn that toggling between all the expectations you need to meet in a single day and still remembering to eat and use the bathroom can leave you feeling zapped. Often, I find myself advising them to leave some room in their day and week for the unexpected, some space for them to breathe and process. Over-commitment is an easy trap to stumble into. I've been there so many times myself. One new teacher who just finished her first week of face-to-face teaching after 70% of her student-teacher placements were online was hit with the reality of my advice when she acknowledged:

"I didn't realise how exhausting it is to be 'on' 24/7."

And so, I suggested re-energising during a weekend. When you're a teacher, you'll need some time on a weekend to do school stuff. Sometimes that will be minimal, such as checking your emails on a Sunday night; at other times that will be more extensive, such as writing your Year 12 reports or lesson preparation. What is vital is that you set a time limit in which to achieve those specific tasks and devote the rest of the weekend to rest, relaxation, recreation and socialising. You need to devote the time to the task that you have available and that will give the best result for the students. I believe it was Sheryl Sandberg in her book *Lean In* who said:

"Done is better than perfect."

I would add that is the case for everyone, except brain surgeons. They, of course, need to get it done perfectly. Two good friends of mine, who have each been teaching for more than 20 years, swear that, on an average weekend, you need two evenings and a whole day free of thinking about or doing anything in relation to teaching. That means no checking emails, no researching a lesson strategy or idea and absolutely no marking! The reason to quarantine this time is that teaching can be all-consuming if you don't intentionally 'turn off' and relax. Thoughts and ideas of teaching involving students, colleagues, lesson ideas, parents and/or compliance requirements will intrude into your weekend time unless you switch it off for a specific time period. It feels like there is never enough time to help your students and colleagues, and so unless you train yourself to do otherwise, you will find that more of your weekend can be taken up by thinking of and/or doing 'schoolwork' than you realise.

> **Switching off is a habit you need to foster to be a sustainable teacher.**

Oh yes, I've seen the memes and heard the jokes: "On holidays, again. I mean, didn't you just go back to work last week?". I've discovered there are two ways to conserve your energy when faced with such holiday envy from friends, family and random people you meet. Number 1: smile and nod. If you really must reply, then number 2 works every time:

"Want to swap jobs?"

I'm yet to receive an affirmative reply. After a quick "No, thanks", they usually start telling me how much they admire teachers and what a tough job we have, etc, etc... I really want to be blunt and say:

"Yes, teachers get more holidays than the average. So what? We earn them and we work on our weekends and during our holidays."

What many people don't understand is how much work teachers do outside the face-to-face teaching hours when students are present in school. The *Gallop Report*, released in February 2021, used research findings from the 2018 report *Understanding Work in Schools*, authored by Susan McGrath-Champ, Rachel Wilson, Meghan Stacey and Scott Fitzgerald, and ongoing research by the Organisation for Economic Co-operation and Development into the work of teachers. This 2018 report drew on the response of 18,234 New South Wales public school teachers, Executives and Principals, stating work hours for, "full-time classroom and specialist teachers – (are) on average 55 hours per week (43 in school and 11 at home)".

This was pre-COVID-19 pandemic and, anecdotally, I would suggest our hours have increased since then, as we respond to health regulations, rapidly shifting government requirements and the needs of our students, families and community. Teachers, Principals, teaching unions, professional organisations and government departments are working on ways to structurally change the system so teachers have fewer face-to-face hours and more time to complete the administrative and compliance demands on their role during school hours. This is a much-needed change, and if we can reduce the 11 hours at home by at least half, it will go far towards improving the working conditions of teachers, which are the learning conditions of students.

There will always be some time we need to spend on schoolwork outside school hours and that means some of it will happen in our 'holidays'. Many people are surprised by this. Holidays for teachers are different from holidays for students. The teacher holiday pie features more than an extended period of leisure or recreation that is the main piece of a student's holiday pie. Scheduling regular appointments like a dental check-up or optometrist appointment during a holiday period saves you work during the term. If I schedule an appointment during the school day, I need to create a lesson plan for a casual teacher (hoping one can be found) and then follow up on what the students did or didn't achieve and how they behaved. If I schedule an appointment during the holidays, I just have to turn up for that 30 minutes or one hour, saving myself a lot of time and energy. Some holidays will feature fewer work activities than others. What will always remain the same is that to be a sustainable teacher, you need to do some schoolwork activities at some stage in the holiday period. It is simply unsustainable not to.

Student holiday pie

Teacher holiday pie

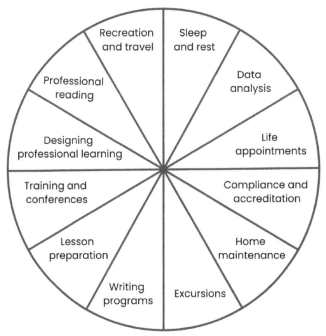

You can and should have that extended break of leisure and recreation, but you also need to intentionally plan your work activities during each 'holiday' to ensure you are on track for a smooth start to each school term. It takes some planning, some good habits and practice being in the moment.

One way you can make the most of the holidays is to plan ahead. Book those trips away as soon as you can. A downside to teaching is that we must take holidays in peak season. We don't get that option to take two weeks at a time when flights and accommodation costs are cheaper and there are fewer tourists around.

> **One of the best pieces of sustainable teaching advice I ever received was: get out of your head and get connected with the Earth and your body.**

So, whether that looks like a week at a friend's farm, 10 days at a beach hamlet down the coast, two weeks in Bali, hiking in New Zealand, a spa weekend, an overseas adventure or a road trip through central Australia, the most important thing is to do something that achieves these three aims and there is minimal decision-making for you. It's no accident that organised tours or resort holidays are popular with many teachers because they are a great way to travel to see new sites, meet people and someone else is making all the big decisions for you.

> **Teachers make hundreds of decisions on a daily basis and by the end of term it's normal to have decision fatigue, so if you have planned ahead and have a holiday organised (whatever shape it takes), it makes it easier for you to enjoy a total break.**

Most people can't afford to travel every school holiday. What's key is trying what my nan called a 'change of scenery' at least twice a year. Prior to the COVID-19 pandemic, I travelled, especially overseas, whenever

I could. I'm also fortunate to be able to go on inexpensive beach or desert holidays, as I've got relatives who live in both locales. Whatever you do, getting away from your normal routine, your everyday environment and seeing or doing new things will help you to recharge for the new term.

The transition between school finishing and the first few days of holiday is an important one. I've never had a slow end of term. They've all been somewhere on the continuum from busy to chaotic. That's just what occurs when you work with a diversity of people in a high-energy environment. What often happens is that I'm more likely to become physically and emotionally run down during this period, and when the adrenaline wears off in those first few days of holidays, I'm more likely to get sick. Adrenaline can be fun and exciting, as you race through all the end-of-term commitments and strive to get things done. But it can also be scary when you're not quite sure whether you'll achieve everything, and when the pressure is off and the adrenaline has dissipated, you're exhausted. So, I've learned to be kinder to my physical and mental health in the last week or two of a school term, to minimise the risk of getting sick. For me, that means healthy eating, regular exercise, sleep and trying to maintain my boundaries around using digital devices of an evening.

Create an automatic 'Out of Office' reply for your work email, and set it for the end of the school day until, if it's a two-week holiday, the last Friday of that break, or if it's the longer Christmas break, a week before you return to school. It's a tiny thing and for some people it's a waste of time, but I believe it's worth it because it is a sign for you and others that you are setting and maintaining boundaries. It helps you to teach more sustainably, as you are intentionally prioritising rest and/or slowing down. Yes, the reality is it's likely you will need to check your email during this period – but it's an option, not a given. I tend to write when I will be totally out of digital contact, for example, a hiking trip in Tasmania, and the period in which I will not be checking my emails regularly. It looks something like this:

> *Hello, I am on school holidays from 17/12/22 and I will not be checking my emails regularly until 24/01/23. I wish you and your loved ones a Merry Christmas and a Happy New Year. I will reply to your email as soon as I can.*
>
> *Kind regards,*
>
> *Melissa*

Turn off work-related notifications on all your digital devices. Those 'pings' or vibrations or messages are distracting, and they affect your health. During the COVID-19 pandemic lockdowns, teachers were receiving more notifications than ever as we tried hard to help our students. When teaching at school, as a teacher, you can respond to one question, the class will hear your reply and then the eight to 10 students who had the same question won't need to ask it because you've already provided them with a solution. When teaching from home, you will receive a notification (for example, Google Classroom message) from each of those students and need to reply. That's stress you need a break from. People I work with have my mobile number, so if something is urgent, they will text or call me. Everyone else can wait until I'm back at work. This gets back to that saying: 'Just because it's urgent for someone else, doesn't mean it has to be for you.'

Some teachers like to spend one to two hours a day for a set period of time completing schoolwork tasks during their holiday break. Others devote two to three days or, in the Christmas holidays, a little more, to knock off everything that needs to get done. What's key is a plan, because I have too many distractions at home and I can easily find myself down a rabbit hole of procrastination as I do other things instead. I plan around my trips away and social functions.

I find it's best to get the previous term's admin tasks done first before you focus on the next. I'm more likely to do the low-priority admin tasks on day when I'm feeling tired, as they don't require that much energy or brain power. I've learned the hard way to be intentional in my planning. I used to leave everything to the last minute, and that meant the last weekend of the holidays and the first one to two weeks of term were super-stressful for no great reason other than me failing to plan. It doesn't matter if you change your plan or you only get through half of the tasks you intended.

> Try to structure your holidays so you avoid a
> 'schoolwork cloud' hanging over you the whole time.
> It stops you living in the moment and enjoying the rest
> and relaxation you so deserve.

New teachers are often surprised when I tell them that I can't sleep the night before I go back to school, after holidays. Sometimes, I have nightmares in which I'm standing in front of a class and I can't speak, or I've forgotten everyone's names, or I haven't done something the Principal asked me to do and I'm in her office getting in trouble. I used to worry that I'd forget how to teach after the holidays, and I'd be really anxious, but I've learned it's a bit like riding a bike. It all comes back to you when you need it. I once thought that getting so nervous after returning from the holidays meant that I just wasn't cut out for the job. That changed when a Head Teacher told me that if I wasn't nervous at the start of a school year, he'd be worried.

> **Nerves mean you care and you're excited for a new year of learning adventures, for caring is the most important quality in a teacher.**

He didn't want teachers who were just turning up to go through the motions and who had lost enthusiasm for their job. He promised me my nerves would dissipate as the week progressed and he was right. So, after more than 20 years of teaching, I still get nervous, especially at the beginning of a school year, and what I have learned is to accept this anxiety as excitement and roll with it. Reframing my perception has made me a more sustainable teacher because I know that these feelings are useful, and I don't waste time overanalysing them and getting stressed.

Discover

When you feed your soul discovering something new or something you love, whether it's soccer, cooking, yoga or dancing, you become (re)energised. To be a sustainable teacher, with good supplies of energy to share, you need to regularly refill your stores of joy, excitement and curiosity.

> **If you don't have a passion or two, outside teaching, then you may too easily become engulfed by the demands of your job as it expands to fill every waking (and sleeping) hour.**

This overwhelming feeling creeps up on you. You find yourself cancelling a Pub Trivia catch-up on Wednesday night because you're exhausted after a tough day at school, or missing indoor netball training because you 'have to' mark Year 8 tests. Before you know it, life is about teaching and family and not much else. Sometimes family activities start to come second to teaching. So many teachers will tell you that they regularly cut bedtime stories short because they need to prepare lessons, or they have left their partner at a social function to go home to write reports. Then comes the guilt. The overwhelming guilt. Social media is littered with posts expressing the guilt teachers feel about missing out on time with family and friends because of the overwhelming demands of teaching.

Everyone is busy and has demands on their time, but there is something quite unique about the profession of teaching and that's the multifaceted combination of our work that can't be done effectively during the work week, under our current conditions. We're all working within our schools, teaching unions and professional organisations to create a more sustainable learning environment for students which, of course, is the working environment for teachers. There are underlying systemic issues that we can't, as individuals, change today but we can, as a collective, change over time.

What we can change today is our individual practices, habits and priorities to be sustainable teachers who enjoy our jobs. To enjoy our jobs, we need energy and enthusiasm, and by making it a weekly, daily and monthly practice to discover a hobby, sport and/or recreational pursuit outside teaching, we renew ourselves so we can give energy to our students, colleagues and the school community. We feed the students' souls, sharing with them wonder in life. Young people are inspired by teachers who do things outside school! By those who have passions and pastimes, which show that they, too, are learners who fail and show resilience by getting back up to try again. By those who enjoy the process of learning as much as, if not more than, the results. They're inspired by teachers who are constantly feeding their curiosity and trying new things. They're not inspired by those who feel overwhelmed, negative and disenchanted with their work and/or life. We all are in that space from time to time, no matter what our job. What's key to sustainable teaching is not staying in that space for too long, as it's exhausting for you and everyone around you. Such negativity makes everyone feel like they're stuck in mud.

Being intentional about discovering your passions and interests, outside teaching, is so important. When you plan time for your passion or new interest, you automatically prioritise it. It's not an afterthought. It's not something that can be easily cancelled or postponed.

> **You prioritise what you value. To be a sustainable teacher, you must value yourself first.**

At the beginning of each year, I revisit my life goals, set new ones and plan time for things that give me joy. I add to my calendar my outdoor group fitness classes, regular social events like Pub Trivia, volunteering gigs, social events, weekends away, theatre/music/art gallery visits, hiking, kayaking, time devoted to doing nothing more strenuous than reading or watching Netflix and/or time for learning something new. Sometimes I do these activities with family and friends, and other times I do them solo. Having solo activities that don't involve family is also important, otherwise – and this is especially true if you have children or other caring responsibilities – you feel that you're constantly 'on call' for everyone else and there is no time for you.

Recently, I asked lots of teacher friends about the time they devote to 'schoolwork' on an average weekend. The common response in those who loved their job and had been doing it the longest is the need to devote *at least* two free evenings and one whole day on an average weekend that is a 'schoolwork-free' zone. They intentionally make it a habit to avoid working during that time. All said that they'd learned the hard way to set and keep boundaries around their time. They acknowledge that, as teachers, we often need to do 'schoolwork' on the weekends or of an evening, but not at the expense of themselves and time with their friends and family.

Classroom teaching by its very design is flexible in many ways. We don't do the 12-hour shifts of the police or the 40-hour week of an office administrator. We can (usually) leave at 4pm to take our child to their guitar lesson or dentist appointment. We do have longer holidays than people in most other jobs. But that flexibility comes at a cost, unless we set boundaries, because we can find ourselves marking essays at 10pm at night, preparing lessons at 5pm on a Sunday afternoon while we keep an eye on our kids in the backyard, or getting up at 5am on a Tuesday morning to finish writing report comments due that day.

> **When we set boundaries and use as many of the sustainable teacher hacks as possible, we can prioritise time to discover all that gives us joy and enriches our soul.**

Daily, we ask students to be challenged in their learning and I feel that to be a sustainable teacher, I need to be learning something new on a semi-regular basis as it helps me to ensure my default setting is positive, practise mindfulness and to be the most empathetic teacher and person I can be. Of course, I am a work in progress, like any of us, and I regularly slip up in my pursuit of this aim. But it's the intention and the habit, which is the most important thing. This is why I encourage you to plan when, how, why and what you do to discover wonder in the world and stick to it! This will help you to maintain your energy for teaching and life in general.

Teacher tips

- "Start your day with something for you, such as exercise, meditation or gratitude. Even five minutes of something for you helps set up your day well and you will feel like you've already achieved something no matter what happens in the rest of your day." Clarinda O – Deputy Principal and PDHPE teacher

- "Buy non-iron clothes." Nadia S – History teacher

- "Try to take on some new challenges each year. As soon as you find yourself doing the same thing from one year to the next, you're bound to get bored. My tip: keep yourself on your toes – keep it interesting!" Michael M – retired English teacher

CONCLUSION

"Everyone else knows what they're doing. No one else looks stressed. I feel like it's all too much and I'll never be good at it." So many times I've heard early career teachers and teachers new to a school say things like this. I get it. I often feel like that when I'm struggling to figure out how to manage a new class or reach a student who is disengaged or unlike any I've met before. I try to reassure them that they've got this! Teaching is learning, and we often pay more attention to being the teacher than the learner because it gives us some sense of control. I've done it myself and still slip into that mindset if I'm stressed or not paying attention.

Years ago, a teacher looked at my (at that early point in my career) very organised desk and said, kindly:

> *"Melissa, you do know that teaching is free therapy for a control freak. No matter how much you try, you will never be in total control of any situation. Relax! You're doing well."*

I think I was about 24 by then and aware of my earnest love of organisation, but I was yet to appreciate the wisdom of his advice. I may have even been a little offended! In the years since, it has resonated. Control leaves little – if any – room for the reality that teaching is about interactions and that I can, and do, learn from the students and their experiences, ideas and values. If I try to be 'in control', I haven't left space for the unexpected magic that occurs when you interact with people.

To be a sustainable teacher, I need to accept that I work within the space between organised and flexible. I need to accept and embrace the idea that I will make mistakes and even look foolish because I'm human. In that space between organised and flexible lies the complex job of teaching in which I feel a mixture of joy, frustration, awe, surprise, humility, wonder, pain, curiosity, paradox, empathy, sadness, excitement, worry and vulnerability.

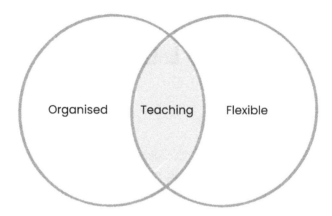

The main difference between early career teachers and people like me is that I've had more practice at making mistakes and learning from each stuff-up, with the support of a network of colleagues, friends and family. If you view teaching like tennis, you're likely to burn out much faster than those who see it like basketball. A Principal I know has a great saying:

> *"If you swim between the flags, we can support you to resolve any challenge in teaching."*

And it's so true. Challenges will happen, and if you're following the school's code of conduct and abiding by the teaching standards, people will be there to support you.

I may have taught more classes than early career teachers and I've had more practice at using techniques and strategies to engage the students in their learning, but I'm just a work in progress – the same as them. I am always unlearning and learning things about people and teaching. Professor Adam Grant, an American organisational psychologist, has written a fabulous book called *Think Again*, in which he highlights the power of rethinking and unlearning. He defines rethinking as a 'kind of mental flexibility'.

Every time I meet a new student or class, or start at a new school, I need to adapt to these new people and a new context. I need to rethink my assumptions and unlearn anything that will no longer be useful to me or the students I teach. Even if I've taught a student before, they grow and change, so I need to establish a new working relationship with them each year, and techniques I have used in the past may no longer work, so I'll need to modify my approach and negotiate a different way of working with them. That's the magical thing about teaching: the wonder of the new.

I'm not a fan of the notion of an expert teacher because it implies a hierarchy which I don't think exists in the real world of classroom teaching today. Some people think that a teacher who has been teaching for 10, 15, 20, 30 years is better at it than someone who has been teaching for three months, one year or two years. I don't think that's necessarily true, because it's not the length of teaching time that gives you the skill to be an effective teacher, it's more the attitude, personal qualities, understanding of context/s, knowledge, reflective thinking and effort applied that makes a difference. You can have those no matter what your age or experience level. Also, you can have them better developed with a certain class or year group than another or, when you teach high school, in a certain subject area. Some years I feel quite confident teaching Year 9, other years I need all the help I can get, and I have no hesitation in asking for it.

The problem I have with a hierarchical approach is that it implies that you become a 'good teacher' by time spent in the job. When you start out in teaching and, especially if you are in a more complex school setting, managing lots of socioeconomic issues as well as developing your teaching skills, you can feel disempowered if you buy into this belief. It appears that everyone else is skilled and you're splashing about trying to keep your head above water. I prefer the notion that I become more skilled at teaching a certain class as the year progresses, within that particular school's context. When I chat with early career teachers, I tell them that I, too, feel like a novice when I meet a new class. It's as I get to know the students and learn which strategies work/don't work with them that I gain confidence and become more skilled. In teaching there is always room for you to grow and change, no matter how many years you've been doing it.

Categorising teachers that way may also suggest that the people who have been teaching longer are teaching 'the right way'. I think a more sustainable approach is to actively value everyone's input whether they have been teaching for four days or 40 years; it's a hive mind in which everyone has ownership and responsibility. We then filter these ideas according to the school and teaching team's values and goals and, most importantly, we trial ideas that best meet the needs of our students before making them part of our teaching toolbox. This team approach and responsibility for, and to, each other is a way to build a coaching culture in which we all find joy and wonder in our work.

I like the sustainable teaching model because the focus is on learning and growing as you care for people in different contexts. It's about creating and maintaining strong relationships. It's about finding joy and wonder to sustain you when the days are tough. It's about working with the tension between organisation and flexibility. It's about unlearning and rethinking assumptions, beliefs and strategies. It's about getting comfy with vulnerability. Above all, it's about conserving time and energy for what matters: helping young people find their possibilities and potential in life through engaging learning experiences.

REFERENCES

Australian Curriculum, Assessment and Reporting Authority (ACARA) (2016), ACARA, viewed 12 April 2023, www.acara.edu.au

Australian Curriculum (2017), 'Learning areas', viewed 12 April 2023, www.australiancurriculum.edu.au/f-10-curriculum/learning-areas

Australian Psychological Society (n.d.), 'Better Access to Mental Health Care: Medicare funded services', APS, psychology.org.au, viewed 12 April 2023, www.psychology.org.au/psychology/medicare-rebates-psychological-services/medicare-faqs-for-the-public

Bennett, T (2020), *Running the Room: The Teacher's Guide to Behaviour*, John Catt Educational Ltd, SL

Brown, B (2010), 'The power of vulnerability', Ted.com, TED Talks, viewed 12 April 2023, www.ted.com/talks/brene_brown_the_power_of_vulnerability

Brown, B (2018), *Dare to Lead: Brave Work. Tough Conversations. Whole Hearts*, Random House, New York

Brown, B (n.d.), Daring Classrooms hub, Brené Brown, viewed 12 April 2023, www.brenebrown.com/hubs/daring-classrooms-hub

Centre for Education Statistics and Evaluation (2021), 'Cognitive load theory in practice', education.nsw.gov.au, viewed 12 April 2023, www.education.nsw.gov.au/about-us/educational-data/cese/publications/practical-guides-for-educators/cognitive-load-theory-in-practice

Commonwealth of Australia Constitution Act (1900), 'The Australian Constitution', ausconstitution.peo.gov.au, Parliamentary Education Office, viewed 12 April 2023, www.ausconstitution.peo.gov.au

Dadvand, Dr B, & Dawborn-Gundlach, Dr M (2020), 'The challenge to retain second-career teachers', Pursuit, University of Melbourne, viewed 13 April 2023, www.pursuit.unimelb.edu.au/articles/the-challenge-to-retain-second-career-teachers

De Bono, E (1985), *Six Thinking Hats*, Penguin Life, An imprint of Penguin Books, London

Dix, P (2017), *When the Adults Change, Everything Changes: Seismic Shifts in School Behaviour*, Independent Thinking Press, Bancyfelin

Downie, AK (2023), 'Could redesigning education end the mental health crisis? A paradigm shift towards a more relevant system', Medium, viewed 7 May 2023, www.medium.com/@andrea-downie/could-redesigning-education-end-the-mental-health-crisis-3c099ec869d3

Downie, AK (n.d.), Andrea Downie, Project Thrive | Well-being and Education Design, viewed 13 April 2023, www.projectthrive.com.au/andreadownie

Dweck, C (2014), Carol Dweck, Ted.com, TED Talks, viewed 12 April 2023, www.ted.com/speakers/carol_dweck

Fullan, M (2010), *Motion Leadership: The Skinny on Becoming Change Savvy*, Corwin; Toronto, Thousand Oaks, Calif

Gallop, G (2021), Reports, New South Wales Teachers Federation, viewed 12 April 2023, www.nswtf.org.au/pages/reports

Grant, A (2022), *Think Again: The Power of Knowing What You Don't Know*, WH Allen, SL

Harris, R (2019), *ACT Made Simple*, 2nd edition, New Harbinger Publications

Headspace (2019), Headspace National Youth Mental Health Foundation, Headspace.org.au, viewed 12 April 2023, www.headspace.org.au

Huffington, A (2017), *The Sleep Revolution: Transforming Your Life, One Night at a Time*, Harmony Books, New York

Institute of Positive Education (n.d.), Institute of Positive Education online shop, Institute of Positive Education, viewed 12 April 2023, www.instituteofpositiveeducation.com

Jobs, S (2017), *Best Product Launch Ever | Steve Jobs Introduces iPhone in 2007 | LeanFlo Inc*, YouTube, viewed 12 April 2023, www.youtube.com/watch?v=t4S6cHZD3x4

Johnson, L, & Bass, R (1995), *Dangerous Minds*, IMDb, viewed 12 April 2023, www.imdb.com/title/tt0112792

Lifeline (2016), Lifeline Australia – 13 11 14 – Crisis Support and Suicide Prevention, Lifeline.org.au, viewed 12 April 2023, www.lifeline.org.au

Lorenz, T (2021), 'What Is "Cheugy"? You Know It When You See It', *The New York Times*, 29 April 2021, viewed 12 April 2023, www.nytimes.com/2021/04/29/style/cheugy.html

Mccrea, P (n.d.), 'Evidence Snacks', Peps Mccrea, viewed 13 April 2023, www.pepsmccrea.com

McGrath-Champ, S, Wilson, R, Stacey, M, & Fitzgerald, S (2018), 'Understanding Work in Schools: The foundation for teaching and learning', *ses.library.usyd.edu.au*, viewed 12 April 2023, https://ses.library.usyd.edu.au/handle/2123/21926

New South Wales Department of Education (2018), 'Department of Education Code of Conduct', nsw.gov.au, viewed 12 April 2023, www.education.nsw.gov.au/about-us/rights-and-accountability/department-of-education-code-of-conduct

New South Wales Department of Education (2020), 'Audiovisual material in schools – procedures for use', education.nsw.gov.au, viewed 12 April 2023, www.education.nsw.gov.au/teaching-and-learning/curriculum/key-learning-areas/pdhpe/child-protection-and-respectful-relationships-education/evidence-based-practice/policy-and-procedures/audiovisual-material-in-schools-procedures-for-use

New South Wales Department of Education (2021), 'Controversial Issues in Schools', education.nsw.gov.au, viewed 12 April 2023, www.education.nsw.gov.au/policy-library/policies/pd-2002-0045

New South Wales Department of Education (2021), 'Positive Behaviour for Learning', education.nsw.gov.au, viewed 12 April 2023, www.education.nsw.gov.au/student-wellbeing/attendance-behaviour-and-engagement/positive-behaviour-for-learning

New South Wales Department of Education (2021), 'Student Behaviour', education.nsw.gov.au, viewed 5 August 2023, www.education.nsw.gov.au/policy-library/policies/pd-2006-0316

New South Wales Education Standards Authority (NESA) (2020), 'NSW curriculum and syllabuses', NSW Education Standards, nsw.edu.au, viewed 12 April 2023, www.educationstandards.nsw.edu.au/wps/portal/nesa/k-10/understanding-the-curriculum/curriculum-syllabuses-NSW

New South Wales Education Standards Authority (NESA) (2022), 'NSW Teacher Accreditation Manual 2022', NSW Education Standards, viewed 5 August 2023, www.educationstandards.nsw.edu.au/wps/portal/nesa/teacher-accreditation/resources/policies-procedures/nsw-teacher-accreditation-manual-2022

New South Wales Education Standards Authority (NESA) (2022a), NESA, nsw.edu.au, viewed 12 April 2023, www.curriculum.nsw.edu.au/home

New South Wales Education Standards Authority (NESA) (2022b), 'Syllabus development process', NSW Education Standards, nsw.edu.au, viewed 12 April 2023, www.educationstandards.nsw.edu.au/wps/portal/nesa/k-10/understanding-the-curriculum/curriculum-development/syllabus-development-process

NIKE (2018), *Look Inside Nike's New House of Go Pop-Up | Nike Chicago*, www.youtube.com, viewed 12 April 2023, www.youtube.com/watch?v=RXyvIYf1tWo

Nottingham, J, & Nottingham, J (2017), *Challenging Learning Through Feedback*, Corwin Press

NSW Government (n.d.), 'NSW legislation', legislation.nsw.gov.au, viewed 12 April 2023, www.legislation.nsw.gov.au/view/whole/html/inforce/current/act-1990-008

O'Leary, TM (2021), *Classroom Vibe: Practical Strategies for a Better Classroom Culture*, Amba Press

Parent Line NSW (n.d.), 1300 1300 52, Parent Line NSW, viewed 12 April 2023, www.parentline.org.au

Perry, B, & Winfrey, O (2021), *What Happened to You? Conversations on Trauma, Resilience, and Healing*, Flatiron Books, New York

Queensland Curriculum and Assessment Authority (2019), 'Australian Curriculum in Queensland', Qld.edu.au, viewed 12 April 2023, www.qcaa.qld.edu.au/p-10/aciq

ReachOut Australia (2019), 'Welcome to ReachOut.com', Reachout.com, viewed 12 April 2023, www.au.reachout.com

Rogers, B (2006), *Cracking the Hard Class: Strategies for Managing the Harder than Average Class*, Paul Chapman Educational Publishing; Thousand Oaks, Calif, London

Rozin, P, & Royzman, EB (2001), 'Negativity Bias, Negativity Dominance, and Contagion', *Personality and Social Psychology Review*, vol. 5, no. 4, pp. 296–320, viewed 12 April 2023, https://journals.sagepub.com/doi/10.1207/S15327957PSPR0504_2

Sahadi, J (2018), 'How Sheryl Sandberg practices "ruthless prioritization"', CNN Business, viewed 12 April 2023, www.edition.cnn.com/2018/10/03/success/sheryl-sandberg-profile/index.html

Sandberg, S (2013), *Lean in: Women, Work, and the Will to Lead*, Alfred A Knopf, New York

School Curriculum and Standards Authority (2014), 'K-10 Outline', k10outline.scsa.wa.edu.au, viewed 12 April 2023, https://k10outline.scsa.wa.edu.au

School Curriculum and Standards Authority (n.d.), 'Years 11 and 12' senior-secondary.scsa.wa.edu.au, viewed 12 April 2023, https://senior-secondary.scsa.wa.edu.au

Schulman, T (1989), *Dead Poets Society*, IMDb, viewed 12 April 2023, www.imdb.com/title/tt0097165

Service NSW (n.d.), Home | Service NSW, www.service.nsw.gov.au, viewed 12 April 2023, www.service.nsw.gov.au

Sweller, J (n.d.), 'Emeritus Professor John Sweller', UNSW Sites, viewed 12 April 2023, www.unsw.edu.au/staff/john-sweller

SXSW EDU (2021), *Oprah Winfrey & Dr. Bruce Perry in Conversation | SXSW EDU 2021*, YouTube, viewed 12 April 2023, www.youtube.com/watch?v=uUAL8RVvkyY

The Neurosequential Network (n.d.), 'NME', NMnetwork, viewed 12 April 2023, www.neurosequential.com/nme

The Smith Family (n.d.), *Learning for Life* program, The Smith Family, viewed 12 April 2023, www.thesmithfamily.com.au/programs/learning-for-life

Victorian Curriculum and Assessment Authority (2019), Home – Victorian Curriculum, Vic.edu.au, viewed 12 April 2023, https://victoriancurriculum.vcaa.vic.edu.au

White, M (2003), *School of Rock*, IMDb, viewed 12 April 2023, www.imdb.com/title/tt0332379

Wiliam, D, & Leahy, S (2016), *Embedding formative assessment*, Hawker Brownlow Education, Moorabbin, Victoria

Woolnough, D (2022), 'Why people are spending so much on emotional support water bottles', *The Sydney Morning Herald*, viewed 12 October 2022, www.smh.com.au/lifestyle/fashion/why-people-are-spending-so-much-on-emotional-support-water-bottles-20220927-p5blcu.html

ACKNOWLEDGEMENTS

There are thousands of people who have trusted me (sometimes reluctantly!) to be their teacher. To each and every student – thank you. You have given me a gift – the opportunity to learn, share, laugh and develop my teaching and human-being skills. These ideas started with you and are written for the benefit of all those who follow you in a classroom: teachers and students.

I've worked with and learned from what feels like a million teachers who have mentored, argued and teased me into becoming my best teacher self. Thank you for the laughs, the listening and the long hours of collaboration. An extra-special shout out to the teaching team at Albion Park High School, especially the English and Languages faculty, Paul, Catherine, Frank, Todd, Neal, Christine and Suzi, and my new team at Edmund Rice College. You provided the spark for this idea and encouraged me at every step.

Thank you to wonderful friends and colleagues who read early drafts, particularly Gemma, Clare, Dionissia, Mick, Nicole, Todd, Belinda, Nadia and Jenny. Your constructive criticism and praise was delivered with wit and encouragement. To all those teachers who offered excellent advice for teacher tips, I value your wisdom and generosity. I owe a depth of gratitude to Summer, who is connection personified. From the moment I opened my mouth, her enthusiasm for this project knew no bounds. And she connected me with Andrea – who is amazing! Together, they provided swift and sensational feedback. Thanks to Michael, who told me I was an entrepreneur at heart and provided much-needed encouragement at the start. To Gilbert, your smorgasbord of book recommendations, wise advice and passion for words inspires me to think my way on to a page. *Danke* for your Berlin brand of encouragement.

I knew Alicia Cohen, Amba Press publisher extraordinaire, was a kindred spirit the moment she introduced herself. She just gets it. With her foresight, support and guidance, this book made it into your hands. A giant thank you. Thanks to my editor, Rica Dearman, who tamed the manuscript into shape, wisely deleting my adverbial explosions and pruning my overwritten paragraphs.

Thank you to my lovely parents and siblings for always encouraging my writing projects. Dad's feedback in the early stages was detailed as we workshopped just how to 'get it right'. Mum's regular check-ins and steadfast support gave me the courage to keep going when I was dancing with the Demon of Doubt, convinced I should give up.

Finally, thank you to my partner, Damian. I love how we give each other space to play with words. You give me strength to believe that my ideas and experiences deserve a wider audience. You encourage me in big and small ways and provide me with the most delicious K.F.C. (Kennedy-friendly cuisine). You check my overanalysis at the door with humour and kindness. And you share Bert, whose kelpie exuberance is the best medicine for someone who occasionally needs to get out of her head!

Oh, and extra-finally, thank you, kind reader. I value your curiosity in diving into this book. I invite you to continue the sustainable teaching conversation, wherever you make the magic of learning a reality for your students.

ABOUT THE AUTHOR

Melissa Kennedy is passionate about sustainable teaching. She is an education leader, published author, speaker and workshop presenter, who believes in helping people to find their possibilities in life through engaging learning experiences. Melissa leads an English teaching team at Edmund Rice College in Wollongong, New South Wales, Australia.

She created this sustainable teaching model to support teachers to thrive rather than merely survive. Teaching is a challenging and rewarding profession, but it's often misunderstood by the community. Too many people don't understand the complexities of the daily life of a teacher. Using the Principles of Sustainable Teaching, Melissa aims to facilitate change from within, empowering aspiring, new and established teachers to become more sustainable in their teaching practice.

Melissa's vision is to build a coaching culture in which we all find joy and wonder in our work as sustainable teachers.

To discuss how Melissa can work with you or your school, email sustainableteacherfiles@gmail.com

ASTROLOGER

Should Have Told You

Stuff Your
ASTROLOGER
Should Have Told You

The brutally honest truth behind
the bad traits of each star sign

DAVID & CHARLES

www.davidandcharles.com

Contents

Meet Alise

When I don't have my head in the stars, I'm a comedian based out of Brooklyn, New York, best known for my years of work writing the Betches Sup Newsletter and my Headgum podcast "Go Touch Grass," where I break down the week's internet news alongside my cohost and dear friend Milly Tamarez. I started my comedy journey ten years ago now, moving to New York after falling in love with improv in college. From there, I moved through the ranks at the Upright Citizens Brigade Theater, eventually joining one of their house improv teams where I performed for several very happy years.

During that time, I also worked on my stand-up and solo career, developing my original live comedy show "The Roast of Your Teenage Self," which toured the country to sold-out crowds and has been featured annually as part of the New York Comedy Festival. It is there that I developed a penchant for light-hearted roasting that eventually led to this book. I truly believe that setting aside time to laugh at ourselves and make light of our shortcomings is one of the best and most healing things a person can do.

In fact, writing the Taurus chapter of this book helped me get out of a rut and move on from a job that was no longer serving me. By roasting myself, I actually helped myself.

In addition to my stage career, I've also been a working actress in film and television for several years, having appeared on shows like Hulu's *Difficult People*, *The Marvelous Mrs. Maisel*, and Stephen Colbert's *Tooning Out The News*. If you can't already tell by the length of this bio, I'm a writer whose work has appeared on Betches, Reductress, PureWow, and Jezebel and in the comedy anthology Notes From The Bathroom Line. My adult puzzle book *Hello, I'm a F****** Puzzle Genius* was released in 2020 and my first astrology book *Zodiac Connections* was released with Thunder Bay Press in 2023. I got my start in astrology while writing for Betches, covering their weekly horoscopes and eventually moving on to write their weekly astrology newsletter, "Blame it On Retrograde."

The road from comedy writer and actress to astrologer hasn't been the most direct, but I've certainly enjoyed the ride. Like many others in my age group (millennial and proud), I started getting interested in astrology several years ago as a diversion from some of the more stressful aspects of my life. Rather than seeing my natal chart, star sign, or horoscope as a prescription to be followed, I've always viewed astrology as an interesting framework through which to view the world. By looking to my star sign (Taurus, by the way) or reviewing my birth chart, I've found that what I'm really thinking about is myself, looking to the future that I'd like to build, and the values that drive what I do.

Also, it's fun! And—despite what I say in this book about my star sign being boring—I do love fun. I hope you have as much fun being roasted by this book as I did writing it. Now if you'll excuse me, I have to get back to work. Like I said, I'm a Taurus.

Alise

Introduction

Greetings stargazer

If you're reading this book, chances are you've decided you need to be taken down a peg or two. Or you're so baffled by the thought that anyone could have anything bad to say about you that you had to pick up this book and watch someone try (*cough*Leo*cough*). Either way, you're welcome.

In these pages you will not find your typical astrological breakdown of the signs, which tends to focus on all the great things each star sign has to offer. Nope. We've seen enough of that. In *this* book you'll learn about the dark side of each sign—from the rageaholics, to the self-important snobs, to megalomaniacal sociopaths masking themselves as "free spirits"—and finally get real about what each sign is *not* bringing to the table. Sure, it may sting to see your sign's flaws laid out so honestly, but at least you're in bad company.

Within these pages you'll find a chapter dedicated to each sign. We start with an overview of each sign's foibles and worst qualities, then dig deeper, outlining exactly what pitfalls they face at work, at home, while traveling, and, of course, in love. Is your sign a commitment-phobe destined to flit between short-term relationships and leave a string of broken hearts in their wake? Or is your sign a serial monogamist clinger who will waste hours—even years—of their life on the wrong person just because they can't bear the upheaval of a breakup? Turn to your star sign's chapter to find out.

Each chapter also comes with a list of five notorious individuals that encapsulate that sign's most nefarious qualities. We all need something to aspire to, right? We also include information about moon signs and rising signs because, despite what Big Astrology may try to tell you, the signs can wreak havoc on your life no matter where they appear in your chart. We end each chapter with information on cusps—those tricky little rascals born at the intersection of two signs that thereby take on some of the negative qualities of each.

Before you begin, it'd probably be best to define some key concepts for the amateur astrologers in the room. Taurus, you may want to take notes. We all know you can be a bit slow on the uptake.

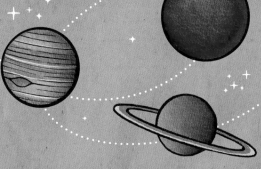

KEY CONCEPTS

Ruling planet

Each sign in the Zodiac has its own planetary master. A sign's ruling planet is key to that sign's personality, and its movements through the cosmos have a big impact on how it interacts with the world. Here's a quick primer on each of the ruling planets and the signs that do their bidding.

Mercury

Mercury rules over Gemini and Virgo and represents communication, changeability, thought, and reason. Mercury is all about thought and intellect, meaning its Zodiac minions are far more infatuated with ideas than people and always speak their mind. (Translation: They hurt feelings and don't even realize it.)

Venus

Venus is the planet of love and beauty and rules over Taurus and Libra. While "love and beauty" may sound nice, Venus's influence often means its charges are overly obsessed with both. These signs spend their whole life in the pursuit of romance, comfort, and aesthetic beauty, but it may all end up a facade. In short, they make great influencers.

Mars

Mars rules over Aries and symbolizes drive, desire, intensity, and aggression. This planet is named after the Roman god of war, so it should come as no surprise that it is combative, survivalist, and slightly animalistic in its influence. In short, the red planet's influence will make anyone a hothead.

Jupiter

Jupiter rules over Sagittarius and is all about expansion and excess (it is the largest planet in the Solar System after all). This gargantuan glutton is obsessed with having a good time and the concept of more, more, more. All that to say, when Jupiter is in the driver's seat, you might want to watch your wallet.

Saturn

Stuffy Saturn rules over Capricorn and all of the Zodiac with an iron fist. It is astrology's disapproving father and is all about strictness, rules, and regulations. It symbolizes structure and hates deviations from the norm. No fun here! Get back to work!

Uranus

Quirky Uranus floats through the
Solar System at a tilt and likes to turn
everything on its head. In modern
astrology it rules over rebellious Aquarius
(to the extent that Aquarius will let
itself be ruled) and symbolizes freedom,
change, and rebellion. When Uranus
appears in the sky, know that things
are going to get weird.

Neptune

Neptune rules over Pisces in modern
astrology and is the planet of idealism,
dreams, and artistry. It puts a hazy veil
over everything, making it hard to discern
truth from lies, dreams from reality.
Think you're getting work done when
Neptune takes the wheel? Think again.

Pluto

Yes, modern astrology still considers
Pluto a planet (sorry scientists), and that
planet is the symbol of transformation,
destruction, death, and rebirth. This
planet rules over Scorpio, accounting
for this sign's intense, slightly dark-sided
nature. It's not their fault! Their planet
makes them that way.

The Sun

The Sun in astrology represents the ego,
vitality, and self, so it's no wonder it rules
over self-obsessed Leo. It sees itself as the
center of the universe because...well...it
is! Hard to argue with that.

The Moon

The Moon symbolizes your internal self
and emotional power and rules over the
sign Cancer. It is all about inner feelings
and depth, making Cancers particularly
susceptible to changing emotions, doom,
and gloom. If you're someone who
always cries at movies, you probably have
the Moon to thank.

Elements

Each of the 12 Zodiac signs can be sorted into one of four elements—earth, water, fire, and air. Your element affects a sign's personality and how it experiences the world. Signs of the same element often see the world through a similar lens, while signs of opposing elements can have difficulty relating to one another.

Earth

Earth signs tend to be grounded folks who experience the world through physical sensations. If it's not right in front of them, they don't believe it, meaning they can be a bit stubborn and unyielding in their worldviews.

Water

Water signs are emotional people who experience the world through their inner feelings. Like an ocean, they want to go deep with everyone and are highly sensitive. Even the smallest disturbance to their emotional state can have ripple effects for days.

Fire

Fire signs are action-oriented people who experience the world through instinct. They are constantly on the go and hate the feeling of standing still. These signs are fun and exciting, but they can often leave others feeling burned out.

Air

Air signs are intellectuals who experience the world through ideas and thoughts. They love a good conversation, but fly away the moment feelings or emotions come into play. They can be high-minded and above-it-all, making them hard to pin down.

Modality

Each of the 12 Zodiac signs is also sorted into one of three modalities, which affects how they handle change. Some signs crave change like oxygen, while others would rather stay in the same place forever than make even the smallest adjustment to their routine.

Fixed

Taurus   Leo   Scorpio   Aquarius

Fixed signs are just that—fixed. They value steadiness above all things and require a lot of coaxing before they'll accept new ideas or ways of doing things. These stubborn signs are endlessly dependable—and frustrating.

Cardinal

Aries   Cancer   Libra   Capricorn

Cardinal signs will accept change, so long as it serves a purpose. These signs are action-oriented and love to be the initiators of change, particularly if it benefits them. Accepting changes brought on by others, however? That's another story...

Mutable

Gemini   Virgo   Sagittarius   Pisces

Mutable signs hate sameness and thrive off changes, big and small. While Virgo is all about making constant little tweaks in the hope of achieving perfection, Gemini is all about big, sweeping changes that upheave everything that came before. In either case, the person you talked to yesterday may be very different to the one you get today.

Opposing sign

The Zodiac is symbolized by a wheel and each sign has its opposite. While opposing signs tend to have very different ways of doing things, they are also typically complementary to each other and can make an amazing team. This is different from your sign's "mortal enemy," which is typically someone you'd have a very difficult time getting along with, even for short periods.

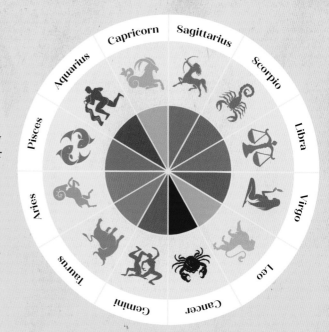

The big three

In astrology, your "big three" refers to the signs that make up your sun, moon, and rising sign in your birth chart (there are a lot of free birth chart calculators online). Your sun sign is the sign most closely identified with your sense of self, and it's the one you would answer with when someone asks, "What's your sign?" However, your moon and rising signs also have a big effect on your personality—sometimes for the worse.

Moon signs

Your moon sign represents your inner life. It rules over your feelings, emotions, and internal self. Basically, it's the version of you that only you know about because you rarely show it to the world.

Rising signs

By contrast, your rising sign is all about how the world sees you. It's your social personality and can tell you a lot about how you come across to other people.

Venus

In this book we've also included information about your Venus sign, which rules how you behave in your romantic relationships. If you're not connecting with the description of how your sun sign behaves in a relationship, it may be because you have a particularly pesky Venus sign at play.

Hello Aries...

Welcome to your burn book, Aries. Are you fuming yet? We're honestly surprised that a hothead like you would allow yourself to be roasted. But then again, you're so cocky you probably think we've got nothing negative to say. As per usual, you couldn't be more wrong. (Not that you'd ever admit it if you were.) Arrogant, insensitive, and impatient, you're the Zodiac's tantrum-throwing permanent toddler. On the bright side, at least you get to say you're number one…in anger, jealousy, and aggression. Your competitive side will love that.

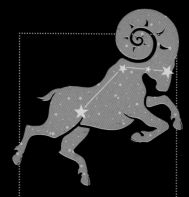

ZODIAC DATES
March 21–April 19

SYMBOL
Ram

RULER PLANET
Mars

ELEMENT
Fire

MODALITY
Cardinal

OPPOSING SIGN
Libra

MORTAL ENEMY
Taurus

PET PEEVES
Passive aggression, coming in second, slow walkers, waiting

5 NOTORIOUS ARIANS

Arians love to brag, so you may have heard them tout their connections to famous figures like Aretha Franklin and Céline Dion, but they might be better represented by these more infamous names:

1 **Giacomo Casanova (April 2, 1725):** Lothario who claimed to have slept with over 100 men and women across Europe. He also successfully escaped from prison on Halloween in 1756.

2 **Clyde Barrow (March 24, 1909):** Depression-era bank robber, murderer, and outlaw known for being one half of the infamous crime duo "Bonnie and Clyde."

3 **Lucrezia Borgia (April 18, 1480):** Femme fatale and daughter of Pope Alexander VI, Lucrezia has been accused of adultery, seduction, and poisoning, and is the subject of countless works of art.

4 **Butch Cassidy (April 13, 1866):** Bank and train robber, and leader of the "Wild Bunch" in the American Old West. His life was immortalized in the 1969 Academy Award-winning movie *Butch Cassidy and the Sundance Kid*.

5 **Vincent van Gogh (March 30, 1853):** Famous for works of art such as *Starry Night* but not in his lifetime. His self-portrait depicts the artist after cutting off his ear in a fit of rage.

Aries in a nutshell

Nice astrologers will call you confident, passionate, and an excellent leader—but we're not nice astrologers, so let's give it to you straight. Confident? More like self-obsessed. Passionate? More like hotheaded. An excellent leader? Only in the sense that you're so competitive you won't stop until you've reached the top (stepping on anyone who dares get in your way, of course).

I'd go on, but you've probably already run out of patience. Good on you for picking up a book, though. Brains over brawn isn't usually your strong suit. Just ask your friends, who are the most likely recipients of your half-baked, rage-fueled rants. They know anytime they take you out there's a high chance the night will end in a fight, usually with someone foolish enough to beat you at pool. We'd say it's a wonder they invite you anywhere, but they're probably too afraid of the epic meltdown that would ensue if you ever discovered they were hanging out without you.

Is this roast making you angry, Aries? Maybe you should take a moment to cool down before reading more. Or you could punch another hole in the wall.

HOTHEADED

Some may say you have a short fuse. We'd say your fuse is nonexistent. Aries are basically the Incredible Hulks of the Zodiac. You won't like them when they're angry. Aries can go from perfectly calm to rage-filled monster in an instant at even the most minor slight. Rams are happy to use their horns to butt heads with anyone and anything, but rarely stick around to deal with the consequences. Once they've calmed down, they move on like nothing ever happened. Their victims, on the other hand, are not so lucky.

ARROGANT

Pop star Demi Lovato once asked, "What's wrong with being confident?" Apparently, she's never met an Aries. What may seem like confidence at first, soon turns out to be arrogance for this sign. Aries are textbook narcissists, only able to see the world through their own narrow lens. Insensitive and inconsiderate, rams spend their life barreling ahead toward their goals, blissfully unaware of all the people they hurt along the way. Not that they would care if they knew. It's Aries' world and we're just living in it. If you can't get with it, it's best to just get out of the way.

COMPETITIVE

Aries is the first sign in the Zodiac, and as far as they're concerned they should be first in everything else too. This sign turns everything into a competition, and there's nothing they won't do to win. If they do, expect to hear them gloating about their accomplishment for years to come. And if they lose...honestly, we don't even want to think about it. Just ask their siblings why they can't even hear the words "family game night" without running for cover. This argumentative sign will never back down or admit when they're wrong, even if the right answer is staring them in the face. Probably why they make such good politicians.

Aries placements

Got Aries elsewhere in your chart? Then you've got a problem. This Mars-ruled sign has a way of dominating the personality of anyone it does business with. And you thought your sun sign was the problem...

MOON IN ARIES

Your moon sign represents your subconscious. If your moon is in Aries, that means your subconscious is impatient, flaky, and trigger-happy. If you've always wondered why you have a hard time sitting still for a meditation or spend hours of your day imagining arguments with strangers, this is why. No wonder you can't stand being alone with your thoughts. They're kind of unbearable.

ARIES RISING

Your rising sign represents how the world sees you, so I regret to inform you that an Aries rising means the world sees you as an aggressive, pushy extrovert with a hair-trigger temper. It's probably why so many invitations have gotten "lost in the mail." Nobody wants a wild card at their birthday party, especially one who might start throwing punches.

VENUS IN ARIES

Just because you're not an Aries sun sign, doesn't mean you're safe from getting burned. Time to meet the Zodiac's resident f'boy: the Aries Venus. Someone with their Venus in Aries thrives in high-conflict relationships. Though "relationships" may be too strong of a word. Fiercely independent, Aries Venuses will resist settling down until the bitter end, preferring to play the field rather than risk getting played themselves. They'll swipe on new matches all day, but when it comes time to meeting up, they go dark. Hopefully they have a library card, because they've been leaving a lot of people on read.

Aries in love

Aries' romantic motto is simple: here today, gone tomorrow. This passion-fueled sign is all about the chase, and rarely wants to stick it out for the long haul. A casual look at their romantic history will unearth a slew of hurt feelings and bitter resentments. Not that Aries cares. They're already onto their next conquest—I mean—relationship.

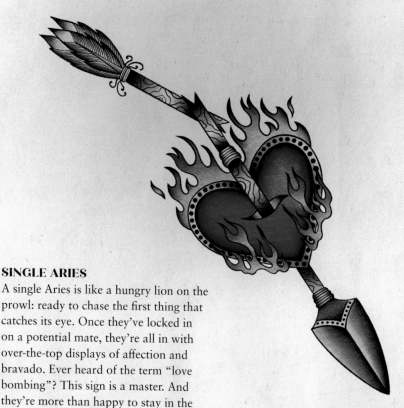

SINGLE ARIES

A single Aries is like a hungry lion on the prowl: ready to chase the first thing that catches its eye. Once they've locked in on a potential mate, they're all in with over-the-top displays of affection and bravado. Ever heard of the term "love bombing"? This sign is a master. And they're more than happy to stay in the "what are we?" phase of a relationship forever rather than make a commitment. Their notch-on-the-bedpost mindset lends itself well to a series of passionate flings that burn hot in the moment, but grow cold the moment their partner starts to catch feelings. Even worse, despite the fact that this love-'em-and-leave-'em sign isn't looking for anything serious, they also can't handle rejection. As far as Aries is concerned, they're the ones who should be doing the rejecting—usually just a matter of moments after using the "L" word for the first time.

ARIES IN A RELATIONSHIP

Think you've gotten an Aries to commit? Are you sure about that? This sign's wandering eye is legendary, and they'll always be more attracted to potential affairs over true partnership. Ever the hypocrite, this sign is also incredibly jealous and probably only committed to their partner to make sure no one else can have them. This impulsive sign is not afraid to go through a partner's phone, and loses their cool at anyone who dares show their partner interest (or even just basic pleasantries). Because of this, Aries' relationships tend to be drama-filled messes that blow up into acrimonious splits. In short? This sign is a divorce lawyer's dream.

Most compatible

Aries + Gemini

Fire and air make an explosive pair with these two. Gemini's constant changeability and go-with-the-flow attitude means Aries will never be bored, and their fire will always be stoked by Gemini's constant gusts of energy and new ideas. On the flip side, Gemini will love the drama that their hot-headed Aries partner brings, and doesn't take their constant conflict too seriously. In fact, they find it kind of funny. Get these two on a reality show ASAP.

Least compatible

Aries + Aries	Aries + Virgo	Aries + Cancer

Aries + Aries

This is a match made in the fiery pits of hell. We've already talked about Aries' infamous competitive streak, so when two rams get together they can't help but butt heads trying to one-up each other at every turn. In arguments, neither side will ever back down. These explosive fights inevitably lead to explosive making-up sessions, much to the chagrin of the neighbors, who are sick of hearing *everything* through the walls. An Aries-on-Aries match may go on forever as the two become stuck in a toxic loop of winning each other over just to break up (loudly, and in public) all over again. They're the epitome of the idea that just because a relationship can last, doesn't mean it should.

Aries + Virgo

When it comes to this pair, opposites attract... and then repel each other. Explosive anger meets slow boiling rage with these two. While Aries is all fire and in-the-moment passion, Virgo is a slow burn. Virgos prefer to lay a solid foundation, prizing stability and consistency above flights of fancy and spontaneous connection. Unfortunately for Aries, flights of fancy are kind of their whole deal. The patience required to bag a Virgo is enough to drive any Aries mad, and the more rams try to barrel ahead with over-the-top gestures and professions of love, the more a Virgo is likely to raise their guard. Ultimately, these two are better off as friends. Or even more likely, as frenemies.

Aries + Cancer

Aries and Cancer go together about as well as you'd expect for fire and water. Insensitive Aries will find themselves constantly at odds with emotional Cancer, a sign that's best known for taking everything very personally. But it's trust issues that will ultimately bring this match down. Cancer will be completely unable to deal with Aries' wandering eye, and unempathetic Aries will be totally unable (and unwilling) to stop. Cancer's need to discuss their feelings douses cold water on Aries' passion. While Aries wants nothing more than to move on, Cancer only feels safe if they can stay put and process. In the end, they should do themselves a favor and stay away from each other.

ARIES AT WORK

A moment of silence for all your coworkers, Aries. We don't envy them. You're not sure why you're always butting heads. All your coworkers have to do is agree with everything you say, shower you with constant praise, and never push back. You have a much easier time getting along with (aka sucking up to) your boss, but that's only to mask the fact that you spend every waking moment plotting how you can steal their job. Unfortunately for you, your big plans always lack follow-through. Coworkers know not to go to you for help or trust you with their ideas—you'll be at the front of the boardroom presenting them as your own by the end of the week. Even worse, you're that coworker who talks loudly in the common areas, microwaves fish, and flies off the handle if anyone dares to complain.

ARIES IN THE FAMILY

If anyone knows how to speak to your hotheaded, competitive side, it's your own family members. You're the one who can't get through a holiday meal without a fight, and you certainly can't get through a simple game of Monopoly without flipping the board over at least once. Even worse is when you win, which will lead to days of non-stop gloating. Siblings, cousins, and basically any family member in your age bracket knows better than to tell grandma about their accomplishments when Aries is around. They just can't help but hijack the conversation to talk about how they did it bigger and better, whether that's actually true or not. Relationships with parents are equally fraught, as Aries' problems with authority are legendary. Nobody can tell them what to do, even their legal guardian. Daddy issues abound with this sign, as they are pathologically driven to supersede the accomplishments of their father, while also desperately seeking his praise and attention. Frankly, you make the antics of the *Succession* siblings look like child's play.

ARIES AT HOME

Does a person live here, or a tornado? The Aries home is defined by one thing: mess. Aries tear through their living space like a whirlwind, and cannot be bothered to put anything back where it belongs. Unworn outfits lay discarded on the floor, half-drunk water glasses stay out until they leave a stain (of course, Aries forgot a coaster), and chaos reigns supreme in the Aries home. As a result, you're constantly losing important items like your glasses, keys, and wallet, leading to fits of rage and more than a few holes punched into the wall. By now you probably have a locksmith on speed dial. Roommates know better than to ask you to lend a hand with the dishes or pick up your old takeout lest they start World War Three. Or is it World War Six? That's why living alone tends to work best for rams. You love nothing more than to start a DIY project, but can never seem to finish them, meaning half-built shelves and haphazardly painted walls abound. You may see no problem with it, but guests and—ahem—overnight visitors will be horrified at the chaos. Best to get a hotel.

ARIES AND TRAVEL

You know those people at the airport who hold up the security line because they didn't take out their ID, left their laptop in their bag, have a pocket full of random items, and somehow managed to leave multiple unauthorized liquids in their carry-on? That's Aries. Aries are basically allergic to planning, meaning when they travel, it is always by the seat of their pants. They're the ones rushing to their gate at the very last minute with a bag full of random crap they threw together last night (meaning they're bound to have left something really important behind.) Worse yet, they make their lack of planning everybody else's problem, and are not opposed to getting in a fight with the gate agent just because a flight dared leave without them. Once they arrive at their destination, they dominate group activities by refusing to compromise on what to eat, what sights to see, and when to head back to the hotel. They're the tourist that shows up in a foreign country and expects the locals to speak their language, accept their currency, and generally cater to their every whim. Basically, they're a viral airport freakout video just waiting to happen.

The two sides of Aries

Aries is considered one of the more masculine signs in the Zodiac (hence the testosterone-fueled fits of rage), but all Aries have both a dark masculine and dark feminine side to them. Regardless of gender identity, which ram you get will depend on what side of the bed they woke up on that day. Here are the different (though still irrationally angry) rams you may have to contend with on a given day, or some toxic combination of the two.

ARIES DARK MASCULINE

When an Aries is situated in their dark masculine side, they are stubborn, impulsive, insensitive, and physically aggressive. When an Aries is operating on a hair trigger and seems to be out looking for a fight, they're situated in their dark masculine. Best to steer clear of rams on these days. Unless you want to end up with a black eye.

ARIES DARK FEMININE

When an Aries is getting in touch with their dark feminine side, they become self-obsessed, hypercompetitive, flaky, and bulldozing. These are the days when they can't feel satisfied unless all eyes are on them, particularly when it comes to romantic prospects. We'd tell you to avoid them on these days as well, but the more you avoid them, the more they'll vie for your attention. Best to just shower them with the praise they crave and move on with your day.

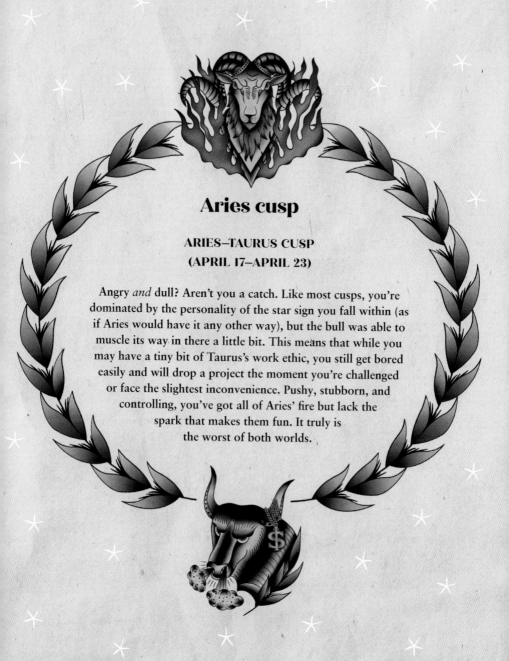

Aries cusp

ARIES–TAURUS CUSP
(APRIL 17–APRIL 23)

Angry *and* dull? Aren't you a catch. Like most cusps, you're dominated by the personality of the star sign you fall within (as if Aries would have it any other way), but the bull was able to muscle its way in there a little bit. This means that while you may have a tiny bit of Taurus's work ethic, you still get bored easily and will drop a project the moment you're challenged or face the slightest inconvenience. Pushy, stubborn, and controlling, you've got all of Aries' fire but lack the spark that makes them fun. It truly is the worst of both worlds.

Hello Taurus...

For someone so materialistic, you sure are dull. I'll give you a second to catch up to what I'm saying here. You're not exactly known for being quick-witted. Fueled by resentment and an insatiable love of money, you put the "bull" in bully in the most boring, average way possible. Some may call you reliable, but the rest of us know the truth: you're stuck in a rut. And you've got nobody to blame for it but yourself.

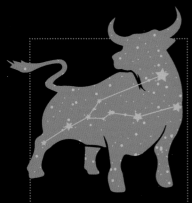

ZODIAC DATES
April 20–May 20

SYMBOL
Bull

RULER PLANET
Venus

ELEMENT
Earth

MODALITY
Fixed

OPPOSING SIGN
Scorpio

MORTAL ENEMY
Gemini

PET PEEVES
Late people, bland food,
being rushed, sudden
changes

5 NOTORIOUS TAUREANS

Sure, Taureans love to discuss how they share a star sign with the likes of William Shakespeare and Janet Jackson, but what about the darker branches of the Taurus family tree? Here are five Taureans who exemplify the worst of this star sign:

1 **Maximilien Robespierre (May 6, 1758):** Pivotal to the "Reign of Terror" during the French Revolution in which political opponents were guillotined for treason with Taurean efficiency.

2 **Catherine the Great (May 2, 1729):** Russian Empress who had her husband murdered to take power. An apocryphal story claimed she once had sexual relations with a horse.

3 **Robert Oppenheimer (April 22, 1904):** American theoretical physicist known as the "father of the atomic bomb" for his role in developing the first nuclear weapons.

4 **Sid Vicious (May 10, 1957):** Punk musician and bassist for the Sex Pistols, Vicious was accused of killing his partner Nancy Spungeon and died shortly thereafter, claiming they'd had a "death pact" to never live apart.

5 **Tsar Nicholas II (May 18, 1868):** Last Russian tsar whose death at the hands of the Bolsheviks marked the start of the 1917 Russian Revolution.

Taurus in a nutshell

Most astrology books will tell you how hardworking you are. They'll tell you how much you love comfort, sensory pleasures, and life's finer things. We'll tell you that you're a stubborn Scrooge, if Scrooge was too stuck-in-a-rut to even consider joining the three ghosts at Christmas. Your obsession with your own comfort blocks out all other concerns, meaning you are that friend who everyone knows will take way more than their fair share of the appetizers during dinner at the too-expensive restaurant you insisted on attending. As for temperament, it's the worst of both worlds for you, Taurus. Too nonconfrontational to get your problems solved, but too judgmental to let it go. You're opinionated, even when the opinion is dull and boring. Sure, you may have a nice house and a fancy car, but what are they worth if your guests are too bored to enjoy it with you?

STUBBORN

Even the most rosy astrological breakdowns will talk about your stubbornness, bull, but let's really talk about it. You hate change, even if it's minor or will make things better in the long run, which is why you look around year after year and find yourself in the exact same place you were when you started. Your inability to be flexible makes you rut-bound, plus you're too opinionated and overbearing to just let others live their lives around you. People can feel the judgment, and they stay far, far away. No wonder you always see bulls in a pen all by themselves. Their "leave me alone" signals are received loud and clear.

MATERIALISTIC

Sure, you got the sharing lesson in preschool, Taurus, but it never really stuck. As one of the most materialistic signs of the Zodiac, your money-and-status obsession borders on tacky. Just because something is expensive, doesn't mean it's actually nice, but there's no use explaining that to you, Taurus. You're that person who needs name-brand everything to feel secure, even if your friends cringe at the sight of the matching Louis Vuitton purse and wallet you take out to performatively pay for everyone's food. It may seem like a nice gesture, but everyone knows your "generosity" is rooted in jealousy and petty resentments. Nobody missed the fact that your ostentatious display of wealth came at the exact same time as Sharon's promotion. You're just not slick enough to pull off being a sneak.

BORING

Yaaaawwwwnnnn—that's my impression of anyone in your presence for more than five minutes, Taurus. Like the bovine you're named for, you're dull, plodding, and frankly boring to be around. Your conservative, traditional values mean there's no chance for surprises with you. Just the same old field, eating the same old grass, day after day. You're the friend who takes the same tacky resort vacation every year and models their wedding after Queen Victoria. Boring!

Taurus placements

While the Taurus sun sign is our focus here, having Taurus as any of your "big three" placements is probably the reason you find yourself stuck in the mud. This slow-moving, stubborn sign has a way of halting the progress of anything in its path.

MOON IN TAURUS

Your moon sign represents your subconscious mind, meaning that your mind is subconsciously sex-obsessed, materialistic, and adverse to change. If you find yourself thinking about the same two things over and over (usually sex or money), your Taurus moon is probably why. We'd tell you to break the cycle, but staying stuck in a loop is kind of Taurus's whole deal.

TAURUS RISING

Your rising sign dictates how the world sees you, and most importantly the first impression you give. So what first impression does a Taurus rising give? A resounding "bleh." Thoroughly unremarkable, a Taurus rising will have to fight to show off their fun side. Maybe on the second impression…if there is one.

VENUS IN TAURUS

Those with a Venus in Taurus will say they're looking for a partner that can provide stability and comfort. Those of us who can read between the lines will say they're looking for a meal ticket. The ultimate gold digger, Taurus Venuses will leverage their sexuality to move up in the world and find a partner who can afford to give them a life of luxury. Their partners can test this theory by uttering the word "prenup" and seeing how fast their beloved sees red.

Taurus in love

Some astrology books will say that the sensual Taurus is something of a stallion in the sack. They may even call you a sex god. We'd call you a sex robot. While you may be methodically pleasing both yourself and your partner with your time-tested moves, Taurus lacks the ability to connect emotionally with their lovers. Once the deed is done, conversation fizzles and Taurus's partners consistently find they have nothing to talk about. Unless, of course, they bring up work, in which case Taurus will drone on and on about the minutiae of their career without any acknowledgment that their partner is bored to tears, or asking them a single question in return.

SINGLE TAURUS

Are you a single Taurus wondering why you're still alone? Probably because you don't play well with others. Taurus wants everything done exactly their way, and will spend their entire life searching for a carbon copy of themselves. This stubborn sign will hold their ground on anything and everything, from how to raise kids to where to go out to eat on a Friday night. They'd rather let a promising partnership fall apart than let go of control, which is why they often do. Their superior lovemaking skills mean Taurus can spend a lifetime hopping from bed to bed, but a deeper connection will elude them until they learn to compromise.

TAURUS IN A RELATIONSHIP

Want to know how to get Taurus to commit? Just stick around. Once a Taurus has established a routine, they'd rather die than upend it. Long-suffering Taureans will stay in a toxic, spark-less relationship for their entire lives simply because they don't want to deal with all the change that comes with a breakup. Anyone unlucky enough to need to shake off their Taurus lover will find the task exceptionally hard, as stubborn bulls will just keep plodding their way back to your door (or into your DMs) for eternity rather than take on the task of moving on.

Most compatible

Taurus + Taurus

Is it any surprise that the best match for Taurus is...another Taurus? This stubborn sign refuses to relent on anything and absolutely hates change, so their perfect partner is someone who sees the world through their same (boring, unoriginal) lens. A Taurus-on-Taurus match will spend their days sitting on the same couch, eating the same food, and having the selfsame conversation over and over again in perfect bliss.

Least compatible

Taurus + Sagittarius	Taurus + Gemini	Taurus + Leo

Sagittarius loves spontaneity, change, and a life of constant excitement. See the problem? While the sexual prowess of Taurus may provide the initial excitement Sagittarius needs, it's their lack of stamina outside of the bedroom that will spell doom for this couple. While Taurus loves nothing more than a night in on the couch, Sagittarius thrives off adventure and trying new things. It won't be long before fiery archers move on from their earth-bound lovers, even if Taurus never does.

Gemini is an air sign that lives life flying high above the clouds. Taurus is an earth sign that prefers to stay stuck-in-the mud. To keep a Gemini's attention, a partner will need to provide a constant stream of intellectually stimulating conversation. Taurus would rather talk about the weather…again. The mismatch here is so stark that this pairing is unlikely to make it past the first date, which will most likely be spent in awkward silence. At least the dinner was good.

A love of materialism will draw these two together, and they may make quite the pretty pair, but their stubbornness will inevitably drive them apart. Both of these signs live by the motto "it's my way or the highway," and will absolutely refuse to budge when their worldviews don't align. This pair may initially dazzle each other with their high-end fashion sense and love of fine dining, but as soon as an issue arises where they'll have to compromise, it's splitsville for these two.

TAURUS AT WORK

Any Taurus who has investigated their sun sign at all will have heard that they're hardworking and dependable. And that's true! To a fault. At work, Taurus is that long-suffering colleague who takes on every task and completes it perfectly, but somehow never seems to move up in the world. Day after day, year after year, Taurus can be found at the same desk, eating the same lunch, plodding away. They may feel anger watching all of their younger, less hardworking colleagues rise in the ranks around them, but it's never enough to actually get them to do something about it. They'll stay in a toxic workplace for years rather than quit and change up their routine, even as they endure the humiliation of watching their former intern suddenly become their boss. Taurus loves nothing more than to be a cog in the corporate machine, and will spend their entire life quietly completing their tasks until the day comes for their tepid, lackluster retirement party—or they simply drop dead at their desk.

TAURUS IN THE FAMILY

On the one hand, a Taurus family member often serves as the root of the family tree thanks to their steady dependability and ability to cook a holiday meal. On the other hand, this tradition-obsessed sign will throw a fit at any hint of change, and cannot help but hold family members to their obsessive and conservative standards. Any attempt to change up the dynamic will be met by fierce resistance from Taurus, who simply cannot imagine why someone would want to live a life that's different from their own. They're the family members who always find faults with their sibling's new partner and can't seem to wrap their head around their artsy cousin's "alternative" lifestyle. Whenever family events come around, Taurus will throw their weight around to make sure everything is planned to their standards, which usually means doing things the exact same way they've been done since their great-great-grandma's days. Vegetarian cousin wants to introduce some new dishes to the holiday table? Get ready for Taurus to fight, push, and pout every step of the way. Mess with the bull, get the horns. Particularly when it comes to the menu.

TAURUS AT HOME

A Taurus's home is truly their castle, and they're happy to raise the gates and stay locked inside for the rest of their days. Home is where Taurus stores all their precious material possessions, so it's no wonder they take interior decorating very, very seriously. Much like with their wardrobe, Taurus has to have name-brand everything. They'll spend hours meticulously decorating their space, and then proceed to never change it, regardless of whether their wallpaper is outdated or carpeting has fallen out of vogue. Houseguests will find that bulls have curated a lovely, comfortable home for themselves…and only themselves. Guests—even ones who pay for room and board—had best conform to Taurus's exacting standards, or feel their host's wrath. Each item has its place and proper decorum must be observed while walking a Taurus's hallowed halls. Dinner guests should brush up on their manners before taking a seat at the Taurus table. Host gifts are expected, and they'll also be judged to Taurus's strict rules. Bring a bottle of wine worth less than $20 and don't expect an invitation back.

TAURUS AND TRAVEL

When a Taurus does decide to venture outside the home, they want to do it exactly their way, which is usually both expensive and unadventurous. They go into a vacation with every hour of the day planned, and cannot abide changes to the itinerary. Unexpected flight delays or changes to the plan will lead to a full-on meltdown, as will basic travel mishaps like a bout of jet lag or a toothbrush left at home. A Taurus is never going to want to go off the beaten path to check out an unmarked local haunt or take a risk on a cheap train or hostel. They'd much rather plod along the same path of millions of other tourists before them, staying in the same hotel chain where they've been accruing travel points for years. By the end of the trip, a Taurus will be telling everyone in their vicinity how much they cannot wait to get home, with a bagful of chintzy souvenirs and photos of themselves pretending to hold up the Eiffel Tower in tow.

The two sides of Taurus

Taurus is one of the feminine signs of the Zodiac, but all Taureans have both a dark masculine and dark feminine side. Regardless of gender identity, which bull you get will depend on a number of factors like stress level, proximity to home, and whether or not they got a good night's sleep. Sometimes it can feel like a simple roll of the dice. Here are the two poles of the Taurus personality, each one as stubborn and unyielding as the last.

TAURUS DARK MASCULINE

When Taurus is falling on the masculine side, they become a work-obsessed, sex-obsessed drone. Try to engage them on a topic other than work, and you'll find them staring blankly in response, or getting angry that you interrupted their daily spreadsheet analysis. The only thing that might pull them away from the monotony of the office are offers of food or sex, which will ultimately culminate in the bull rolling over to fall asleep without a word—unless you count loud, methodical snores as conversation.

TAURUS DARK FEMININE

When a Taurus is feeling particularly feminine, their exacting, judgmental side comes to the forefront. They become obsessive in their home life, and cannot help but try to bully family and loved ones into living life the way they think is best. Like the stepmom from hell, they impose their obsessive materialism on everyone around them and are unrelenting in their expectations of manners and decorum. Elbows off the table, you lout!

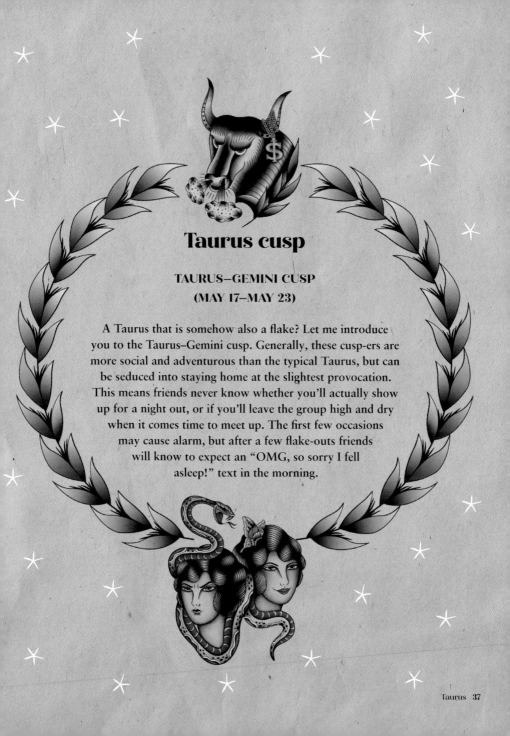

Taurus cusp

TAURUS–GEMINI CUSP
(MAY 17–MAY 23)

A Taurus that is somehow also a flake? Let me introduce you to the Taurus–Gemini cusp. Generally, these cusp-ers are more social and adventurous than the typical Taurus, but can be seduced into staying home at the slightest provocation. This means friends never know whether you'll actually show up for a night out, or if you'll leave the group high and dry when it comes time to meet up. The first few occasions may cause alarm, but after a few flake-outs friends will know to expect an "OMG, so sorry I fell asleep!" text in the morning.

Hello Gemini...

We're honestly surprised you could pay attention to one book long enough to make it this far. Though, let's be honest, you probably just skipped right to your own chapter. You are the main character of the universe, after all. You may have fooled the rest of the world into thinking you're smart by knowing a little bit about everything, but we know the truth. You're the epitome of the phrase "jack of all trades, master of none." Once somebody decides to dig deeper, your sparkly personality loses its shine faster than you lose interest in a romantic partner—or five.

DATES
May 21–June 20

SYMBOL
Twins

RULER PLANET
Mercury

ELEMENT
Air

MODALITY
Mutable

OPPOSING SIGN
Sagittarius

MORTAL ENEMY
Other Geminis

PET PEEVES
Boring
conversations,
serious people,
fixed schedules,
being interrupted

5 NOTORIOUS GEMINIS

Movie stars, dictators, and philanderers—Geminis
can count them all in their illustrious ranks. It
would honestly be easier for us to create a list of
famous Geminis who aren't in some way notorious,
but here's a sampling of just five:

1 **Marilyn Monroe (June 1, 1926):** Beautiful
actress and sex symbol of Hollywood's Golden
Age, Marilyn's magnetic sexuality led to
multiple high-profile marriages and affairs.

2 **Marquis de Sade (June 2, 1740):** French
nobleman and philosopher whose sexually
graphic novels gave rise to the term "sadism."

3 **Errol Flynn (June 20, 1909):** Hollywood
heartthrob, womanizer, and on-screen
swashbuckler, Flynn is infamous for a life
of hard drinking, failed marriages, and
legal troubles.

4 **Henry Hill (June 11, 1943):** American
mobster whose life of crime at the behest
of the Lucchese crime family in New York
City inspired Martin Scorcese's 1990
movie *Goodfellas*.

5 **Wallis Simpson (June 19, 1896):** American
divorcee, lover, and wife of King Edward VIII.
Their relationship eventually led to Edward's
abdication from the throne. The pair went on
to live in exile in France and were said to have
developed Nazi ties.

Gemini in a nutshell

You've spent your whole life being praised for your wit and intellect, but we're done with all that. Gossipy, devious, and thoroughly unreliable, Gemini draws people in only to leave them disappointed (and potentially heartbroken) just a short while later. Consummate con artists, Geminis will steal candy from a baby only to decide they don't actually want candy and toss it in the trash a moment later.

Think a Gemini is your friend? Not for long. Gemini friendships may burn bright, but they also burn out quickly, as this air-headed sign is always looking for the next best thing. As a Mercury-ruled sign, you probably see yourself as a top-notch conversationalist. In reality, you dominate the dialogue by waxing poetic about your favorite topics while simultaneously looking over your conversation partner's shoulder to see if someone cooler has come along. A roguish social climber, you tend to bring a "use-'em-and-lose-'em" mentality to your friendships, and your love of gossip means you've probably made more than a few enemies on your way to the top.

UNRELIABLE

What's the worst way to get a Gemini to do something? Ask them to do it. The ultimate commitment-phobe, Geminis are pathologically incapable of keeping their word. In fact, the more firm a commitment they make, the less likely they are to actually follow through. You'd much rather spend your life chasing the latest shiny object than be bothered with trivial things like "keeping your word." Coworkers know better than to expect you'll meet important deadlines, and friends are used to having you flake out on important events like birthdays, baby showers, and engagement parties. To be honest, they're not even sure you'll show up to your own wedding.

TWO-FACED

Geminis are known as "the Twins," so is it any wonder they tend to have two faces? Geminis love gossip, and their only loyalty is to their ability to tell a good story. Loved ones learn quickly not to share a juicy secret with you, as it'll be plastered across several group chats by morning. Forever the charmer, Geminis will make a person feel as if they're the best of friends when they're in conversation, then turn around and trash-talk them to whoever will listen as soon as they leave the room. You may be fun to hang out with at a party or a night out on the town, but your shifty sign will never actually show up for a friend when the going gets tough for them—unless you need fodder for your ever-expanding rotation of party stories, that is.

IMMATURE

Whether they're eight or eighty, Geminis spend their whole life searching for the fountain of youth and only finding Botox. Forever a slave to trends and fads, Gemini lives suspended in a state of arrested development. This restless, fickle-minded sign hates to be tied down by "adult" expectations like showing up to work on time or paying the bills. You may try to spin being a "child at heart" as a good thing, but those closest to you will quickly grow tired of your silly antics and inability to take life seriously. The childishness often gives way to full-on temper tantrums when you're called to account for your bad behavior. This behavior may have worked in elementary school, but as you grow older you'll find more and more people are willing to simply leave you in the sandbox.

Gemini placements

The Gemini sun sign may be the main focus in this chapter, but having the Twins as any of your "big three" means you may find yourself at the mercy of their flaky, unpredictable ways. This verbose sign is known for dominating conversations...and any birth chart where it may appear.

GEMINI RISING

Tell people about your Gemini rising sign, and they might respond by saying that's why the world sees you as witty and intelligent. What they're not saying is that they also see you as a shallow social climber who's not to be trusted. You've probably spent your whole life hearing about your "sparkling personality," but most people also get the impression that your shine and substance do not go hand in hand.

MOON IN GEMINI

Can't seem to settle your thoughts? Meditation leaving you frustrated and restless? You can thank your Gemini moon, which is characterized by a deep and abiding fear of boredom. With their head perpetually in the clouds, Gemini moons find it nearly impossible to live in the present. They'd rather spend their life losing themselves in elaborate fantasies, usually about world domination. Unfortunately however, you need self-discipline for that.

VENUS IN GEMINI

Got your Venus in Gemini? No wonder you can't commit. You're a master at getting potential partners interested, but your heart's teeny-tiny attention span means you're always battling your own wandering eye. Gemini Venuses are perpetually awash with romantic possibilities, meaning they always have someone waiting in the wings when their current relationship fizzles out. These placements love the start of relationships—when everything is fun and carefree—but will run the moment the romance starts to turn serious or their partner wants to impose expectations.

Gemini in love

We'll start with the good stuff, Gemini. You're a really good flirt. Like, really good. Don't believe us? Just ask one of the multiple partners you're probably juggling as we speak. Your double-crossing sign is all flirt and no follow-through, meaning you have no problem maintaining multiple romantic partners—or professing love to them all. Once it comes time to actually defining the relationship, suddenly your sign has nothing to say. What's that, Gemini? Commitment got your tongue?

SINGLE GEMINI

In many ways, a single Gemini is a happy Gemini. This air sign hates to be tied down, and would much prefer to float from fling to fling than deal with someone else's suffocating relationship standards. As a master communicator, you have no problem lingering in the "texting phase" of a relationship and never actually meeting up for a date. In fact, the will-they-won't-they of flirting is your favorite part of the process. Once things move from the realm of "what ifs?" you start getting bored. And once you start getting bored, you quickly make your exit. The ultimate player, Gemini has no problem charming the pants off someone one night, only to forget about them by morning. No wonder so many people have blocked you on the apps.

GEMINI IN A RELATIONSHIP

As the Zodiac's ultimate commitment-phobe, you may technically agree to be in a relationship, but you'll never truly settle down. Even when partnered up, you prefer to keep your options open, and any beau of yours will have to be okay with your penchant for flirting with anything that moves. Or not! It doesn't bother Gemini. In fact, you prefer a relationship in which a constant cycle of making up and breaking up is just part of the deal. It helps to keep things interesting—and "interesting" is Gemini's *raison d'être*. If you do settle down over the long term, it'll probably be with someone whose wealth and status helps to elevate your own. All the better for when you take half and run.

Most compatible

Gemini + Aquarius

Gemini's ultimate match is Aquarius. As a fellow air sign, Aquarius is too caught up in their own lofty ideals to try to pull Gemini back to earth, and their status as the Zodiac's resident "weirdo" means they'll always keep the Twins on their toes. This heady sign is happy to keep things intellectual rather than emotional, and the two can spend hours exchanging ideas about everything under the sun. Aquarius's emotional distance is perfect for Gemini, as they'll never get attached enough to be hurt by Gemini's wandering eye or complete inability to commit. In fact, they may not even notice when Gemini is gone.

Least compatible

Gemini + Capricorn

Earth-bound Capricorns are way too frigid and serious for light-hearted Gemini, and will quickly leave them feeling suffocated and restrained: two emotions the Twins simply cannot abide. Capricorn is all about commitment, which is something Gemini will never be able to provide. Even worse, Capricorns remember every promise and will expect Geminis to stick to what they say—a nearly impossible task for a sign whose moods change with the time of day.

Gemini + Sagittarius

This air and fire pairing is bound to be explosive. At first, they'll be drawn to each other's fun-loving lifestyles and ability to match wits. Plus, Sagittarius's recklessness will provide Gemini with the sense of adventure they crave. Unfortunately, adventure also spells danger for these two, as they'll egg each other on and inflame each other's worst tendencies. They could end up stuck in the makeup-and-breakup cycle that Gemini craves, but ultimately Sagittarius's tendency to call Gemini out when they're wrong will spell the end for this combustible couple.

Gemini + Taurus

Sensual, material Taurus may be able to attract a Gemini with their brand-name clothes and reputation for being good in the sack, but simply put, Taurus is way too dull to keep Gemini around for more than an evening. Taurus's total disinterest in intellectual pursuits will leave Gemini bored to tears the moment their initial attraction fades. As soon as the conversation lulls—usually moments after the two have finished doing the deed—Gemini will find themselves making any excuse to get out of Taurus's bed. Not that Taurus minds. They have work in the morning.

GEMINI AT WORK

A job? Gemini? Not for long. Your sign is not one for steady employment. Sure, your mastery of the skill of "faking it till you make it" means you often wow during the interview stage, but you quickly lose interest and disappoint your boss once it comes to actually doing the job you've been hired for. Similarly, you'll probably dazzle your coworkers with your water-cooler chitchat, but that great first impression will quickly fade once they learn about your real job: purveyor of office gossip. Once a Gemini finds a job they actually do like, their devious nature will kick into high gear and they'll double-cross and manipulate anyone they can to climb the ladder. If only you could put some of that energy into doing your actual job. But that would be way too boring for Gemini, who needs constant stimuli to stop from jumping out of their skin. This sign is more suited to a "non-traditional" job—con artist, influencer, and double agent come to mind.

GEMINI AT HOME

Given your long history of ghosting romantic partners, it's kind of fitting that your home looks like nobody's lived there in years. Geminis hate to sit still and rarely spend their waking hours at home, meaning their living space tends to look more like a hostel than a home. If Gemini does manage to decorate, their interior design philosophy can usually be described as…incoherent. Your preferred décor usually consists of an assortment of shiny objects that you've collected on your travels randomly scattered across haphazardly installed shelves. These magpie-like tendencies can make living with Gemini a nightmare, as housemates never know when they'll come home to another musty furniture item (or even a live animal) that Gemini has pulled off the street to care for.

GEMINI IN THE FAMILY

No matter where you actually fall in the birth order, you always want to be the baby. And what Gemini wants, Gemini gets. Especially since you know exactly what to say to charm the pants off grandma while simultaneously putting in the bare minimum at birthdays, holidays, and other important family events. Is your presence not present enough? Gemini loves to roll up to the family reunion and collect accolades for their own (heavily embellished) accomplishments, while also retaining almost nothing about what everyone else has been up to. Unless, of course, there's some juicy gossip. You're always the first to blast the family business far and wide so long as it makes for a good story, and your siblings will probably go to their grave waiting for an apology for that time you told the whole school about their little bed-wetting problem. As you grow older, the younger generation will love your silly "fun aunt" antics, but adult family members know better than to call you for babysitting duty unless they want to come home to a freaked-out kiddo (thanks to the R-rated scary movie you let them watch) who's hopped up on candy (in place of dinner) and up way past their bedtime (what bedtime?). Ultimately, you're happy to accept a perpetual seat at the kids' table rather than deal with all the responsibilities that come with joining the adults.

GEMINI AND TRAVEL

On the one hand, you love the idea of travel. On the other, you hate doing the things that are required to make travel happen like booking flights, finding a hotel, or—worst of all—packing a bag. In theory, your love of adventure should lend itself to being a good travel partner, but in practice you become immediately overwhelmed by all the possibilities your destination holds, while also refusing to be tied down by things like "hotel checkout times" and "dinner reservations." Rather than following a prescribed plan, you'd rather wander the streets of your new locale and just see what happens. As a result, you'll often leave without having seen any of the sites your destination is famous for but with at least two new international lovers who think they are your one true love.

The two sides of Gemini

Gemini is considered one of the masculine signs in the Zodiac, but all Geminis have dark masculine and dark feminine tendencies within them. No matter where you fall on the gender spectrum, you may find yourself flipping between either of these two versions of Gemini on any given day. Actually, let's be honest, you may find yourself flipping between the two even within the same hour. They don't call you "the Twins" for nothing, do they?

GEMINI DARK MASCULINE

Reckless. Thrill-seeking. Player. All three adjectives can be used to describe a Gemini who is getting in touch with their masculine side. When they are in touch with their dark masculine, Geminis have an intense desire to show off. They become braggarts who absolutely must be the smartest person in any room they enter. And if someone arrives who threatens their intellectual dominance? Get ready to start swinging.

GEMINI DARK FEMININE

When a Gemini is in touch with their dark feminine they become a charming heartbreaker and incorrigible flirt. The ultimate scammer, these femme fatales have no problem using their charms to get ahead and get what they want, then dip as soon as things start to get serious— or the check arrives. Paying the bill? Gemini? Not a chance.

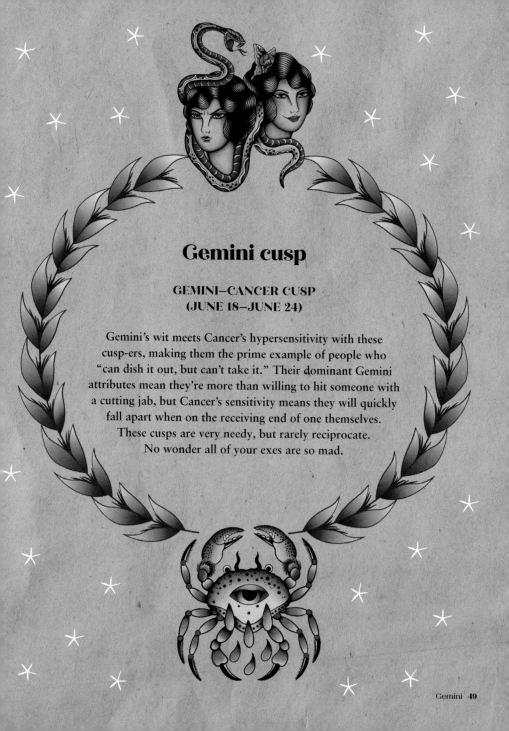

Gemini cusp

GEMINI–CANCER CUSP
(JUNE 18–JUNE 24)

Gemini's wit meets Cancer's hypersensitivity with these
cusp-ers, making them the prime example of people who
"can dish it out, but can't take it." Their dominant Gemini
attributes mean they're more than willing to hit someone with
a cutting jab, but Cancer's sensitivity means they will quickly
fall apart when on the receiving end of one themselves.
These cusps are very needy, but rarely reciprocate.
No wonder all of your exes are so mad.

Hello Cancer...

It's your turn to get roasted Cancer—*and* you're already crying. No surprises there. Your watery, moon-ruled sign could fill an ocean with the tears you shed on a daily basis over everything, from a slight inconvenience to a decades-old playground brawl you haven't gotten over yet. We'd ask you to forgive us for what we say in this chapter, but forgiving isn't really your thing. Neither is forgetting. In fact, you crabs love nothing more than to stay holed up in your shell, counting grudges like precious jewels. At least that means you won't be out ruining another birthday party with your legendary ability to bring down the mood.

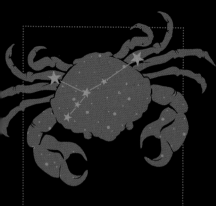

DATES
June 21–July 22

SYMBOL
Crab

RULER PLANET
The Moon

ELEMENT
Water

MODALITY
Cardinal

OPPOSING SIGN
Capricorn

MORTAL ENEMY
Sagittarius

PET PEEVES
Insufficient gratitude, egotistical people, forgotten birthdays, endings

5 NOTORIOUS CANCERS

Sure, Cancers may be able to boast about counting beloved figures such as Meryl Streep, Nelson Mandela, and Princess Diana among their big-hearted ranks, but what if we told you these people were the exception, and not the rule? Moody and vengeful, these hypersensitive signs are far better represented by the following infamous individuals:

1 Henry VIII (June 28, 1491): Infamous monarch who started the Church of England just so he could get a divorce. He would go on to have six wives, two of whom he beheaded.

2 Mike Tyson (June 30, 1966): American boxing champ and felon best known for biting off one of his opponent's ears during a match.

3 Lizzie Borden (July 19, 1860): American ax murderer who was accused of killing her father and stepmother with "forty whacks" from an ax in their family home.

4 Julius Caesar (July 12/13, 100 BC): Roman ruler whose dictatorial style led to his assassination by members of his own senate on March 15, 44 BC.

5 John Dillinger (June 22, 1903): American Depression-era gangster who robbed 24 banks and four police stations as leader of the Dillinger gang. He was imprisoned multiple times and escaped twice.

Cancer in a nutshell

Most astrologers will tell you that your big emotions are your strength, but that's not the whole truth. Your moody, secretive, grudge-holding sign will waste its life away mulling over pointless worries, perceived slights, and worst-case scenarios. It's no wonder that you're represented by the crab, because your constant bad mood can often cause you to snap, leaving a serious bruise on anyone who dares get in your way.

Your sign loves to wallow in the negative and has not yet found a doorstep it can't darken with its constant catastrophizing. Even worse, your moon-ruled sign changes moods like the tides, so loved ones never know which version of you they're going to get: the weepy, overly needy clinger or the aloof, standoffish wallflower. Either way, they know every conversation is going to revolve around you and your myriad problems, real or imagined. Though, let's be honest, we all know it's the imagined ones that really get you going.

MOODY

Gloomy Cancers live their life enslaved by their ever-changing moods, which usually range from "lightly downtrodden" to "exceedingly devastated." This is where your crab-like nature can really get the best of friends, coworkers, family, and anyone else within snapping distance. It is impossible for others to know what might trigger one of your notorious moods, probably because you hardly know for yourself. As one of the most pessimistic signs in the Zodiac, you have a way of infecting any situation—even a child's birthday party—with your "What's the point?" outlook. With Cancers, the glass isn't just "half empty," it's "half empty and about to explode."

MANIPULATIVE

Cancers are known for being in tune with their own emotions, which makes them experts at manipulating those of others. Crabs will do anything to get their emotional needs met, even if they have to tell a few lies or keep a few secrets to make it happen. These signs project so much emotional neediness it can blind those around them to how cold and calculating they truly are. Masters of the passive-aggressive note, sullen sigh, and backhanded compliment, moon-ruled Cancers have a way of manipulating the emotions of everyone around them with its invisible pull. In the end, they'll have gotten everything they wanted and everyone else will be left feeling drained and bamboozled. No wonder this sign hates spending time in the Sun. They're emotional vampires.

VINDICTIVE

Quick, Cancer! List every person who has ever wronged you. We know you can. Vengeful, vindictive Cancers love nothing more than to snap their claws onto a grudge and hold on for dear life. This overly sensitive sign takes everything personally and will never forget when someone crosses one of their many invisible lines. Given their ever-expanding list of enemies, a happy Cancer is one who gets to exist in a constant state of *schadenfreude*—the German word for "pleasure derived from someone else's misfortune." Uh-oh! Facebook says Cathy just lost her dream job? Well, maybe she should have thought about that before pegging you with a dodgeball in seventh grade…

Cancer placements

Even when you don't have Cancer as your sun sign, these manipulative crabs have a way of getting their claws in any chart where they appear. Bad vibes are kind of infectious that way.

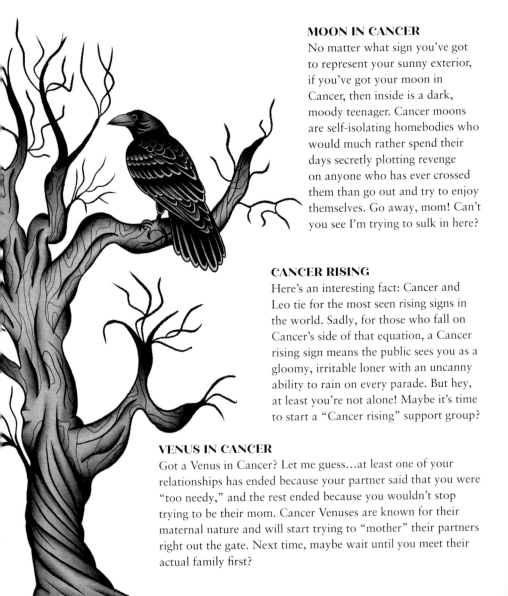

MOON IN CANCER

No matter what sign you've got to represent your sunny exterior, if you've got your moon in Cancer, then inside is a dark, moody teenager. Cancer moons are self-isolating homebodies who would much rather spend their days secretly plotting revenge on anyone who has ever crossed them than go out and try to enjoy themselves. Go away, mom! Can't you see I'm trying to sulk in here?

CANCER RISING

Here's an interesting fact: Cancer and Leo tie for the most seen rising signs in the world. Sadly, for those who fall on Cancer's side of that equation, a Cancer rising sign means the public sees you as a gloomy, irritable loner with an uncanny ability to rain on every parade. But hey, at least you're not alone! Maybe it's time to start a "Cancer rising" support group?

VENUS IN CANCER

Got a Venus in Cancer? Let me guess…at least one of your relationships has ended because your partner said that you were "too needy," and the rest ended because you wouldn't stop trying to be their mom. Cancer Venuses are known for their maternal nature and will start trying to "mother" their partners right out the gate. Next time, maybe wait until you meet their actual family first?

Cancer in love

Mariah Carey's hit "Obsessed" may have been about a Libra (the rapper Eminem), but it should have been about you, Cancer. Obsessively loyal, Cancers will hold onto a relationship long past its expiration date simply because things like "letting go" and "moving on" are not in their repertoire. Once a crab lets someone inside their shell, there is no going back. On the off chance someone is able to extricate themselves from Cancer's grip and become their ex, they'll have made an enemy for life. Cancer does not take emotional betrayal lightly. They're still not over the time their middle school infatuation danced with somebody else.

SINGLE CANCER

Single Cancers love to play hard to get, but it really is just that—a game. They'll ignore a person's texts while simultaneously lurking on their social media and following their every move. And if they just happen to show up at the very same coffee shop their crush just posted about going to every day? Well, isn't that just one more sign from the universe that they're meant to be together? Cancers are the sign most often to find themselves locked in a "situationship" because of their penchant for pursuing the unavailable. They'll waste years pining away over an unrequited love rather than moving on to pursue someone attainable. Then what would they have to complain about?

CANCER IN A RELATIONSHIP

We don't know about crabs, but Cancers mate for life. Once they're in a relationship (either real or imagined), Cancers are almost impossible to break up with. Try, and you'll be met with a moody, passive-aggressive guilt-tripper who won't allow the relationship to end until they get "closure," usually in the form of multiple hours-long conversations that leave the other party too emotionally drained to follow through with the split. As a partner, Cancer is jealous and secretive. They'll go silent at dinner and leave it up to their beau to figure out why. (Hint: It probably has something to do with the "flirty" server who refilled your breadsticks.)

Most compatible

Cancer + Capricorn

Are you a Cancer looking to make things work for the long haul? Then you're gonna want to find yourself a Capricorn. These tetchy signs will bond over their shared negative outlook and love of staying home. Cancer will never have to worry about Capricorn's ability to commit (it's what they do), and Capricorn will have no problem putting in the work required to get Cancer to open up. Once these two homebodies pair up, they'll never leave each other—or the couch.

Least compatible

Cancer + Sagittarius

Water and fire? Yeah…
that's gonna cause some
problems. Sagittarius's
unserious nature and
penchant for ribbing
loved ones will get under
Cancer's hypersensitive
skin in an instant. Even
worse, Sagittarius's
inability to stay in
one place or make a
commitment will drive
Cancer crazy as they try
in vain to get their archer
partner to settle down.
Let this relationship
go too far, and Cancer
might spend their whole
life pining after this sign
even though they know
it won't work—maybe
even because they know it
won't work out.

Cancer + Aries

Another fire sign, Aries
likes to get hot and heavy
fast, whereas Cancer
prefers to take things
slow and allow emotional
bonds to develop over
time. This slow-moving
pace will infuriate
Aries, who will in turn
overwhelm Cancer with
big shows of affection
right out the gate. If they're
able to get over the initial
mismatch, trouble will
still arise from Aries'
wandering eye, which will
fuel Cancer's jealousy and
cause them to lash out.
Once they do, Aries will
be more than happy to
let the argument explode
rather than talk things
through rationally. Avoid
this pairing unless you
want yet another ex you
refuse to be in the same
room with.

Cancer + Gemini

When needy Cancer
gets together with
commitment-phobic
Gemini, there are bound
to be some tears—on
Cancer's end, that is.
Gemini has what it
takes to charm their way
through Cancer's hard
shell, but by the time they
do they'll probably have
moved on to their next
romantic pursuit, leaving
Cancer feeling exposed
and betrayed. Empathic
Cancer will be driven
mad by Gemini's ever-
changing emotions, and
Gemini will be bored to
tears by Cancer's need to
constantly discuss heavy,
emotional topics. Let's just
say these two are better off
as friends. If they can even
manage that…

CANCER AT WORK

You know that coworker who silently fumes in the corner of the meeting and never says a word, but sends an extremely detailed, passive-aggressive email later that day about everything that was wrong? That's you, Cancer. The Zodiac's constant buzzkill, coworkers know not to come to you with a new idea or project unless they want to hear all the ways it could go awry. Depressing and unproductive to be around, you've probably noticed the way people avoid your desk like the plague, lest they be drawn into one of your lengthy mope sessions about the boss who never listens or the coworker who wronged you. Speaking of coworkers who wronged you, you keep a detailed list of them in your desk and spend at least half the workday fantasizing about when you will exact your revenge. You love nothing more than to feel superior at work, and will often take jobs you're overqualified for just to complain about how overqualified you are. The same goes for working late, which you'll volunteer to do mostly for the sulking rights they afford you later. When annual review time comes around, your boss knows to be prepared for a meltdown, as you take even the most constructive criticism very, very personally. Honestly, someone should probably check your desk for voodoo dolls the next time you're out of the office.

CANCER IN THE FAMILY

Mom? Is that you? Maternal Cancer loves to take on the role of matriarch, whether or not they actually are one. You are obsessed with family in a way that starts off as endearing but ends up creepy to anyone who bears witness to hours-long phone calls home. Relatives know to expect an incoming of texts about how much you "miss" them any time they don't make family their top priority. You love nothing more than to take on the role of the long-suffering sibling who stayed home to take care of mom and dad, just so you can guilt-trip anyone who dared move away. This fierce loyalty to family often means you're the in-law from hell for anyone who dares enter the clan, and you're not above delivering a slightly too-long weepy wedding speech about how the bride or groom to be is "taking your baby away."

CANCER AT HOME

There's a reason Cancer is represented by an animal that carries its home on its back. For your sign, home is everything. No wonder it's so difficult to get you to leave. Cancer's home is the place where you feel most comfortable to be yourself, which is why it's always a little bit depressing. Windows closed, shades drawn, and a pile of blankets to show where you last wallowed in your own despair, the Cancer residence is a sanctuary for your own moodiness. When the rare guest is allowed inside the den, the dreary-yet-elaborate surroundings will leave them feeling more like they just stepped into a haunted mansion than a person's living room. On the bright side, your obsession with domesticity means you are clean and meticulous when it comes to keeping house. Unfortunately, your solitary sign keeps *chez* Cancer locked up tighter than a bank vault, so there's rarely anyone around to admire your handiwork.

CANCER AND TRAVEL

Leaving the house? Cancer? We'll believe it when we see it. Cancers hate to be without their creature comforts, so the hurdle required to actually get them to go anywhere can often be insurmountable. When you do decide to take a trip, you bring your doom-and-gloom attitude along for the ride and cannot help but draw attention to everything that might go wrong. What if your luggage gets lost? What if you get lost? What if your hotel is hit by an asteroid? It's all on the table for your pessimistic star sign. Even the most minor travel delay or language barrier will send you into a homesick spiral. Cancers have a knack of finding the worst in everything, especially accommodation, which will never match up to the haven they've built at home. And you're not happy to just privately pout, either. You must bring everyone down with your constant complaining. With Cancer, every vacation is turned into a guilt-trip, since you love nothing more than to "compromise" with the group, only to hold it over their heads later. You'll spend an entire dinner silently seething that you didn't get your choice of restaurant and taking passive-aggressive jabs at your table mates. In short, everyone would be better off if you just stayed home and watched the Travel Channel.

The two sides of Cancer

Watery, emotional Cancer is considered one of the Zodiac's "feminine" signs, but their temperamental nature means they can swing into their masculine at any moment, regardless of gender identity. Those on the receiving end of one of your mood swings might feel like they're dealing with two completely different people, but underneath it all is just the same gloomy crab out to ruin everyone's day with their bad vibes.

CANCER DARK MASCULINE

Moody and aloof, a Cancer who is engaging in their dark masculine side may think they appear strong and stoic, when they're actually just being a curmudgeon. Getting this version of Cancer out of the house is an even more Herculean task than usual, as they are typically feeling solitary and antisocial. Probably for the best. No one needs that kind of a cloud over their night out anyway.

CANCER DARK FEMININE

Naturally femme Cancer will often find themselves engaging in their dark feminine side, which is just as moody and gloomy as their dark masculine but with an extra dose of neediness and passive aggression. The ultimate martyr, a Cancer situated in their dark feminine loves to "sacrifice" for their loved ones, but only so that they can play the role of the long-suffering mother for weeks after. Poor, unfortunate crab. You have it so hard.

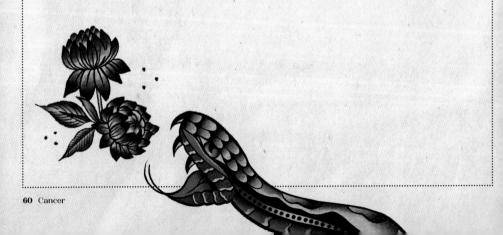

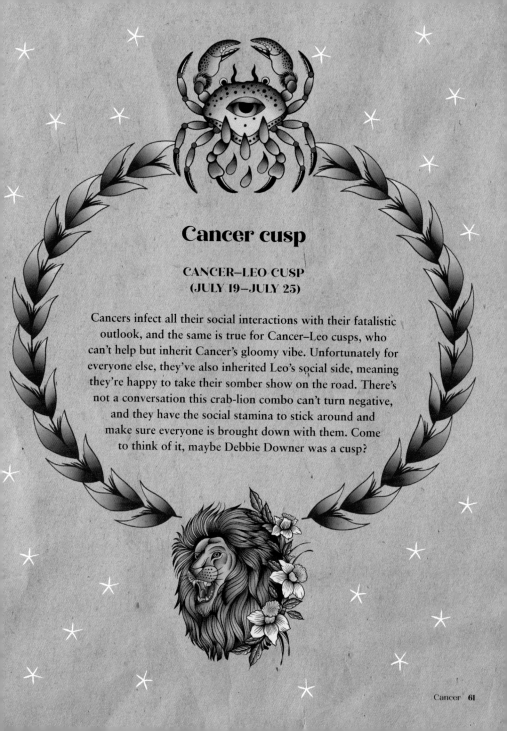

Cancer cusp

CANCER–LEO CUSP
(JULY 19–JULY 25)

Cancers infect all their social interactions with their fatalistic outlook, and the same is true for Cancer–Leo cusps, who can't help but inherit Cancer's gloomy vibe. Unfortunately for everyone else, they've also inherited Leo's social side, meaning they're happy to take their somber show on the road. There's not a conversation this crab-lion combo can't turn negative, and they have the social stamina to stick around and make sure everyone is brought down with them. Come to think of it, maybe Debbie Downer was a cusp?

Hello Leo

You're so vain, you probably think this chapter is about you. And for once, you're actually right. Not that you'd ever admit it if you weren't. You're represented by the lion, aka the king of the jungle. Fitting really, since you tend to think your word is law. There isn't a mirror in the world you can't get lost staring into—and you haven't found a flaw yet. Probably for the best, since your image-obsessed sign is all about how you look on the outside. Unfortunately, that leaves little room for self-improvement or introspection. In the end, your obsession with appearances leaves you blind to what people really see when they look your way: a gaudy, self-obsessed know-it-all who'd rather chase fame and fortune than work toward something real.

5 NOTORIOUS LEOS

Fame-loving Leo can boast many A-list names among its ranks, from Jennifer Lopez to Mick Jagger to Whitney Houston, but it's the dark side of Leo that truly represents what this sign has to offer. Here are five notorious Leos who have changed history, sometimes for the worse:

DATES
July 23–August 22

SYMBOL
Lion

RULER PLANET
The Sun

ELEMENT
Fire

MODALITY
Fixed

OPPOSING SIGN
Aquarius

MORTAL ENEMY
Taurus

PET PEEVES
Being ignored, public callouts, back talk, bad dressers

1 Elizabeth Bathory (August 7, 1560): Hungarian countess known as "Countess Dracula" due to her love of human blood. According to legend, she used to bathe in blood, believing it would keep her young.

2 Mata Hari (August 7, 1876): Dutch exotic dancer and courtesan who was convicted of using her feminine wiles to spy for Germany in World War I and executed by firing squad.

3 Napoleon Bonaparte (August 15, 1769): French Emperor and general who conquered much of Europe during his reign. He was forced to abdicate the throne twice and lived his final days in exile on a remote island.

4 Alfred Hitchcock (August 13, 1899): American filmmaker who directed some of the most iconic horror movies. His obsession with "icy blondes" like Grace Kelly and Kim Novak is visible throughout his movies.

5 Coco Chanel (August 19, 1883): French fashion designer whose signature style gave us the Chanel suit. After the liberation of Paris in 1944, she was accused of serving as an informant for the Nazis when her affair with a German officer became public.

Leo in a nutshell

We're not even going to bother going over how nice astrologers typically say you are, Leo. You praise yourself enough as it is. Instead, we're going to get right to the heart of the matter. Leos are narcissistic, entitled megalomaniacs who see nothing beyond their own myopic worldview. Your preening sign is as shallow as they come, and has the garish fashion sense to prove it. You build your entire life around your "look at me!" mentality. And—good news—people are looking. Though they don't necessarily like what they see. At a party, you're the person who sucks up all the oxygen by prattling on about everything on your mind, blithely unaware that your friends may also have something to contribute to the conversation. And by friends, we really mean followers. King Leos would much rather surround themselves with sycophants than risk allowing someone into their inner circle who might actually tell them like it is. Unfortunately for you, that's our job. Let's get started, shall we?

VAIN

Quick, Leo! When was the last time you looked in the mirror? Just kidding. You're probably looking in one right now. Your image-obsessed sign can't help but spend every waking moment crafting what they consider the perfect exterior. A quick trip down Leo's social media page will likely reveal an endless scroll of perfectly posed pictures and filtered selfies. Not pictured? Friends, family, or a single hobby other than smiling for the camera. Leos may think of themselves as irreproachable objects of envy with a mighty roar, but one simple question will leave them totally undone—did you know there's something in your teeth?

SELF-OBSESSED

When your ruling planet is the Sun, it's hardly a surprise that you think the world revolves around you. Leos are typically concerned with just three things: me, me, and me. Other people's thoughts and feelings are simply not their concern. In fact, they probably don't even register as you mindlessly move along on your never-ending quest for world domination. And who better to rule the world than you, the best, smartest, and most beautiful person ever to walk the Earth? Unfortunately, even if you do succeed on your mad quest, you'll have no one to share your spoils with, thanks to all the feelings you've hurt along the way. For your sign, it truly is lonely at the top.

CONDESCENDING

Leos know best. At least, they think they do. And they're willing to say so—loudly and often. Pompous and overbearing, you can hardly conceive of a world in which someone else's opinion would be worth considering. Your puffed-up sign has no problem deriding anyone whose thoughts differ from your own, even if the facts are on their side. In fact, the more you're proven wrong, the more likely you are to dig in, employing childish insults, adolescent eye rolls, and toddler-inspired tantrums to bully naysayers into agreement. At least the mean girls of the world are impressed.

Leo placements

In the same way that Leo takes over any room it enters, so it takes over any birth chart in which it appears. Got Leo as one of your "big three"? Well, then you may as well have it at the top of your chart because this sun-ruled sign has a way of outshining all of the others.

MOON IN LEO

Leo moons are spotlight chasers, obsessively fixated on making sure all eyes are on them. They spend every waking moment strategizing new ways to get attention, and aren't above petty tricks like bursting into tears or "losing" an earring to make it happen.

LEO RISING

If being seen is your goal—and let's be honest, it is—then congratulations! You are seen. As a conceited, tacky, blow-hard with little to offer outside your impeccable photo-editing skills. You always said you wanted to get people talking. You just didn't realize that it would be behind your back.

VENUS IN LEO

Got your Venus in Leo? Then be prepared to spend your whole life searching for a partner who is as obsessed with you as you are. Venus Leos are great at initially attracting partners with their shiny magnetism, but often repel them later with their high-maintenance tendencies and inability to retain information about anyone other than themselves. It's one thing to ask someone if they have any siblings on a first date, but after a year of dating it's kind of another story...

Leo in love

Leos enjoy living their lives in love with exactly one person: themselves. Everyone else, even their partner, comes second. When it comes to searching for a life partner, Leos need someone who is exactly as in love with themselves as they are and willing to go along with whatever they say without question. They need a partner who is happy to shower them with a constant stream of praise and leave no doubt as to the level of their devotion. Leos would date themselves if they could, but a fawning doormat will do just as well.

SINGLE LEO

Single Leo is all about quantity over quality. You'd much rather surround yourself with a gaggle of adoring potential suitors than put in the work it takes to find an equal partner. Plus, an endless parade of first dates lets you indulge in two of your favorite activities: getting dressed up and talking about yourself. Hours can go by before you notice you haven't asked your date a single question, and you hardly care if they're enjoying themselves...so long as they pick up the check. Once you part ways, it's out of sight, out of mind. Probably why you're one of the rare people who has never been ghosted. You'd have to save their number for that.

LEO IN A RELATIONSHIP

Once Leo finds someone who is sufficiently enamored with them, their romance tends to burn hot and heavy. Leos are high-maintenance lovers who expect nothing less than complete loyalty from their partner, who they regard more as an accessory than a full human. This is probably why you tend to go for people who can add to your own status and allure (or are just plain rich). You want someone powerful and influential, with the important caveat that they never become more powerful or influential than yourself. The moment they do, you'll kick them to the curb—usually without doing them the courtesy of informing them that it's over.

Most compatible

Leo + Libra

Leo's ultimate match is a Libra. Air fuels fire when this match gets together, and Leo will love the way beauty-obsessed Libra gasses them up with praise for their physical appearance. These front-facing signs love all the same things: style, socializing, and being seen. Plus, Libra's indecisive nature means they'll have no problem letting Leo make all the decisions. Just how Leo likes it.

Least compatible

Leo + Capricorn

The mismatch between social butterfly and homebody will stop this pairing dead in its tracks. Flashy Leo and low-key Capricorn have almost nothing in common and will find themselves constantly at odds on how to spend their time together. While Capricorn would love nothing more than to stay at home and watch their favorite comfort show, Leo sees no point in getting into a relationship if they can't show it off to the masses. Capricorn will chafe at Leo's need for outside approval, while Leo will find themselves constantly cringing at Capricorn's lack of social graces. The moment Capricorn embarrasses Leo at a party by not knowing who everyone's latest reality TV obsession is, they'll be out the door for good.

Leo + Cancer

Leo can't stand anyone who wants to rain on their parade, and gloomy Cancer will do just that. These two will butt heads constantly over their opposing worldviews, and overly cheery Leo will always come off as fake to pessimistic Cancer. Leo's navel-gazing will mean they'll never put in the work needed to get through Cancer's tough exterior, and their inability to consider other people's feelings will send hypersensitive Cancer into an emotional tailspin. Ultimately, all the ugly crying and emotional vulnerability will give Leo the ick faster than Cancer can say, "What are we?"

Leo + Aries

Aries' hot-and-heavy and obsessive approach to love will certainly get Leo's attention at first, but once the novelty wears off and Aries' eye starts to wander, it'll be constant clashes for these two. This fire-on-fire pair will lead to explosive fights as neither will ever want to compromise. Plus, competitive Aries will always try to one-up Leo, something lions absolutely cannot tolerate in a partner. Leo may allow themselves to get caught up in a vicious makeup-and-breakup cycle with Aries, but only for the attention that the constant emotional turmoil will then bring.

LEO AT WORK

In the workplace Leo bravado mixes with an acute case of imposter syndrome to create a toxic situation for everyone involved. On the one hand, you believe you should be the boss, regardless of where you actually stand in the chain of command. On the other hand, you're desperate to hide even the smallest insecurities from your coworkers, and act out of a constant fear they'll discover you have no idea what you're doing. The mix of insecurity and ego means you go overboard projecting an air of confidence, even when the whole team would be better served if you just sat back and listened. Leo is that coworker who makes a big show of how busy they are, but when push comes to shove people will be hard pressed to figure out what exactly it is that you do all day. The answer? Scrolling social media and keeping jealous tabs on all the people you can't help but compare yourself to. It's a tough job, but somebody's gotta do it!

LEO IN THE FAMILY

For spotlight-loving Leo every day is the Leo show. And boy, do your family members know it. As far as you're concerned, every family member is the spare to your heir, and you tend to see them more as loyal servants than equals. And sure, Leos are known for being extremely generous with family and loved ones…if they agree to get on their knees and kiss the ring. Your showboating sign hates to share anything, even DNA. This can lead to a competitive streak with siblings, cousins, and even your own grandma if she's getting too much attention. Who said her 90th birthday party should be about her, anyway? Like most monarchs, you keep a jealous eye on all of your next of kin, just in case one of them gets any ideas about stealing the throne. At the first whiff of dissent, you'll have your ill-fated family member locked up in the tower faster than they can muster troops for a rebellion. Ruthless to a fault, you have no problem putting their head on a spike in front of the family vacation home to send a message to any other young upstarts (aka your nieces and nephews) who may consider coming for your crown. Long live the king!

LEO AND TRAVEL

Leo's preferred method of travel is probably palanquin, but barring that, first class will do. Your "go big or go home" ethos goes triple for travel, and you see no point in booking a vacation to anywhere other than the lap of luxury. From hotel rooms to restaurants, Leos need everything to be five-star. Any attempt to shrink expenses by their travel companions will be met by Leo's signature scorn. Speaking of travel companions, they'd better be okay with being conscripted into Leo's personal photography team. You take "pics or it didn't happen" to a whole new level when you travel, and need to make sure every outfit—which you bought specifically for the trip and planned weeks in advance—is meticulously documented. For Leos, travel is less about enjoying the vacation than it is about making sure

other people can see that they're enjoying their vacation. That's why half of your friends secretly mute you any time they know you're about to go away, lest their feeds are flooded with an endless stream of perfectly posed photos alerting them to your every move. And if your Trevi Fountain sunset pics come out less than stellar, there's always Photoshop. Your fans—I mean friends—expect perfection.

LEO AT HOME

Gold toilets, velvet tapestries, and richly upholstered chaises—is this the Playboy Mansion, or *chez* Leo? Leo sees their home as their own personal Versailles, and decorates accordingly. Most people would feel a little odd putting their own portrait up on the wall, but you're not most people, are you, Leo? You subscribe to a strict "bigger is better" policy, especially when it comes to your home. You won't be truly happy until you're pacing your palatial floor plan, watching a massive flatscreen from your equally enormous sectional, and sleeping the

night away on a mattress that could fit a small family. You'd probably describe your taste as "high-end" to whichever unfortunate interior decorator you employ to execute your vision, but they'll soon find that "gaudy" is a lot more like it. The concepts "stealth wealth" and "quiet luxury" are foreign to your sign, which puts the ability to show off above all other concerns. Unfortunately for you, fame chaser, this is exactly why the true elites will always steer clear of your gold-encrusted path.

The two sides of Leo

As a fire sign, Leo tends to fall on the masculine side of the Zodiac.
But within every Leo lies a dark masculine and dark feminine side,
lurking and waiting to be unleashed. Not sure which side of the
king-size bed you woke up on today? Here's how you can tell
Leo's dark masculine from its dark feminine.

LEO DARK MASCULINE

Talk about a Napoleon complex—a Leo that's
situated in its dark masculine is confident to
the point of megalomania. They see the whole
world as one big kingdom to be conquered,
and they have no problem stepping on lesser
mortals to get to the top. Move over Louis
XIV, the real Sun King has arrived.

LEO DARK FEMININE

When a Leo is expressing their dark feminine
side the whole world has to stop and stare.
They'll stop at nothing to get all eyes on them,
even if their loud, garish behavior earns them
more than a few dirty looks. So what? As long
as it's your name that's on people's lips, dark
feminine Leo is happy. Just be sure you don't
hear what anyone is actually saying.

Leo cusp

LEO–VIRGO CUSP
(AUGUST 19–AUGUST 25)

Fire and earth make a deadly combination for these cusps.
While loud, aggressive Leo still dominates your personality,
it's tinged with Virgo's perfectionism and judgy behavior.
Virgo's influence sends your standards sky-high, while Leo's
self-obsession ensures that you're the only person who can meet
them. Combine that with Leo's tactlessness, and you get an
overly critical narcissist with zero filter.
Your poor coworkers…

Hello Virgo...

You may think nobody can be harder on you than you are on yourself, Virgo, but we're not worried. You may love nothing more than to impose your rigid standards on everyone around you, but the fact of the matter is you're far from perfect yourself. Not only are you famous for letting perfect be the enemy of the good, you take it one step further and turn "perfect" into a dam that stops all progress. Your pathological need to go over minute details ad nauseam makes you a menace to everything from morning meetings to friendly game nights. You just can't help yourself. You have to ensure that every rule of Monopoly is followed to the letter, even if that gets in the way of fun. Luckily, "fun" is not something you'd ever be accused of being.

DATES
August 23–
September 22

SYMBOL
Virgin

RULER PLANET
Mercury

ELEMENT
Earth

MODALITY
Mutable

OPPOSING SIGN
Pisces

MORTAL ENEMY
Sagittarius

PET PEEVES
Missed deadlines, typos,
tardiness, mess

5 NOTORIOUS VIRGOS

Let's get this out of the way right now: yes, Beyoncé is a Virgo. But when this perfection-chasing sign goes wrong, it goes way, way wrong. Here are five famous Virgos who used their sign's analytical powers for less than noble means:

1 **Ivan the Terrible (August 25, 1530):** The first tsar of Russia who callously executed thousands of people during his reign and even killed his own son for trying to go against his will.

2 **Louis XVI (August 23, 1754):** French monarch and husband of Marie Antoinette who failed to endear himself to the French people. His unfortunate reign ended with the French Revolution and the removal of his head via guillotine.

3 **Caligula (August 31, 12 AD):** Roman emperor known for his cruel and unusual behavior. During his short reign he was accused of torturing senate members who disagreed with him.

4 **Elizabeth I (September 7, 1533):** The "Virgin Queen" of England who famously reigned without marrying in order to hold onto power. She eventually named James I as her heir, but not before beheading his mother—Mary, Queen of Scots—for treason.

5 **Whitey Bulger (September 3, 1929):** American crime boss who was sentenced to two life sentences. Despite being #2 on the FBI's Ten Most Wanted Fugitives list in 1999, he evaded capture for over a decade until an anonymous tip led to his arrest in 2011.

Virgo in a nutshell

How does it feel to be the Zodiac's consummate buzzkill? By now you've probably gotten used to the wave of side-eyes that greet you anytime you walk into a room. The moment Virgo enters, everyone knows the party is officially over.

It's not often that someone is as outwardly critical and inwardly self-hating as you. You should honestly give yourself some credit for being as mean to yourself as you are to others—not that you'd ever outwardly praise yourself for anything. You'd much rather toil in private, tinkering away at your masterpiece but never revealing it to the public for fear that it's "not good enough." Unfortunately for those around you, you don't limit these harsh critiques to yourself. Your penchant for meanness under the guise of "truth telling" means your friends learned to stop asking your opinion long ago, but that's no matter. You're a master of unsolicited advice, and will share your critiques whether they're asked for or not. This is probably why your social circle is so small. Those who can't take the heat got out of the kitchen a long time ago.

PERFECTIONIST

"What's wrong with perfection?" You say this to yourself, as you pore over the 50th draft of a company-wide email about the proper way to label a file. As one of the Zodiac's fixed signs, you hate change, and you use your perfectionism as a cudgel to make sure it never happens. Nothing is ever good enough for you, which means you spend your days constantly revising old work rather than moving on to something new. Your analytical eye makes you an excellent editor (or tax collector), as you love nothing more than to obsess over a lengthy document of errors. Actually, there is something you love more—telling the author about all of the errors you found…in the harshest terms possible.

PEDANTIC

When your perfectionism isn't enough to grind the gears of progress to a halt, your pedanticism will. Those who know you realize that getting trapped in a conversation with you will mean an endless cycle of minor corrections that will be enough to bring any real conversation to a halt. You just don't know how to let a misused word or an inelegantly phrased sentence go, even if the speaker's meaning was clear to everyone else. You see every conversation as an opportunity to show off your impressive intellect and make others feel small in the process. By the time you're done picking apart their story, your coworker will rue the day they decided to tell you about their weekend. Serves them right for saying "literally" when they actually meant "figuratively." Rude.

PESSIMISTIC

When critiquing a project to death isn't enough to stop it moving forward, you pull out the final tool in your arsenal: a detailed list of everything that could go wrong. Sure, your impressive powers of analysis might be used for something like solving world hunger, but why do that when you could instead use it to ideate incessantly on all the ways solving world hunger would contribute to the Earth's overpopulation issue? You're a master at finding the downside to everything, from trying a new restaurant to your friend's decision to adopt a dog. You just can't hold back telling them about the time your aunt adopted a dog only to discover it had an incontinence problem that could only be solved with expensive surgery. What's that? You're just trying to help prepare them for the inevitable...

Virgo placements

Virgo tends to be a more subtle sign, but if it appears in one of your birth chart's "big three" there's no way you're not going to feel the effects. Virgo does its work under the surface, meaning it will get under your skin eventually.

MOON IN VIRGO

If you're born with your moon in Virgo, it means that your inner monologue is a constant stream of critiques. You may look like you're engaged in conversation, but you're really clocking every single thing that could be improved about your surroundings (those fire escapes aren't up to code), your companions (Theresa's new haircut is a little crooked), and, most importantly, yourself (Why did I just say that? Do these people even like me? I bet they don't like me...). Honestly, we're depressed for you.

VENUS IN VIRGO

People with their Venus in Virgo like to say they're "realists" when it comes to love. We'd like to say they're cynical defeatists obsessed with looking for reasons it can't work. Virgo Venuses hate all the things most people find romantic, like passion, affection, and spontaneous gestures. Instead, they prefer a person who can methodically check boxes off on the "perfect partner" spreadsheet they've been maintaining since they were ten years old. At least nobody can ever accuse them of not knowing what they want.

VIRGO RISING

When your rising sign is in Virgo it means the world sees you as an anal-retentive control freak in desperate need of a chill pill. Sure, they may also know they can rely on you for anything work- or organization-related, but that doesn't typically translate to being included in many social events later on. Maybe you should become a party planner? Then they'll have to invite you.

Virgo in love

A Virgo's love language is simple: critique. Your perfection-obsessed sign expects nothing less than the very best from everyone, and your unfortunate romantic partners are no exception. Those who enter into a relationship with you can expect a partnership that's low on physical affection, but high on nitpicking and castigation. It's not that you don't *like* physical affection—you just like it performed in a highly methodical way. (And you will require a shower both before and after.) As a Virgo you prefer to whip your partner into shape and, as an added bonus, they get a front-row seat to your constant negativity and pessimistic obsessing. No wonder so many of them end up as sad as you.

SINGLE VIRGO

In many ways, a single Virgo is a happy Virgo. (If there even is such a thing as a happy Virgo.) You'd rather be alone forever than have to put up with someone who can't meet your sky-high standards. And you've yet to find anyone that can.

Being single also reinforces Virgo's negative self-image, which already says you deserve to be alone until you've finally achieved true perfection. In this case, misery does not love company.

VIRGO IN A RELATIONSHIP

In a relationship with a Virgo? Then you may be entitled to financial compensation. Virgos love to turn their critical eye toward those closest to them, and who is closer than the person who shares your bed? (Which, by the way, you forgot to make properly.) The closer Virgo and their partner get, the more constant the stream of admonishment becomes. Virgos say they prize "truth" above all else in a relationship, but it just so happens that the "truth," as they see it, never involves them being in the wrong. In the end, they'd rather cut and run than budge when differences arise. The relationship was just a distraction from their quest for perfection anyway.

Most compatible

Virgo + Pisces

Fantasy meets reality when these two pair up, and the results are actually a loving, stable relationship. Dreamy Pisces' rose-colored glasses mean they see Virgo's constant stream of criticism for what it is: an expression of love. So long as Virgo provides a stable foundation (which they will), Pisces' legendary insecurity won't be triggered, leaving only their best qualities to come into play—compassion, empathy, and optimism. They can help Virgo break out of their glass-half-empty shell, while Virgo will provide Pisces with the structure they need to follow through on some of those big ideas. Anyone who thinks a dreamer and a realist can't make it work simply hasn't seen these two in action.

Least compatible

Virgo + Gemini

Geminis are simply far too messy and unpredictable for you, Virgo. You may initially be attracted to them, thinking they're a "fixer-upper" you can mold to your standards, but you'll quickly find that Gemini is a sign that cannot be tamed. Geminis have no problem challenging every aspect of your worldview, without realizing that arguments they see as simply an intellectual exercise actually cut you to your very core. Not to mention the fact that their tolerance for dirty dishes will have you out the door the moment you first step foot in their apartment.

Virgo + Sagittarius

Someone who is meaner to you than you are? No thanks. When Virgos and Sags get together, both sides are in for a nasty tongue lashing (and we don't mean in the bedroom). Both of these signs pride themselves on "truth telling" via cutting remarks, meaning they are bound to end up in a clash of below-the-belt insults. They may start out thinking that they're just matching wits, but they'll end up hurting each other's feelings. Steer clear of this partnership. You're hard enough on yourself as it is.

Virgo + Aquarius

Aquarius and Virgo fail to connect because they see the world from totally different perspectives. On the one hand, Aquarius is an optimistic big thinker who always has their eye on a distant, idealistic future. On the other, Virgos are pessimists who are consumed with the imperfections of the here and now. These mismatching worldviews mean they'll each drive the other crazy. Virgo will be totally unable to hear Aquarius's vision for a better world, and Aquarius will never stop daydreaming long enough to help with the things that need to be done in the present—like bringing in the groceries or folding the bed sheets.

VIRGO AT WORK

Work is where Virgo thrives—and is at its most deranged. On the one hand, there's no one who can claim you aren't a hard worker. On the other, you take that "hard work" ethos to the point of delusion. In your mind, no one is as thorough, smart, or logical as you, meaning no one else's opinion matters. Even your boss is just an obstacle on the way to true perfection, and you have no problem disregarding their wishes if they contradict your own. Coworkers know to add an extra hour onto any meeting with you, as you cannot help but pepper them with an endless stream of questions and clarifications. They also know better than to come to you for advice or help on a project, since your legendary red pen will surely leave them feeling more demoralized than inspired. You may love critique, but "constructive criticism" is simply not in your wheelhouse. Plus, your obsession with following rules makes your peers want to spend as little time with you as possible, lest you catch wind of any violations. They may come to you when it's time to reorganize the break room, but there will be an office-wide eye roll the next day when they open up their email to a tome from you on proper supply usage and lunch storage protocol.

VIRGO IN THE FAMILY

The perfect family member does not exist, but Virgo will certainly try. The ultimate parents' pet, Virgo will stop at nothing to be the most accomplished, helpful, and service-oriented member of the family. Sure, this makes you the apple of your mother's eye, but it also turns every family gathering into a low-simmering competition. Unlike Aries, who makes their competitive streak known with loud boasting and overt plays for attention, Virgo loves to play the modest martyr while secretly believing they're better than everyone else. If any cousins or siblings offer to help clear the table alongside you, you'll swiftly make them regret that decision by drowning them in a sea of criticism and nitpicking. As much as you love to portray yourself as a humble, family-centered helper, you really see your family members as pawns you can use to display your own perfection and superiority. The ultimate overachiever, you take a family member's choice to live their life outside your own standards personally, and will do everything in your power to correct them into submission. If someone who shares your DNA can have fun, does that mean you can too? You can't even begin to imagine it.

VIRGO AT HOME

Simple, clean lines. White (or off-white) paint. Some people may call the Virgo décor style "minimalist." We call it boring and sterile. Virgos love to live in an environment where they can see how clean things are, which means they prefer to keep everything blindingly white. From their couch to the walls to their always-starched sheets, Virgos like a home that looks like no living creature has ever stepped foot in it, let alone lived there. They cannot abide clutter, meaning every item has a carefully chosen place and must be returned there the moment it is out of use. Every item in the Virgo kitchen is labeled, even if they live alone. Guests will be met with an immediate onslaught of anxiety, as Virgo will never trust an outsider not to ruin the place with their dirt and carelessness. Even minor spills can bring an entire dinner party to a halt as Virgo leaps into action with their five-part spill-cleaning routine. When it comes to the Virgo home, you are not only crying over spilled milk, you're having a full-blown meltdown.

VIRGO AND TRAVEL

Why hire a travel agent when you can just travel with a Virgo? (Answer: because the travel agent won't tag along and anxiously ensure you follow their itinerary to the letter.) Virgos live in a constant state of preparing for the worst, and when traveling that tendency is amplified to the max. You're that person at the airport who checks and rechecks their ticket every 15 minutes (it's still exactly where you left it) and keeps their passport strapped to their chest at all times. Once Virgos arrive at their accommodation, they cannot unpack until they have checked every nook and cranny for dirt and grime, stripped the mattress to look for bugs, and ensured that the front desk is ready to give them a wake-up call promptly at 6am so that they're not late for the early morning museum tour they booked months in advance. For Virgos, vacationing is about efficiency, not relaxation. This means you typically spend more time meticulously planning every moment of your break than you do enjoying it, and leave disappointed because there will always be something that didn't go exactly as you planned. At least you won't be filling anyone's feeds with sugar-coated travel grams anytime soon. You're too busy writing a sternly worded review for your hotel regarding its underwhelming towel softness for that.

The two sides of Virgo

Virgo naturally falls on the feminine side of the Zodiac, but that doesn't mean that its masculine side won't come out to play every once in a while. And by play, of course, we mean work. This is Virgo, after all. Here are the two sides of the Virgo coin onto which anyone can fall depending on the day.

VIRGO DARK MASCULINE

When a Virgo is situated in its dark masculine, they are all business and low-simmering ambition. They have no problem barking orders at lesser mortals (read: everyone) and wear their pet peeves clearly on their sleeve. Like a cold, distant father who is impossible to please, dark masculine Virgos often exist in a state of stoic silence. They don't really have anything nice to say, and so they don't say anything at all.

VIRGO DARK FEMININE

When a Virgo is in their dark feminine, you'll only find out what they're feeling through a series of passive-aggressive actions and telling gestures, such as rewashing the dishes after you've already done them because the work was not up to par. A dark feminine Virgo spends their days obsessively organizing and reorganizing their living space, only to do every task all over again the moment a new speck of dust appears. Introverted and shy, dark feminine Virgos will never tell a guest outright to take their shoes off in the hall, but they'll get the hint when they hear the faint sounds of scrubbing the moment they walk out the door.

Virgo cusp

VIRGO–LIBRA CUSP
(SEPTEMBER 19–SEPTEMBER 25)

Earthy Virgo loves to hang back and keep a watchful eye on the world, while airy Libra wants nothing more than to stay above the fray. When they combine, you get a chilly, detached observer who loves standing on the sidelines and feeling superior. These cusp-ers have lots of opinions on how things should be done, but they'd never let themselves get emotionally involved enough to share them. Instead, they turn their critical gaze inward and spend their days perfecting their appearance with the meticulousness of a physician prepping for brain surgery. Too bad they're actually just trying to figure out what shoes will go best with their top.

Hello Libra...

Don't give us that doe-eyed "who me?" look. It's not going to work here. You may have the rest of the world fooled into believing your helpless maiden act, but we know the truth. You're not the unassuming, impartial ditz that you pretend to be. In reality, you're a calculating game-player who hangs about on the sidelines and waits until a winner is declared, then pretends you were with them all along. Your legendary indecision comes less from wanting to be "fair" than it does from an intense desire never to miss out. Your air-headed sign would rather spend its life floating from shiny object to shiny object than get bogged down by things like "commitment" and "loyalty." But hey, at least you're pretty.

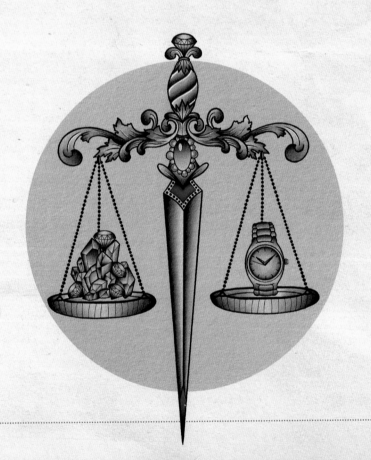

DATES
September 23–
October 22

SYMBOL
Scales

RULER PLANET
Venus

ELEMENT
Air

MODALITY
Cardinal

OPPOSING SIGN
Aries

MORTAL ENEMY
Capricorn

PET PEEVES
Fighting, ugly décor,
binding contracts,
being left out

5 NOTORIOUS LIBRAS

Glamorous Libras certainly have some glitzy names in their ranks, from Serena Williams to Bruce Springsteen, but the sign is perhaps better represented by these equally eye-popping but slightly more notorious names:

1 **F. Scott Fitzgerald (September 24, 1896):** American novelist famous for *The Great Gatsby*. He pulled inspiration (and exact dialogue) from his glamorous wife Zelda's diaries before eventually leaving her in a psychiatric hospital.

2 **Bonnie Parker (October 1, 1910):** American bank robber who followed her partner Clyde Barrow into a life of crime in pursuit of money and fame. They even posed for pictures—rifles and all.

3 **"Squeaky" Fromme (October 22, 1948):** Attempted assassin and "Manson Family" member. She was sentenced to life in prison in 1975 for attempting to assassinate US President Gerald Ford.

4 **Kim Kardashian (October 21, 1980):** Trendsetting reality star who skyrocketed to fame with a *special* tape after humble beginnings as Paris Hilton's best friend and closet organizer.

5 **Richard III (October 2, 1452):** The final Yorkist king of England who was portrayed as a hunchbacked tyrant by William Shakespeare in his eponymous play. Many believe Richard may have ordered the deaths of his two young nephews to keep his crown.

Libra in a nutshell

Ditz, air-head, lightweight—these are all words you've probably heard used to describe you, Libra. And those are the people who are being nice. In reality, your charismatic sign is a master manipulator who only plays dumb in order to shirk responsibility. The ultimate people pleaser, your sign loves to tell people what they want to hear while keeping your true feelings a mystery. Libras are often called the Zodiac's "peacemakers," which may sound like a good thing, but we know it comes from a deep-seated and singular obsession with maintaining the appearance of tranquility, whether it matches reality or not. You'll do everything in your power to placate those around you in an effort to maintain "good vibes," even if it means completely changing your opinion to fit in with whoever you're talking to. This makes you a master of first impressions, as you're able to charm just about anyone with a glance. But that impression wears off quickly on your second meeting—and third, and fourth—when you reintroduce yourself and reveal you're blissfully unaware that you've ever met. No wonder you've had to perfect the art of the childish giggle and endearing "Oopsies!" You need it.

INDECISIVE

Even the most generous astrological breakdown will mention Libra's indecisiveness. You spend your life in a constant state of FOMO (fear of missing out). When faced with a decision, you'll procrastinate and vacillate, totally immobilized by the fear of what you'll miss from choice A if choice B goes forward. Libra's enemy is the buffet line. You'll literally starve in the face of a feast because you can't decide which entrée to sample first. This inability to make a choice is only amplified when it comes to interpersonal disputes. Friends know better than to try and pin you down on an opinion. You're a master of evasion and will use every trick in the book to avoid being cornered into taking a firm stance—from flirting, to pouting, to straight-up lying.

SHALLOW

Libras are the epitome of style over substance as they are only concerned with how things appear on the surface. So long as things seem beautiful and tranquil at first glance, they can hardly be bothered with digging deeper to discover how things actually are. Libra is represented by the scales, which gives the appearance of fairness and equilibrium. Whether or not that's really the case is none of Libra's concern. You are a master at sweeping dust and grime under the rug before guests arrive, then getting distracted by your own reflection and forgetting the dirt was ever there to begin with.

JUDGMENTAL

Is it any wonder a sign that's wholly concerned with appearances judges them so harshly? Whoever said not to judge a book by its cover clearly never met you. As far as Libra is concerned, the cover is all that matters. Every new person you meet gets the once-over from your exacting eye, and you will make a mental note of each and every hair that's out of place. Your singular obsession with beauty means you harshly judge any person, place, or thing that you find unsightly or plain. Diamonds really are Libra's best friend. The shinier, the better.

Libra placements

Sparkly Libra tends to command the attention of everyone in the room, so if you've got it as one of your "big three" there's no way you won't see its influence shining through. Here's a surface-level understanding of what Libra means for your birth chart. That's all they really care about, anyway.

VENUS IN LIBRA

Venus is Libra's ruling planet, so anyone who has their Venus in Libra is basically Aphrodite incarnate. Beautiful, selfish, and fully capable of starting the Trojan War on a whim, then turning around and acting like it was all Helen of Troy's fault. Your flirtatious romantic magnetism will mean many champions would happily die for a chance at your hand. Unfortunately for poor Achilles, he doesn't realize your irregular attentions are a bigger threat to his well-being than that heel will ever be.

LIBRA RISING

Got Libra as your rising sign? Then the world likely sees you as a social-climbing, ditzy flake who'd rather spend all day making inconsequential small talk than express an opinion or go deep on a topic. Sure, this can mean they also see you as fun and easy to be around—a total lack of substance will do that—and you're always invited when it's party time. But when a friend is in need of an honest opinion or deep discussion they'll scroll right past your name and onto someone they can actually trust to keep it real.

MOON IN LIBRA

A Libra moon's thoughts are simple: me, myself, and I. Consummate navel-gazers, a Libra moon means your interior life is concerned with yourself, your goals, your reputation, and pretty much nothing else. You're constantly calculating how to impress those around you, and will gladly change key parts of your personality to make this happen. This can often leave you feeling unmoored and directionless, since you're continually changing course to suit wherever the wind blows. At least you're charming!

Libra in love

Self-obsessed Libras will always be more in love with their own reflection than they are with anyone else. In an ideal world, Libra would spend their whole life collecting admirers like precious jewels rather than ever settling down. Settling down would involve making a choice, after all. Masters of flirtation and flattery, Libra has an innate sense of how to beguile anyone and everyone with just one glance. Lovers will be dazzled by your ability to stare deeply into their eyes. What they don't realize is you're actually just checking out your own reflection in their irises.

SINGLE LIBRA

A single Libra is never really single; they're just floating blissfully through a state of noncommitment with a host of potential suitors. Your indifferent sign loves to live in the "What are we?" phase of a relationship, and will grow frustratingly evasive any time their partner tries (and fails) to demand an answer. The more they push, the more cold and heartless Libra becomes until they pull the ultimate move in the Libra arsenal: disappearing without a word. Shiny, transparent, and lacking in substance—is it any wonder Libra is the Zodiac's ultimate ghost?

LIBRA IN A RELATIONSHIP

It takes a determined person indeed to actually pin a Libra down to a commitment, usually via a steady stream of gifts and praise. Libras are high-maintenance partners who want to be treated like a housecat, pampered, petted, admired, and with no expectation they'll provide anything in return. No matter how "committed" your relationship appears, you'll always have one foot out the door, constantly scanning the horizon for a better option. Just as you were won over by gifts and admiration, so you can be quickly lost the moment a shinier object comes along. No wonder you've developed such an impressive collection of engagement rings. They just look so pretty on your finger!

Most compatible

Libra + Sagittarius

Air and fire generally make a great combination, so it's no surprise that Libra's best match is a Sagittarius. Both signs share an interest in being social, and Sagittarius's sense of humor will ensure all their conversations stay exactly where you like them: totally unserious. Archers love the thrill of the chase, meaning they'll actually find your indecisiveness and constant will-they-won't-they-ing attractive. As an added bonus, Sagittarius's carefree nature means they won't take it personally when Libra goes back on their word or refuses to commit, which is pretty much a prerequisite for anyone who wants to make it work with the master of scales.

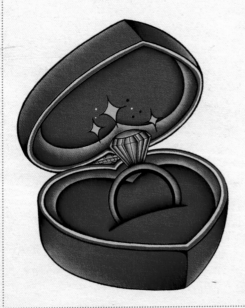

Least compatible

Libra + Virgo

These two perfection-oriented signs may find themselves initially attracted to each other, as Virgo will appreciate Libra's flawless outward appearance and Libra will appreciate Virgo's spotless surfaces (all the better for seeing their own reflection). That initial attraction will quickly wither, however, once you dig a bit deeper and find two diametrically opposed worldviews that lead to feelings of frustration and betrayal for Virgo and dismissive disinterest from Libra. Virgo's obsession with commitment and literal interpretation of promises and opinions (you know, they expect you to stick to them) will repel Libra, who hates being called to account for anything, especially their own opinions.

Libra + Aries

Aries' direct and confrontational vibe is simply too much conflict for light and breezy Libra. While you may initially love the adoration Aries pours on you during the courtship process, that feeling will quickly sour when Aries' jealousy and your conflict avoidance finally meet. The moment Aries realizes how many other admirers their flirty Libra keeps in tow, they'll be ready for a fight. Unfortunately for them, Libra sees even the slightest hint of a conflict as their cue to leave—usually without saying so much as a goodbye.

Libra + Libra

How can two navel-gazers even look up long enough to notice each other? A Libra will never be able to provide another Libra with the constant stream of adoration they require. They are both too busy looking in the mirror to realize their partner is even there. But it's the communication issues that will really do this couple in as neither partner will be capable of telling the other how they really feel, leading to a lifetime of long-simmering resentments and passive aggression. These two won't trust each other either, and for good reason. They know from experience just how easy it would be to convince their faithless partner to stray. Probably because they both already have.

LIBRA AT WORK

Lazy Libra knows how to appear busy when the boss comes around, but a brief glance at their computer screen will show that the "work" they've been "so busy" with all day was actually an online shopping spree. Libra's ultimate job would be something between a trophy wife and a courtesan, and they tend to view their job as a way to bide time until their meal-ticket reveals itself. Libra, your charming, easygoing nature often makes you a favorite with coworkers— until they need you to finish a task or give an opinion. Libras will worm their way out of ever delivering a verdict, even if that means leaving important tasks in permanent limbo. When workplace tensions finally bubble to the surface, you'll find Libra hiding in the break room hoping no one notices they've been playing both sides all along. In the event that you are the one in the hot seat, you'll bat your eyelashes, self-deprecate, and even unleash a flood of crocodile tears to make sure your poor HR rep can hardly remember why they called the meeting in the first place. Mission accomplished!

LIBRA IN THE FAMILY

As the family's Libra, you're definitely the one person everybody gets along with... but only because they don't know how you actually feel about anything. You're definitely the one that can be counted on to diffuse any family reunion flare-ups or placate that uncle at the dinner table. What nobody realizes is the Miss. Nice Niece act is all a ploy to make sure that once inheritance time comes around your name is at the top of everyone's list. Nobody knows this better than your siblings, who learned long ago that while you may swear up and down you'll help keep them out of trouble, you'll be singing a very different tune once your parents actually walk into the room. Your penchant for people pleasing is always at its peak when mom and dad are around. When tensions get too high, you revert to Plan B: avoidance. You have absolutely no problem skipping a holiday (or seven) if it means you'll be able to avoid a tough conversation.

LIBRA AT HOME

Beauty-obsessed Libras love nothing more than to decorate a space to their exact tastes and specifications, then to show off their handiwork via a series of lavish parties. As far as Libra is concerned, they are the definitive voice when it comes to art, music, and design, and they're basically doing the world a favor by inviting those with inferior taste over to see how it's really done. This makes you the ultimate silent critic any time you step into someone else's space, as you cannot help but make note of every outdated furnishing or—worse yet—slightly crooked wall art. Home is all about creating an environment of peace and symmetry for you, Libra, which is why you cannot abide a noisy neighbor or unkempt lawn. While you'd never confront them in person, you have no problem wielding the power of your neighborhood homeowners' association to keep the rest of your block in line, then serenely feigning ignorance when the nice old lady across the street asks why she's suddenly being fined for an "eccentric mailbox" violation.

LIBRA AND TRAVEL

Libra may seem like an easygoing travel companion, but anyone who has actually traveled with you knows the truth: holidaying with Libra is infuriating. While you may claim you have no opinion on accommodations, restaurants, and the itinerary, your travel companions will quickly realize that's not the case when they get a glimpse of your sourpuss face the moment you see something that's not to your liking. Even worse, you'll make sure the entire group wastes valuable sightseeing time hemming and hawing over every possible decision, from where to eat to what useless trinket to buy at the gift shop. You make friends wherever you go, which sounds nice enough. What people don't realize is that your "friendly" demeanor is also coupled with a complete lack of discernment when it comes to pickpockets, ne'er-do-wells, and scammers. One minute you're having the nicest chat with a too-friendly tour guide outside the Louvre, the next minute you're at the embassy trying to figure out where everyone's passports have gone. I guess that's just what you get for traveling with the Zodiac's ultimate air-head!

The two sides of Libra

It may surprise you to hear that Libra is one of the masculine signs of the Zodiac—probably because they wield their feminine wiles like a weapon of war. With that in mind, it should come as no surprise that within every Libra there is a dark masculine and dark feminine side just waiting to get out.

LIBRA DARK MASCULINE

Insecure, unreliable, and insensitive—when a Libra wakes up on their dark masculine side of the bed they embody all three. They're the type to make a date, confirm multiple times, then abruptly cancel at the last minute, even though they know the other person is already on their way.

LIBRA DARK FEMININE

A Libra that's expressing their dark feminine side may come off as bemused and empty-headed, but that's actually just an act. Dark feminine Libras are master manipulators who will do anything to get their way. Except, of course, actually telling someone what it is they want. Instead, they'll lay out a series of traps—I mean hints—for their unsuspecting partner to pick up on and see if they pass the test. Unfortunately for everyone involved, they rarely do.

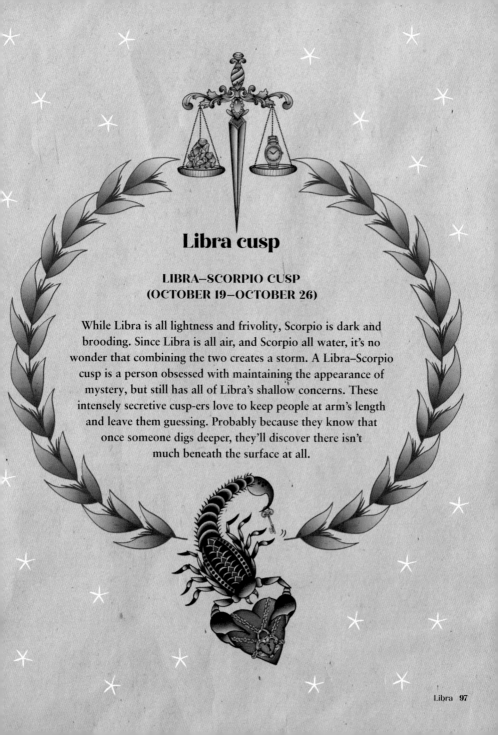

Libra cusp

LIBRA–SCORPIO CUSP
(OCTOBER 19–OCTOBER 26)

While Libra is all lightness and frivolity, Scorpio is dark and brooding. Since Libra is all air, and Scorpio all water, it's no wonder that combining the two creates a storm. A Libra–Scorpio cusp is a person obsessed with maintaining the appearance of mystery, but still has all of Libra's shallow concerns. These intensely secretive cusp-ers love to keep people at arm's length and leave them guessing. Probably because they know that once someone digs deeper, they'll discover there isn't much beneath the surface at all.

Hello Scorpio...

Your sign often gets a bad rap—and that's exactly how you like it. It's not hard to write about your dark side, considering it's the only side you've got. We'd call you an evil mastermind, but you'd probably take it as a compliment. There is no secret too salacious, no act too depraved, or torture too twisted for your ruthless sign to enjoy. In fact, you love nothing more than to watch other people squirm. A spiteful master of mind games, you use cruelty and intimidation to make sure no one gets close enough to see who you really are: a deeply insecure child in scorpion's clothing. Luckily, thanks to your noxious personality, nobody ever wants to.

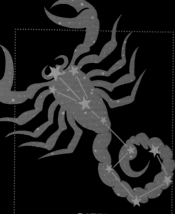

5 NOTORIOUS SCORPIOS

All Scorpios aspire to fame and it's little wonder there are so many names to choose from. Your ruthless sign wants notoriety by any means. Here's a sample of the Scorpios who attained your sign's ultimate goal: infamy:

DATES
October 23–
November 21

SYMBOL
Scorpion

RULER PLANET
Pluto

ELEMENT
Water

MODALITY
Fixed

OPPOSING SIGN
Taurus

MORTAL ENEMY
Pisces

PET PEEVES
Small talk, air-heads, canceled plans, broken promises

1 **Marie Antoinette (November 2, 1755):** The last Queen of France who had a love of finery and was insensitive to the problems of her people. She was executed at the height of the French Revolution.

2 **John Gotti (October 27, 1940):** American gangster and head of the Gambino crime family in New York City, famous for being one of the most powerful and ruthless crime bosses of all time.

3 **Larry Flynt (November 1, 1942):** American publisher who founded *Hustler* magazine and three pornographic news channels. His obsession with notoriety led him to push the envelope, including publishing nude photos of Jacqueline Kennedy sunbathing in 1975.

4 **Christopher Columbus (October 31, 1541):** Italian explorer who "discovered" the New World by stealing land from the native population. His exploration took him across the globe and led to the decimation of several indigenous societies.

5 **Kris Jenner (November 5, 1955):** "Momager" of the Kardashian clan, Jenner successfully managed the lives of her entire family leading to a popular meme declaring, "The devil works hard, but Kris Jenner works harder."

Scorpio in a nutshell

Not gonna lie, Scorpio, we're a little scared to roast you, knowing the pleasure you take in plotting revenge, but your tactics of intimidation won't work here. The Zodiac truly enters its villain era with you, since you love nothing more than scaring the pants off everyone you encounter. Your brooding, sex-obsessed sign is known for its unparalleled ability to make others feel uncomfortable, and there is no taboo that's too hot for you to touch. You've perfected the art of the menacing glare, which you gleefully employ on anyone who tries to get too close. Whatever friends you have know much better than to try and probe too deeply into your interior life, despite the fact that you're always pressing them to divulge their deepest, darkest secrets for your unholy collection. If someone does make it past your hard exterior and into your inner sanctum, they'll soon notice that the doors have locked behind them. You see those closest to you as possessions to be jealously guarded at all costs, and will keep them close by force if necessary. We'd say life with Scorpio is "'til death do us part," but you probably have more than a few tricks up your sleeve to ensure you'll still be able to get in touch from beyond the grave as well.

POSSESSIVE

Let us guess, Scorpio, your first word was "mine." As the most possessive sign in the Zodiac, once you get your hands on something you are never letting go, no matter how hard it may struggle against your constrictor's grip. This possessiveness also makes you intensely jealous. You have no problem going from zero to green-eyed monster the moment you feel that someone is encroaching on the territory you've claimed. Stage-five clinger? Lovers and friends wish you were that lax. You're more like a stage ten, and will lie in wait to lash out in private the moment you feel that their attentions are divided. How dare your BFF be caught texting another friend in your presence! As far as you're concerned, you should be the only number on their phone.

SECRETIVE

Scorpios love nothing more than collecting other people's secrets, but that shouldn't fool others into thinking you'll ever divulge one of your own. Scorpios love to maintain an air of mystery at all times, and would much rather leave a series of tantalizing breadcrumbs about their "dark" past than reveal themselves to another person. In your twisted mind, the truth makes you vulnerable, which is something your sign can never abide. People confide their secrets to you because they know you'll keep them... until they cross you, that is. Then, you'll use everything in your power to exact your revenge—the slower and more painful, the better. As much as you love exploring everyone else's dark underbelly, you protect yours with the viciousness of a cornered scorpion. Anyone who gets close can expect to feel your sting.

POWER-HUNGRY

Scorpios are known for their lust for power. Unfortunately for the rest of the world, you tend to define "power" in the most Machiavellian terms possible. Fear and intimidation are the name of your game, and you have no problem being ruthless or downright cruel to get what you want. Sure, you've mastered the art of subtle manipulation, and really love the feeling of intellectual superiority it can provide. But when that doesn't work, you're not above beating your foes into submission and will happily employ the most dastardly tactics imaginable in your quest for world domination.

Scorpio placements

If you've ever wondered why people's hair stands on end any time you're around, having Scorpio at the top of your chart is probably the reason. Unsettling Scorpio doesn't need to be your sun sign to creep in and spread darkness throughout your chart. Here's what to expect if you've got the scorpion as any of your "big three."

MOON IN SCORPIO

Having your moon in Scorpio means your internal life is spent living on the dark side of the dark side. Your inner monologue is mainly concerned with plotting, manipulation, and pouring over a treasure trove of dark secrets. You're that friend who can bust out an encyclopedic knowledge of serial killers and their methodologies and is always up for a seance (and knows how to perform one). We wouldn't be surprised to hear most of your thoughts are spoken in tongues. Frankly, just thinking about them scares us.

SCORPIO RISING

Got a rising sign in Scorpio? No wonder people tend to run away screaming whenever you arrive. Your public persona is that of a dark, intimidating, super-human who may or may not have made a deal with the devil to gain unearthly powers. Sexy, spooky, and suspicious, people may be slightly intrigued by your mysterious aura, but their terror and the unease you inspire will keep them away.

VENUS IN SCORPIO

Be honest, you only bought this book to try and find your perfect match, didn't you? Scorpio Venuses are obsessed with love and finding a soulmate. They dive heart-first into all of their love affairs and have no problem exploding with passion the moment they feel a spark. The instant a romantic connection is made, you're all in, and expect nothing less than the same devotion in return. In short, don't be surprised if you have a shotgun wedding—or several—in your future.

Scorpio in love

The line between love and hate is never blurrier than in your twisted heart, Scorpio. On the one hand, your passionate sign loves love and is constantly on a quest to find its perfect partner. On the other, your deep sensitivity and jealous tendencies mean you can easily turn your lovers into enemies the moment they cross one of your many invisible lines. Scorpios need intensity in all aspects of their life, so it's no surprise that they're attracted to intensely sexual, highly emotional relationships. It's almost as if your entire sign read *Fifty Shades of Gray* and thought, "Challenge accepted."

SINGLE SCORPIO

Sex-obsessed Scorpios have no problem enjoying everything the single life has to offer. Your astronomical levels of lust and constant need to push boundaries in the bedroom borders on nymphomania, and you have no problem spreading your passions far and wide. You also have no problem spending a wild night baring your soul (and a few other things) with a stranger, only to follow your passions to another bedroom the next night. Given how protective you are of your own heart, you would think that you'd be less careless with other people's. Unfortunately, for your growing list of one-night stands, that's not the case.

SCORPIO IN A RELATIONSHIP

Unlike their scorpion mascot, Scorpios mate for life. Your possessive and obsessive sign loves to pursue deep connections and sees all partners as a potential soulmate. Unfortunately for them, your definition of "soulmate" means that two become one, even at the expense of your own independence. Your secretive nature can also lead to trust issues, and any perceived slight will cause you to lash out. You love to set secret tests for your partners to assess their loyalty, then subject them to a lengthy silent treatment when they fail. In the bedroom, your lusty sign loves to push boundaries, and you're going to need a partner that's along for the—ahem—ride. An immunity to rope burn is also preferred.

Most compatible

Scorpio + Cancer

Scorpios aren't just looking for a soulmate; they're looking for a partner in crime. Luckily, they've found it in their fellow water sign, Cancer. Cancer will have no problem giving everything to their Scorpio partner and will gleefully answer all of Scorpio's probing questions. Plus, this introverted pair will love nothing more than to spend long nights at home together planning their future...and plotting their revenge.

Least compatible

Scorpio + Leo

When water meets fire there are bound to be problems. There's no compromise when it comes to this power-hungry pair. Both sides will always want to be right and would give up the relationship rather than give up control. Jealous Scorpio will hate Leo's attention-grabbing tendencies, and naturally extroverted Leo will loathe Scorpio's need for one-on-one time. Even though Scorpio's sexy, mysterious vibe and Leo's shiny personality may lead to an initial attraction, this mismatch will be pretty hard to overcome.

Scorpio + Libra

Light and bubbly Libra loves to live a life of peace and tranquility, which sounds like nothing so much as a snooze-fest for intrigue-obsessed Scorpio. While Libra strives to keep all their social interactions pleasant and conflict-free, Scorpio loves nothing more than to make it weird and watch the mess unfold. Libra's changeability will always be at odds with Scorpio's need for stability, and their trust issues will be forever triggered by the Libra partner's flirty nature. Scorpio will find themselves forever chasing their flighty Libra partner, leading to intense frustration…and more than a few voodoo dolls.

Scorpio + Aquarius

Heady Aquarius is all intellect, while Scorpio is all emotion. These two may initially bond over their shared hatred of conventionality, but their differing worldviews will inevitably lead to conflict. Aquarius is always trying to make the world a better place, while Scorpio would much rather spend time probing the dark corners of humanity's basest pursuits. Independent-minded Aquarius will never give Scorpio the undivided attention they need from a partner, and Aquarius will grow frustrated with Scorpio's need to turn every conversation toward emotions. While they may respect each other's complete disregard for the ordinary, these two are better off as friends.

SCORPIO AT WORK

Your ideal career would either be as a secret agent or a police interrogator. Barring that, ruthlessly moving your way up the corporate ladder while silently sabotaging your coworkers' ambitions will have to do. Your covetous sign cannot abide being an underling, meaning you quickly develop a deep and abiding hatred for any "boss" or "manager" that stands in your way. You'll stop at nothing until your name is the first one on the masthead, not because you actually care about success in your field, but because you crave power over others. In fact, you spend half your work hours secretly searching for other jobs while plotting ways to take down the company with your exit. But while you may have absolutely no loyalty, you also have no patience for treachery from a colleague. Your scorpion-like tendencies are on full display the moment you feel wronged in the workplace, and you have no problem lying in wait and collecting secrets until the ideal time comes for you to strike. Did your "work bestie" actually think they'd get a promotion over you? All it'll take is one anonymous email to the boss detailing their deepest, darkest secrets to make them realize your work friendship was as fake as their resume.

SCORPIO IN THE FAMILY

While most people spend their energy trying to avoid family conflict, you love nothing more than to stoke it. You know exactly which button to push to send every one of your family members over the edge. And you'll gladly push— preferably moments after dinner is served at a holiday. Despite your devil-may-care attitude, your intense jealousy means you also want to be the favorite, and you have no problem manipulating emotions behind the scenes to make that happen. You know exactly what to do to pit family members against each other while using your collection of family secrets as an insurance policy to ensure nobody will ever do the same to you. While you love nothing more than to find out everyone else's business, your secretive nature means you never let your guard down long enough for them to get to know you in return. Even with family, your true feelings remain hidden behind a labyrinth of insurmountable walls, leaving you feeling eternally lonely and your family members with an unshakable feeling that they'll never know what's really going on behind your sly smile. Probably because it's the truth.

SCORPIO AT HOME

The ideal Scorpio abode is more like a dungeon than a living space. The shades are always drawn, both to discourage visitors and to keep prying eyes from seeing the depraved acts going on inside. Scorpios thrive on darkness and will want that to be reflected quite literally in their décor. As far as you're concerned, there's no such thing as too much black—from the sheets to your clothes to the color you splash on the walls. The few guests you do allow into your den of depravity shouldn't be surprised to see occult items strewn about, or sexually charged art hanging in the communal areas, just daring them to ask what it is you get up to in your off hours (not that you'd ever tell). Your gothic heart will be reflected in the materials you bring into your home, and you're no stranger to metallic furniture or stone floors. As for the thermostat, you like to keep your home roughly the same temperature as your heart—just above freezing.

SCORPIO AND TRAVEL

Scorpios like to travel alone—preferably to a dangerous location where they don't speak the language. Vacationing Scorpios eschew tradition and are way more interested in seeing a city's seedy underbelly than the typical sites. While Scorpio's travel companions will spend their days taking in the usual tourist traps, you choose to sleep the day away and save all your energy for sampling the destination's nightlife. Any attempt from fellow travelers to impose a plan will be met harshly, since you'd much rather explore based on intuition alone. Scorpios prefer to travel on the edge of danger, instead of in the lap of luxury, and love nothing more than arriving at the dingiest hostel in town with only a few coins and an outdated travel book, then seeing what happens. For some that sounds like the premise of a horror movie, but for you it's the perfect vacation itinerary.

The two sides of Scorpio

Scorpio is one of the Zodiac's feminine signs, but that's not to say
this sign doesn't have two dark sides to choose from. These sex-obsessed
water signs tend to be fluid in their gender expression, but here are the
two poles every Scorpio has inside.

SCORPIO DARK MASCULINE

Lavish displays of passion and romance
are accompanied by intense bouts of
possessive jealousy for Scorpios that
are situated in their dark masculine.
A Scorpio that's expressing its masculine
side does everything with a hint of
violence and intimidation, and there's no
telling when they might lash out. Thought
the average Scorpio was guarded? Just
wait until you meet one that's expressing
its dark masculine side. They're way
more likely to be hiding a secret family
than to show vulnerability with the
ones they love.

SCORPIO DARK FEMININE

Scorpios love to live in the feminine,
which is their natural state of existence.
Dark feminine Scorpios are sensual
to the point of making others feel
uncomfortable, which only turns them
on even more. On the flip side, Scorpios
that are expressing their feminine side
are also more likely to be vindictive, and
have never felt a grudge they couldn't
hold on to for dear life. They know how
to take down anyone with a cruel word—
or even just a single icy glance.

Scorpio cusp

SCORPIO–SAGITTARIUS CUSP
(NOVEMBER 18–NOVEMBER 24)

The Scorpio–Sagittarius cusp is called the Cusp of Revolution, and there's no convention these cusps won't challenge. Sagittarius's vicious wit mixes with Scorpio's love of watching people squirm in these folks, giving them an almost supernatural ability to cause discomfort. There's no fight from which these cusps will back down. It's good you've inherited Sagittarius's near-pathological independence, since you'll often find yourself alone.

Hello Sagittarius...

Life is just one big joke to you, isn't it? Well, we're deadly serious when we say you're the Zodiac's obnoxious know-it-all. You may fancy yourself a philosopher, but in reality you're a blowhard doomed to repeat the same stories and jokes for the rest of your life. It's honestly impressive the way you can go on and on, blissfully unaware that you're not impressing anyone at this party—which you totally crashed, by the way. Your foolhardy sign lives its entire life in search of fun, burning through connections and guzzling up experiences at a pace so quick you never really enjoy them. You may rack up some good stories along the way, but you'll spend your whole life cycling through people to hear them.

DATES
November 22–
December 21

SYMBOL
Archer

RULER PLANET
Jupiter

ELEMENT
Fire

MODALITY
Mutable

OPPOSING SIGN
Gemini

MORTAL ENEMY
Scorpio

PET PEEVES
Rules, emotions,
predictable situations,
sensitive people

5 NOTORIOUS SAGITTARIANS

Archers spend their whole lives hunting excitement, so it should be no surprise that the pursuit has turned up more than a few unsavory characters, including these five infamous folk:

1 Patrizia Reggiani (December 2, 1948): Italian socialite and matriarch of the Gucci family who had her ex-husband shot after he divorced her for another woman.

2 Lucky Luciano (November 24, 1897): American gangster who helped develop the American organized crime syndicate in the 1930s. He was convicted of running a prostitution ring in 1936 and fled to Cuba, where he continued to serve as a mob leader until his deportation to Italy in 1946.

3 Emperor Nero (December 15, 37 CE): Notorious Roman emperor known for executing his enemies, including his own mother, and for his persecution of early Christians. His reign was marked by tyranny and extravagance, and for the great fire that destroyed much of Rome in 64 CE.

4 Pablo Escobar (December 1, 1949): Colombian drug lord and leader of the Medellín Cartel, Escobar amassed massive wealth as the so-called "King of Cocaine." He was killed by police after escaping house arrest at the elaborate mansion prison he built for himself known as "La Catedral."

5 Mary, Queen of Scots (December 8, 1542): The life of this queen of Scotland was marred by a series of disastrously bad decisions. She was eventually executed after being caught plotting against her cousin, Queen Elizabeth I.

Sagittarius in a nutshell

Party's over, Sagittarius. Your gluttonous sign lives for excess. Your sex, drugs, and rock 'n' roll ethos might seem exciting from the outside, but you'll turn up empty-handed when it comes to the things that really matter in life. Introspection? Nope. Commitment? Nada. Intimacy? Not so much. You're represented by the archer, meaning you love to portray yourself as a straight shooter. But it's easy to take shots when you keep everyone at a distance. That's why you burn through relationships well before any form of real attachment can be developed. Friends know they can always count on you to get the party started, but they also know they'll always come second to your never-ending pursuit of a good time. You'll spread their secrets far and wide if they make for a good story, and have no qualms using your sharp wit to stab them in the back if it'll help you feel superior. Ultimately, in the hunt for true friendship, you archers rarely hit your mark.

RECKLESS

You take devil-may-care to a whole new level, Sagittarius, and often end up paying the price. Your lust for novelty, and obsession with spontaneity, often blind you to any potential consequences your actions may bring, landing you in more than a few sticky situations. Your impulsive sign is totally incapable of thinking ahead, and will blindly follow your every whim only to end up shocked at the wreckage later. Your long-suffering parents are used to late-night phone calls from you pleading with them to bail you out of your latest easily avoidable emergency. You try to play this trait off as a hilarious quirk of your spontaneous lifestyle, but after the third phone call from jail most people will discover you're actually the one thing you hate most in the world: thoroughly predictable.

TACTLESS

One of your favorite mottos is "truth hurts." Unfortunately for those around you, an archer's truth typically comes in the form of a shot through the heart. Your zero-filter sign never stops to think about the effect your words may have on others, and is often blithely unaware of the hurt feelings you create. Your complete lack of tact means you often leave people feeling offended, which you quickly write off as just another example of someone being "too sensitive" for your rapier wit. But how many "too sensitive" people does someone have to meet before they take a look at how their own behavior affects others? For undiplomatic archers, the limit does not exist.

OBNOXIOUS

Loud, garish, ham-fisted Sagittarius loves nothing more than to take over an entire room with their explosive energy. You may think this makes you the life of the party, but more often than not you're just annoying everyone. Your over-the-top behavior guarantees that the attention is on you at all times, and you can hardly conceive of a world in which that's actually a bad thing. Your clueless sign has never met a party it couldn't crash, and will typically just assume you were left off the guest list by accident. Who wouldn't want to hear you loudly recounting your lengthy stories while everyone else is trying to sing "Happy Birthday?" You simply can't imagine.

Sagittarius placements

Just as the obnoxious personality of Sagittarius takes over every room it enters, so the archer takes over every birth chart it appears in. You may think you dodged a bullet avoiding Sagittarius as your sun sign, but if you've got this domineering dandy as any of your "big three," you're in for some problems—not that you'd ever stand still long enough to realize it.

MOON IN SAGITTARIUS

Sagittarius moons think about the future so much they're incapable of living in the moment. Their obsession with the next best thing means they're totally lacking in introspection, and their thoughts move at such a rapid pace they never stop to appreciate what they have. People can tell you spend every conversation thinking about what you're going to say next instead of listening. That's probably why they rarely bother to tell you anything of particular note.

SAGITTARIUS RISING

If you've got Sagittarius as your rising sign it means the world sees you as an over-the-top extrovert obsessed with having a good time. They probably think of you as the ultimate party-hopper, good for getting on a VIP list, but far too impulsive and narcissistic to be trusted. When others talk, they can literally feel you not caring. Your habit of scanning the room to see if someone more exciting has arrived doesn't help either.

VENUS IN SAGITTARIUS

Those with their Venus in Sagittarius are frenzied romantics who love to sweep someone off their feet only to leave them without a leg to stand on. These "free-love" advocates would have done well in the swinging sixties, but struggle with monogamy and settling down. Lucky for you, we hear polyamory is on the rise...

Sagittarius in love

Those born under the sign of Sagittarius spend their entire life chasing excitement, and what is more exciting than love? Until the other person starts making demands, of course. You love the start of relationships, but are easily spooked the moment your beloved starts to have expectations of their own. Fiercely independent Sags will do anything to maintain their autonomy, and lash out at anyone who they feel is trying to take it from them. It's probably a good thing you love your freedom so much—you may very well end up alone.

SINGLE SAGITTARIUS

Single Sags love to burn through hot-and-heavy flings at a frenetic place, then leave their one-night-only partner with their head still spinning. Your declarations of love may be true in the moment, but the feelings tend to burn out by morning—just like the candles you lit to set the mood. In many ways, Sags are designed for the single life as they don't want to be tied down by anyone and can't bear the idea of a life without as many sex-capades as possible. In the bedroom, you may think of your "wham, bam, thank you ma'am" style of lovemaking as passionate, but it can often end up coming off as frantic to those on the—ahem—receiving end of your frenzied advances.

SAGITTARIUS IN A RELATIONSHIP

Sags naturally want to roam free, so in order to settle down you'll have to find the right jockey for your inner wild horse. Sags often make very callous partners as their brutal honesty and independence can mean they often have a hard time taking their partners' feelings into account. You take very little seriously, Sagittarius, and see everything as merely an intellectual exercise, meaning emotions, especially those of other people, are rarely at the forefront of your mind. You seek novelty over stability and would rather have a series of passionate affairs than a committed relationship. Good thing you're not one to get lonely.

Most compatibile

Sagittarius + Leo

For the rare Sagittarius that actually does want to settle down, your best match is fellow fire sign Leo. "Look-at-me" Leo knows how to keep someone's attention, even yours. Their fun and flirty extroverted side means life will always be exciting, plus they're way too obsessed with themselves to bother with putting rules and restrictions on their partner. So long as you shower them with passionate kisses and admiration when you are around, they won't be worried about what you get up to when you're not. A willingness to take lots of cute-couple photos is also a plus.

Least compatible

Sagittarius + Scorpio

Sagittarians and Scorpios may find themselves initially attracted to each other, thanks to Scorpio's mysteriousness and Sag's air of danger, but the relationship will fizzle out the moment Scorpio's possessiveness comes out to play. Sagittarius's inability to take emotions seriously will enrage their Scorpio partner, while Scorpio's jealousy and need for reassurance will only push Sag farther and farther away. Ultimately, this pairing is way more likely to end up in lifelong enmity than become a perfect match.

Sagittarius + Taurus

Boring, steady Taurus will never be able to keep a Sagittarius's attention long enough to sustain a relationship. Sure, Sag will be happy to hop into bed with Taurus every once in a while after they hear about their notorious sexual prowess, but bulls will never be able to keep archers' attention for more than a few hours. Taurus is just far too stable for chaos-loving Sag. As for Taurus, the moment Sagittarius turns up late for a dinner date and causes them to lose a reservation, thoroughly turned-off bulls will be out the door. At least neither of them will feel the need to say goodbye!

Sagittarius + Cancer

Cancer is a homebody. Sagittarius is an adventurer. See the problem? Restless Sagittarius will never sit still long enough for cozy Cancer's liking. Sag's complete lack of tact will never fly with sensitive Cancers, who are known for taking everything personally. But the real death knell for this match is their differing worldviews. Sagittarians are bon vivants who love life and all it has to offer, while Cancers are naturally gloomy pessimists who would rather spend the day at home with their feelings. These two can barely see eye to eye, let alone go through life side by side.

SAGITTARIUS IN THE FAMILY

When was the last time you called your grandmother, Sagittarius? Actually— scratch that—have you ever called her? Flighty Sagittarius can hardly be bothered to pick up the phone, meaning most of your family members tend to learn about your major life events through social media. As with all your other relationships, you're happy to show up for the family reunion (especially if there's free food and drink), but your unsentimental sign is not one to put maintaining familial connections at the top of their to-do list. When you do show up for the odd holiday or birthday party, your lack of tact usually puts you at the center of whatever squabble is threatening to ruin the day for everyone. You just can't help but ask Aunt Marge about her divorce proceedings, or point out cousin Katie's new nose. The more boring or mundane the family affair becomes, the more likely you are to light little fires for the pure amusement of watching them burn. Who says pop-pop's retirement party can't double as an episode of *Family Feud*?

SAGITTARIUS AT WORK

Working 9–5? No thanks. Your novelty-loving sign chafes against even the most mild routine, and you'd much rather juggle five jobs that you're mediocre at than settle in and do one job well. Coworkers know the only thing they can count on you to show up for is happy hour, and your ability to turn even the tamest office holiday party into a debauched bacchanal is the stuff of office legend. Your love of hearing yourself talk is on full display in an office, which you view less as a place of work and more as a venue for you to test out your best jokes and stories. Meetings, in particular, are unbearable with you. While you may see your colleagues as a captive audience, they'll feel more like hostages, forced to listen to your constant interruptions when they really just want to go to lunch. Not only are Sagittarians completely lacking in professional decorum, but they'll also lose their temper at anyone who tries to impose the rules, even if that person is the boss. In fact, the harder the powers-that-be try to rein you in, the more outrageous your behavior will become. That's probably why your list of firings could fill a novel, while your list of professional references barely fills a page. Oh well, you are a fire sign, after all.

SAGITTARIUS AT HOME

Home? You mean that place you store your underwear between trysts? Any address associated with wanderlusty Sagittarius is usually more of a pit stop than a home base. For you, "home" is just a place where people can send your mail—and even then, you're way more likely to let it pile up on the kitchen counter than you are to actually open it. Sagittarius never wants to feel like they've settled down, and what's more settled than a permanent residence? You'd much rather spend your life couch surfing than put down roots. You're always on the move—literally—which is why your "home" is filled with half-unpacked boxes that will stay that way until you relocate again. Your fridge is a resting place for decaying takeout and your bedroom is almost as messy as your love life. Your extroverted sign is always on the go and barely ever spends any time at home, so you really can't understand why your landlord is so angry you forgot to pay the rent (again). Chill out, bro. You'll get to it next time you're around— probably in a month or two.

SAGITTARIUS AND TRAVEL

Risk-chasing Sagittarius is the most travel-obsessed sign in the Zodiac. In your ideal world, you'd never have time to unpack your carry-on between trips. You're a self-proclaimed travel expert and bring a "Sagittarius-knows-best" vibe to any group trip you attend, regardless of how much you actually know about your destination. This makes you an extremely condescending travel partner, despite the fact that you're also the person most likely to completely disregard important cultural norms about dress, behavior, and speaking volume. (You only have one setting: loud.) You're that tourist who will pretend that they speak the language when actually you're just parroting phrases you learned from a guidebook with an accent so wrong you accidentally end up saying something offensive. But hey—if you end up with a black eye, that's no problem. Nothing bores you more than a trip that goes according to plan. Anyone who joins you on one of your jaunts should be prepared for you to roll up to your flight five minutes before takeoff, coffee in hand and a phone with one percent battery, totally unphased that you almost ruined the trip for everyone. What? You'll just sleep at the airport and fly out the next day. Not like you haven't done it before…

The two sides of Sagittarius

Sagittarius is a masculine sign, but that doesn't mean archers don't have both masculine and feminine sides to contend with. Like every other sign, Sagittarius has a dark masculine and a dark feminine side that they can tap into on any given day. Here's what to watch out for from both.

SAGITTARIUS DARK MASCULINE

When Sagittarians are expressing their dark masculine side, their recklessness comes to the fore even more than usual. These impulsive hotheads have no problem starting fires just for the rush of watching other people put them out. Dark masculine Sags will bulldoze their way into any conversation just to hear themselves talk, and love to initiate a battle of wits with anyone who dares try to get a word in for themselves. Unfortunately this verbal sparring can turn into physical fights faster than you can say "devil's advocate."

SAGITTARIUS DARK FEMININE

Sagittarians expressing their dark feminine side love to spend a night out on the town flirting with everyone they come into contact with, regardless of that person's feelings or relationship status. They'll happily break up a marriage just for the story, and have no problem inviting multiple suitors to the same party so they can watch them all duke it out for their affections. Those on the receiving end of their coquettish ways may be left with the distinct impression that these Sags get off more on the drama than they do on the romance. They'd be right.

Sagittarius cusp

SAGITTARIUS–CAPRICORN CUSP
(DECEMBER 18–DECEMBER 24)

A mutable fire sign meets a cardinal earth sign with these cusp-ers, meaning they are constantly fighting an internal battle between Sagittarius's reckless thrill-seeking and Capricorn's prudent practicality. This toxic pairing creates someone who is hyperfocused on themselves and their own ambitions with a complete lack of sensitivity to how their single-minded pursuit of success might affect those around them. In short, you're the ultimate evil genius.

Hello Capricorn...

Sorry to interrupt your workflow with something as trivial as introspection; we promise this won't take long. Your stuffy, spiritless sign is represented by a goat— probably because of your unique ability to destroy any playground you come upon. Your "all-work-and-no-play" sign simply doesn't have time for things like "fun" or "enjoyment." You're far too busy methodically working your way through your checklist for world domination. Yes, that's right, we know about your plan. Others may think you're simply another cog in the corporate wheel, but we know better. Underneath your unassuming demeanor and buttoned-up shirt is a ruthless, power-hungry tyrant carefully working through a 100-step plan to impose your will on the masses.

5 NOTORIOUS CAPRICORNS

Capricorns seek power, not the limelight, so will fly under the radar as second-in-command, but this hasn't stopped your sign producing internationally recognizable figures like Catherine Middleton and Dolly Parton—or these famous names:

DATES
December 22–January 19

SYMBOL
Sea goat

RULER PLANET
Saturn

ELEMENT
Earth

MODALITY
Cardinal

OPPOSING SIGN
Cancer

MORTAL ENEMY
Aquarius

PET PEEVES
Unserious people, broken protocols, wasted time, children

1 **Al Capone (January 17, 1899):** Prohibition-era gangster prominent in organized crime as the Chicago Outfit boss. He ruthlessly organized the infamous St. Valentine's Day Massacre, but was only charged with tax evasion before spending the rest of his life in Alcatraz.

2 **Marie Lafarge (January 15, 1816):** French husband-killer convicted of using arsenic to poison her spouse in 1840 (the first conviction due to forensic toxicological evidence), she wrote her memoirs in prison, doggedly proclaiming her innocence.

3 **J. Edgar Hoover (January 1, 1895):** American FBI director who launched witch hunts against so-called communists, "deviants," and civil rights leaders, all while allegedly hiding his own "deviant" lifestyle.

4 **Edgar Allen Poe (January 19, 1809):** American writer whose macabre works put the "goth" in "Gothic." His methodical mind led him to invent the detective story, but he is best known for works involving untimely deaths, tell-tale hearts, and prophetic ravens.

5 **Howard Hughes (December 24, 1905):** Wealthy American manufacturer, aviator, and film producer better known as a recluse. Severe obsessive compulsive disorder meant he spent much of his later years in exile in luxury hotel rooms across the United States.

Capricorn in a nutshell

You may think we're here to call you boring, Capricorn, but we know that's all an act. In fact, we'd actually say that you're the most interesting sign of all. Sociopaths are interesting, after all. Your conservative, no-frills appearance masks an inner tyrant quietly biding their time until they can seize power and rule with an iron fist. Your unsuspecting demeanor is just a front for your true self: a petty, cruel absolutist who spends their gloomy life silently convinced that they're better than everyone around them. Sure, there are plenty of other signs that see themselves as perpetually in the right, but they lack the stamina needed to actually enforce their views on the world. Not you. Your domineering sign is a master of quiet influence, and you'll stop at nothing until you're calling the shots. Friends—to the extent that your work schedule will allow you to have friends—know that they will always come second to your ambition, especially if they have nothing material to bring to your master plan. Who has time for things like weddings and birthdays when there is work to be done?

RIGID

If you don't bend you'll break...unless of course you have a will of steel. Capricorns know there is exactly one optimal way to do things, and it's the way they've always been done. The ultimate disciplinarian, your sign has no patience for loosened restrictions, lax behavior, or—horror of all horrors—casual Fridays. Your complete and total adherence to protocol makes you every boss's dream and every coworker's nightmare, as you clock and report even the slightest deviation from the norm to the appropriate authorities. Your religious devotion to the status quo makes it almost impossible for you to take in new information or consider alternative paths for doing things, and you have no problem expressing your disdain for anyone who colors even slightly outside the lines. The 1950s called. They want their mentality back.

PETTY

Anyone who thinks there are things too small to be complained about hasn't met you, Capricorn. Your petty sign is the master of making mountains out of molehills. You can hardly go out to eat without sending at least something back to the kitchen because you found the dish to be too salty/not salty enough/too cold/too hot. In social interactions, there's no grudge too small for you to hold onto, and you're notorious for taking unnecessary jabs at anyone who crosses you (or dared to cross you ten years ago). You take any opportunity you can to express your disapproval, which is constant. Have you ever considered a career as one of Bravo's Real Housewives? You'd fit right in.

CHEAP

You may describe your financial philosophy as "sensible" or "frugal," but anyone who has ever had to split a check with you would probably describe it a bit differently. You're cheap. Your Scrooge-like sign looks for every possible opportunity to pinch pennies, even if it comes at the expense of those around you. You'll happily deduct ten percent off a waiter's tip for inefficient water delivery and have no problem subjecting your travel companions to the most barebones accommodation if it means saving a buck. For you, the least expensive option is always best and you'd rather live a life of Spartan austerity than ever be caught spending a penny more than is absolutely needed. This makes you an excellent money manager for any business you're a part of, but an absolute nightmare when the office tries to plan anything fun. Who needs balloons on their birthday? The unencumbered air is free!

Capricorn placements

Low-key Capricorn may not be the star of your birth chart, but it doesn't need to be. Capricorn would much rather assert its subtle influence via some of the lesser placements until it brings you to heel over the course of years. Suddenly, you look around and your life is all Capricorn, whether you want it to be or not.

MOON IN CAPRICORN

Your moon sign represents your internal life, and when your moon is in Capricorn it means you spend all your energy trying to find new ways to be productive. You have no time to spin your wheels on intellectual pursuits, frivolous hobbies, or fruitless emotions. Instead, you are singularly focused on the next step you need to take to make it to the top. Some may say you're quiet, but really you're just biding your time. Soon they'll see... they'll all see!

VENUS IN CAPRICORN

Those with their Venus in Capricorn are looking for one thing and one thing only: commitment. Summer flings, one-night stands, and brief flirtations are of no interest to them as all of that is simply a waste of time. They conduct their romantic life like a series of job interviews for the role of "life partner," all the way down to checking a potential partner's LinkedIn before making a date. Nothing says romance like a well-formatted resume.

CAPRICORN RISING

If you've got Capricorn as your rising sign it means the world sees you as a stuffy sourpuss who only cares about work. Some may say you're just shy or stoic, but in truth the perception tends to match reality. You *are* a stuffy sourpuss who only cares about work. There are only so many times you can turn the dinner conversation to annual expense reports before you stop getting invited out by anyone.

Capricorn in love

Is a Capricorn ever actually in love? Or are they only briefly allowing themselves to feel a love-like emotion because getting married is part of their ten-year plan? Either way, potential partners should know not to expect a shower of romance from you. Your practical sign sees love and marriage as something to cross off your to-do list in lifelong pursuit of the status quo. Anyone who hopes to be brought on at Capricorn Inc. will need to present their resume and qualifications before being considered for the role. If they're a fit, they'll hear from you in three to five business days. If not, they shouldn't expect to hear anything at all, since you've already moved on to more suitable candidates.

SINGLE CAPRICORN

Single Capricorns are not overly preoccupied with their single status. They're married to their work as it is. If they are dating, it's more because that's just what people do than it is the result of a genuine desire for romantic companionship. This will be immediately apparent on a first date, which will always feel to the other person more like a job interview than a night out. You're not one to waste time and will want to hear how they answer your list of necessary preliminary questions before you agree to go on a second date—or even have a second drink.

CAPRICORN IN A RELATIONSHIP

Any potential partner for your high-achieving sign will have to be okay with always coming in second to work in your ambitious heart. If they can handle the late nights and constant office talk, you will agree to provide them with a stable yet emotionally distant companionship that will technically meet all of the requirements of a romantic relationship. They shouldn't seek out lavish displays of emotion, but they can expect that the bills will be paid and the house will be clean. Once the appropriate relationship milestones have been met, they can look forward to an uninspired proposal, traditional wedding, and subsequent production of 2.5 children as per the most recent census. Well, it worked for your grandma!

Most compatibile

Capricorn + Scorpio

Once a Capricorn has reached the stage in life where they have decided a partner is necessary to achieve the remainder of their goals, they should set their sights on a Scorpio. You may think traditionalist Capricorn and boundary-pushing Scorpio would never work, but in this case water and earth mix to make a mud that both partners can wallow in. Capricorns are loyal and stable partners, meaning Scorpio will never have to worry about the trust issues that plague their other relationships. Scorpio will love the fact that under Capricorn's mild-mannered persona there is an immense and slightly terrifying dark side to explore, and introverted Capricorn won't have any problem spending time in Scorpio's lair divulging dark secrets. Unless there's work to be done, of course.

Least compatible

Capricorn + Aquarius

Free-thinking Aquarius and status-quo obsessed Capricorn see the world through two very different lenses. Capricorn will find themselves forever frustrated by their Aquarius partner's inability to commit to anything, especially a conventional job. Meanwhile, Aquarius will tune out the moment they hear the words "ten-year plan." The end goal of a Capricorn relationship is a classic wedding—frills and all—while an Aquarius would be much happier eloping to Vegas while wearing their favorite Halloween costume. It's just not a match, is it?

Capricorn + Libra

Noncommittal Libra will drive Capricorn crazy, and Libra will grow to resent their Cap partner's constant attempts to hold them to what they say. Capricorns are ultra-direct and simply cannot understand Libra's passive-aggressive communication style, or why their opinion keeps changing based on who they're talking to. Capricorn is also one of the only signs that is totally immune to Libra's flirtatious charms, as they're much more concerned with substance than style. Meanwhile, Libra will head for the hills the moment they realize their no-frills partner doesn't even own a full-length mirror for them to primp in.

Capricorn + Leo

Leo and Capricorn may initially find themselves attracted to each other for their social status, but the relationship will quickly dissolve over one simple snag—they'll never be able to agree on what to do. Leo is the ultimate extrovert and will want to show off their six-figure Cap partner as much as possible at parties, dinners, and networking events. Understated Capricorn will find all of Leo's bragging obnoxious and would much rather spend a quiet evening at home gearing up for the workday ahead. They don't need a gloating partner to pump them up. Unfortunately for them both, gloating is what Leo loves best.

CAPRICORN AT WORK

Capricorn at work? Don't you mean their happy place? Capricorns live for work and work to live. To you, the office is the one place where the world actually makes sense. It's the one place where your ceaseless ambition doesn't make you a sociopath, it makes you a boss. Or at least, it will once you complete your ten-year plan to take over the company and run it the way it actually should be run. You love efficiency and cannot stand to see valuable resources wasted on slacking employees, office happy hours, or—worst of all—team-building activities. You get to the office early every day just to make everyone else feel late, and your coworkers know you'd ban all chitchat and smiling if you could. You bring a distinct "not-here-to-make-friends" attitude to the workplace that makes you the perfect person to heartlessly conduct a mass layoff on the boss's behalf. Colleagues see you as the ultimate brown-noser, always sucking up to the boss and acting as their little informant on the floor. You never question authority, mainly because you intend to be the authority one day. Your introverted sign hates the spotlight, so your ultimate goal is always to be the power behind the frontman. That way, someone else can take the blame (and the fall) while you act as the quiet puppet master, holding the strings and the power.

CAPRICORN IN THE FAMILY

Quick question, Capricorn. How many times have you heard the phrase "You're not my dad!" at a family event? Too many to count? That's what we thought. Capricorn is the ultimate father figure, regardless of where they actually fall in the family tree. You're a natural provider who relishes in doling out resources to help your bloodline thrive. But those who accept your assistance should beware. These handouts often come with a closed fist and tight leash, as you'll also expect anyone who takes your help to abide by your rigid standards. Your house, your rules. Capricorns see the success of their family members as a reflection of their own achievements, and you have no problem making your disapproval known to any artsy cousins who are still "figuring things out." Your tough-love approach to familial relationships means you're often the one the younger generation dreads being seated next to at family events, especially if they know their latest report card isn't up to snuff. But hey, at least you can always be counted on to execute your great-great-grandma's pecan pie recipe to perfection!

CAPRICORN AT HOME

Some people fill their home with signs that read "live, laugh, love" or "gather." Your home says "Don't touch." Stuffy, conservative Capricorn wants their living quarters to feel more like a museum than a home. As far as you're concerned, a house is a place for people to display their heirlooms and refuel before returning to work. Capricorn's décor is stiflingly old-fashioned, either passed down in their family by generations or acquired at an estate sale. You couldn't care less about trends, and guests who step over a Capricorn's threshold often feel like they've been transported back in time. So what if your wallpaper is from a previous century? If it worked for the Victorians, it'll work for you. The Capricorn home checks all the boxes of a classic domicile, but lacks any of the warmth to make it feel really lived in—probably because it isn't. If home is where the heart is, then your home is the office building where you spend the majority of your day. You just maintain a separate residence because sleeping in your cubicle is against company policy.

CAPRICORN AND TRAVEL

"Capricorn" and "travel" are two things that generally do not mix. If you can be persuaded to take your vacation days, you'd much rather spend that time at home, contemplating when you can get back to work again. In your mind, travel is a frivolous, expensive endeavor only undertaken by dilettantes who are not currently in the midst of a methodical plan to take over the world. If you do travel, usually at the behest of a partner or family member in desperate need of fun (Why? You don't know), you'll budget the entire thing down to the penny, leaving no room for spontaneity or reckless spending. There will be no five-star dinners or trips to the shopping district when you're around. If you do plan something to do on your trip, it's probably because you were able to finagle a discount or find a coupon. You'd fly in the cargo hold if it meant a cheaper ticket, and refuse to stay anywhere but the most budget accommodation. If you end up with bedbugs, then that's just another sign that you never should have left home to begin with.

The two sides of Capricorn

Despite their dad-like energy, Capricorn is one of the Zodiac's feminine signs. That said, a dark masculine and dark feminine side exists within every Capricorn, silently plotting until they can make their intentions known. Any Capricorn can find themselves grappling with one of these two identities on a given day. Here's how to spot which one has taken over.

CAPRICORN DARK MASCULINE

A Capricorn that's situated in its dark masculine takes their "emotionally distant father" dial and cranks it up to an 11. Hard-nosed, domineering, and totally unconcerned with anything that is not a verifiable fact, dark masculine Caps often come off as rude or cold. Probably because they are actively choosing to be rude and cold. You can attempt to tell them about your day if you want, but they'll most likely just be watching your mouth move while they think about something at work.

CAPRICORN DARK FEMININE

Detached dad, meet overbearing mom. Capricorns situated in their dark feminine are perpetual cynics who aren't happy keeping their worldview to themselves. Instead, they try to impose their way of thinking on everyone around them, believing wholeheartedly that if the world could only see things their way, it would be a much better—and more organized—place. They treat everyone like children in need of a firm hand and have no problem dispensing advice to those who they feel need it, which just so happens to be everyone they've come into contact with.

Capricorn cusp

CAPRICORN–AQUARIUS CUSP
(JANUARY 17–JANUARY 23)

Practical, conservative Cap meets idealistic rebel Aquarius
to create an aloof, judgmental radical who simply cannot
understand why the rest of the world is not on their
intellectual level. These cusps have solved all of society's
problems several times over and can't help but judge their
fellow man for failing to get with the program. The natural
loners are always one step away from becoming a woodland
hermit and spending the rest of their days toiling over
a manifesto that nobody will ever read. At least it
keeps them from ruining another party with
one of their lectures.

Hello Aquarius...

Or whatever other-wordly greeting you would prefer. As the Zodiac's resident space alien, we're sure you'd be more than happy to hear all about how "weird" and "non-traditional" you are. But that's not what we're here to talk about. Instead, let's talk about how your obsession with aloofness and rebellion keeps you trapped in an ice palace of your own making. It's easy to look down on others from your satellite on Mars, but real changemakers are the ones who come down to earth and get their hands dirty. How many hermits do you know who actually publish their manifesto?

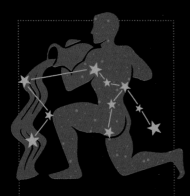

5 NOTORIOUS AQUARIANS

Aquarians love to point to the changemakers and artistic innovators in their sign, like Oprah Winfrey and Harry Styles, but that's not all this Zodiac sign has given us. It's one thing to be offbeat, but these five infamous Aquarians are downright notorious:

DATES
January 20–February 18

SYMBOL
Water bearer

RULER PLANET
Uranus

ELEMENT
Air

MODALITY
Fixed

OPPOSING SIGN
Leo

MORTAL ENEMY
Pisces

PET PEEVES
Tradition, rules, people who say they're "not political," the status quo

1 **Grigori Rasputin (January 21, 1869):** Russian mystic who ingratiated himself with the Romanov family since he could magically "heal" the tsarevich Alexei's hemophilia. He survived many attempts on his life before being drowned in the Neva River. His influence over the royal family is thought a factor in the eventual Russian Revolution.

2 **Elizabeth Holmes (February 3, 1984):** Tech entrepreneur who claimed to have invented a device for multiple blood tests from a single finger prick. She was found guilty of fraud when it was discovered her device never worked and sentenced to 11 years in prison.

3 **David Lynch (January 20, 1946):** American filmmaker whose boundary-pushing work, including *Twin Peaks* and *Blue Velvet*, is known for its often disturbing imagery that can leave audience members feeling uneasy.

4 **Lord Byron (January 22, 1788):** English poet who enjoyed various scandalous relationships, including a rumored affair with his half-sister's daughter. One lovelorn ex described him as "Mad, bad, and dangerous to know."

5 **Paris Hilton (February 17, 1981):** American heiress to the Hilton hotel fortune, often regarded as the first "influencer." Her public behavior in the early 2000s made her a tabloid staple and led to run-ins with the law.

Aquarius in a nutshell

Aquarius loves its reputation as the Zodiac's rebel, but riddle us this: does it really count as being a rebel if your "rebellion" is so predictable? At a certain point your loved ones all learn to roll their eyes at your eccentric style and constant chafing against the status quo. If you're able to maintain any loved ones, that is. Constantly analytical and aloof, you rarely put in the emotional work necessary to maintain real connections. Instead, you'd much rather keep other humans at arm's length, observing them as if you're an extraterrestrial tasked with reporting back to the mothership about human life. And sure, you have lots of ideas about how to make this strange planet called Earth a better place, but they usually stay just that: ideas. Your independence-obsessed sign is totally incapable of asking for help to put your plans into action, and will never admit when someone else has knowledge or expertise that exceeds your own. Instead, you'll spend your entire life with your head in the clouds, pontificating about what the world could be if you got your way. Sadly, everyone else is just too boring and pedestrian to understand the true genius behind "no-pants Wednesdays." Dullards!

DISTANT

So close, yet so far away. For as much as you claim to be a humanist, connecting with other humans one-on-one isn't really your strong suit. Instead, Aquarians like to keep everyone in their life at a distance. They prefer to keep their conversations intellectual, not emotional, and will lean heavily on their talent for sarcasm the moment anyone tries to get close. With your arms crossed and your head in the clouds, you laugh in the face of anyone who tries to get you to engage with human emotions. While you love thinking about the big picture, you can often find it hard to connect with what is happening right in front of you. But how exactly do you plan to change the world if you refuse to actually live in it?

PROUD

It's one thing to believe in yourself. It's another to believe in only yourself. Aquarians live their lives with their nose in the air, totally assured that they are better in all things. It's part of the reason why you're so committed to marching to the beat of your own drummer—you're convinced that they're playing the superior tune. For as much as you hate rules, you are totally rigid in your adherence to your own ideas about how things should be. You would rather die than ask for help because that would mean admitting there might be someone else on the planet whose intellectual capabilities match your own. If it's true that pride goeth before a fall, then you'd better keep a first-aid kit handy.

LONER

Who needs other people when you've got all your big ideas to keep you company? Aquarius is the Zodiac's lone wolf—and you like it that way. Nothing gives you a bigger thrill than to spend an entire party standing in a corner looking interesting. If someone is smart enough to come over and ask you a question, then good for them. They've passed your test and have earned the right to be regaled with your latest idea for how to achieve world peace (usually without being able to get a word in themselves). If nobody approaches and you spend the whole party in stoic silence, so be it. You didn't even want to come, anyway. You have no problem flying solo because you see it as a testament to how unique you really are. But is it really your "uniqueness" that keeps people away? Or do you just give off bad vibes?

Aquarius placements

High and mighty Aquarius doesn't need to be your sun sign to exert its influence. This air sign can blow anyone in its idealistic direction, especially if it appears in another one of your birth chart's "big three." Eccentric weirdos just know how to make a splash that way.

MOON IN AQUARIUS

If your moon is in Aquarius, then your emotional life is...thoroughly unemotional. You'd much rather spend all your time pouring over big ideas than big feelings. Unfortunately for you, the distance you create with yourself also creates a distance with others, who can't help but feel there's a lot hiding behind your detached expression. No wonder so many of your closest relationships only exist online.

VENUS IN AQUARIUS

Those with their Venus in Aquarius thrive in long-distance relationships. Physical touch is not your love language, and neither is showering your beloved with attention every second of the day. You don't need much from a partner and want someone who won't expect much from you in return. Meeting up once a month to howl at the full moon is fine with you.

AQUARIUS RISING

The good news? If you've got your rising sign in Aquarius, you want the world to see you as different—and they do! The bad news? It's in less of a "cool rebel living their best life" kind of way and more of a "creepy loner who lives in the woods" kind of way. Maybe it's your distant stare. Maybe it's your general "alien on a business trip" vibe, but either way, other people feel like something is just a bit off about you. If only they knew you come in peace! Sort of...

Aquarius in love

Partnership does not come naturally to you, Aquarius. You'll always be more in love with your own ideas than another human. When you do find someone whose freak flag flies as high as yours, you'll still only open up once they've passed through your gauntlet of mind games, thought experiments, and riddles. More often than not, the person will just give up rather than suffer through another lengthy text exchange about a hypothetical scenario when all they asked was where you want to go for dinner.

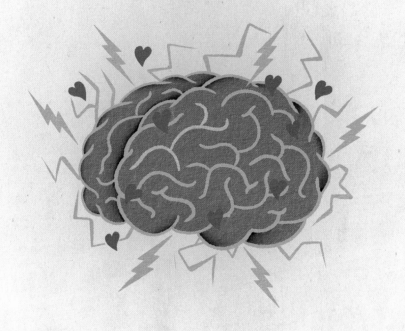

SINGLE AQUARIUS

A single Aquarius has usually been that way for a while and barely even noticed. You prefer to spend your life alone contemplating what an ideal match would be like if—and that's a big if— you were to engage in one. You're the definition of a sapiosexual, aka someone who has to be attracted to a person's mind before they could possibly consider a romantic relationship. Until such a mind-connection is met, you're happy to get your rocks off through sex parties and online encounters—the less "vanilla" the better.

AQUARIUS IN A RELATIONSHIP

Thanks to your feelings of superiority, you tend to be highly selective when considering a potential partner, and will only agree to enter into something as normative as a committed relationship with someone who you feel can match your wit and intellect. Outward appearances mean very little to you. In fact, you're much more likely to fall for the unconventionally attractive weirdo everybody tells you to stay away from than you are the local heartthrob. You know the girl in the YA novel who falls madly in love with the pale quiet guy despite the fact that she's 99.9 percent sure he's a vampire? She's definitely an Aquarius.

Most compatibile

Aquarius + Aries

Want to actually make a relationship work? Find yourself an Aries. The doer and the thinker meet with this pair, as each fuel each other's best tendencies. Detached Aquarius is far too above-it-all to trigger Aries' competitive streak, while Aquarius's constant stream of eccentricities will be just enough to keep Aries' wandering eye interested. Aquarius will love the fact that passionate Aries will always have the enthusiasm to put their ideas into action, and Aries will love that flighty Aquarius will never get angry when they burn out and move on to the next thing. This is a partnership made in half-finished-project heaven. Just don't ask them to actually plan a wedding.

Least compatible

Aquarius + Cancer

Differing worldviews, values, and needs make this match a nearly impossible one to make work. Emotional Cancer wants a partner who will stick around all day and wallow in feelings. Then you have heady Aquarius, who finds nothing so boring as discussing base emotions and finds the needs of others totally stifling of their independence. One is a gloomy pessimist primarily concerned with the here and now, the other is a heady optimist with their eyes permanently focused on the horizon. It's hard to imagine these two having a successful conversation, let alone a relationship.

Aquarius + Virgo

An Aquarius–Virgo relationship can best be categorized as a hamster wheel of criticism. Virgo will criticize Aquarius for their messiness and unpredictability and Aquarius will hammer Virgo for their obsession with perfection and order. Virgo will hate the way Aquarius constantly questions their way of doing things, which they consider to be the product of perfectly sound logic and research. Meanwhile, Aquarius will be left feeling like their every move is being noted by a live-in hall monitor. Relationships are built on mutual affection, not judgment.

Aquarius + Pisces

Sentimental Pisces is one of the worst possible matches for heady Aquarius, as these two will simply never be able to give each other what they need in a relationship. Pisces will take all of Aquarius's sarcastic remarks to heart, and Aquarius will never even try to understand why Pisces' feelings are so perpetually hurt. A notorious grudge-holder, Pisces will build up a well of resentment for their Aquarius partner, while Aquarius will be so busy with their own thoughts they won't even notice anything is wrong. Eventually, it'll boil over into an epic Pisces meltdown—usually because Aquarius forgot to get Pisces a birthday present (again).

AQUARIUS AT WORK

The three favorite words of Aquarius: work from home.
You love nothing more than to toil away in solitude on your
latest project, and hate engaging in mundane office politics and
small talk. Your tech-obsessed sign loves to conduct all its business
virtually, away from the prying eyes and small ideas of your oh-so-
normal coworkers. Once you rise through the ranks to become the boss
yourself, employees know to expect you'll get totally derailed anytime
some shiny new piece of tech comes your way. You're all about innovation
for innovation's sake, and are perpetually chasing the next best thing, even
if the old way of doing things was perfectly fine. Your constant desire to be on
the cutting edge means you rarely stop to think about whether or not change is
necessary—just that it's available. This obsession with novelty means you often leave
projects half finished as you float from shiny new idea to shiny new idea. In meetings,
you love ideating endlessly over the big picture, but when push comes to shove you
just cannot bring yourself to dig into the little details that actually make the big picture
happen. As impressive as you are when you're standing on your soapbox, it doesn't
take long for coworkers, bosses, and clients to realize you're really just a lot of hot air.

AQUARIUS IN THE FAMILY

Every family has its eccentric, and
Aquarius, that's you. You're that
weird aunt/cousin/sibling who nobody
really understands and never RSVPs to
anything but always shows up (late) to
tell everyone about their latest big idea,
invention, or cause. It's not that you don't
care about your family—in many ways
you feel like they're the only ones who
truly understand you—but you're not one
to let it show. The only way for a family
member to know you love them is if you
let them talk. Thinking someone is smart
enough to be listened to is the highest
form of compliment from Aquarius.

Otherwise, you have no problem
dominating the dinner table conversation
with every "taboo" topic under the sun,
from politics to religion to whether or not
there is life on other planets. (The answer
is yes, and you are their representative.)
You love to pick out your stodgiest and
most conservative family members, then
keep pushing their ideological buttons
until they eventually break. This tendency
has put you at the center of more than
a few holiday blowouts, but you don't
mind. At this point your relatives know
to duck for cover the moment you start
"just asking questions."

AQUARIUS AT HOME

The Aquarius home cannot be constrained by the normal trappings of art and design. If you want to put a bed in the middle of a living room and a couch in your kitchen, then that's what you're gonna do. You don't care about things like "matching" and will use any color you want anywhere you want. Some people might need a seizure warning before walking through your door, but that's not your problem. If your guests don't find the décor overwhelming, the beeps and boops from your various machines might be the thing that sets them over the edge. Your tech-loving sign would live in a fully automated Smart House straight out of an episode of *Black Mirror* if they could. You love nothing more than to show guests the new computer you built, or how you can turn the lights on and off with a clap. And sure, maybe this means Big Tech can hear your every move, but as far as you're concerned that's just one more person to listen in on all your brilliant ideas.

AQUARIUS AND TRAVEL

Aquarians love to travel...alone. In fact, you'd love nothing more than to spend your days roaming to the Earth's most far-flung locations, making notes on your fellow man as a detached observer of the human condition. Those who try to organize travel with you will find that you cannot be constrained by things like "itineraries" or a "return ticket." You're much more interested in the locals than you are in your travel companions, and are prone to wandering off for hours, then turning back up at the hotel just when everyone was about to call the police. Friends and family know better than to expect to get a call or an update from you when you're abroad, as home is the last thing on your mind. In fact, you see every new place you visit as an exciting opportunity to become an expat. Why not? You're an outsider wherever you go anyway. There is no food too adventurous or custom too foreign for you to explore, and you will rebel against any tour guide or tourism board that tries to tell you what to do—even if it's for your own safety.

The two sides of Aquarius

Detached Aquarius is one of the Zodiac's masculine signs, but this does not mean they don't have a feminine side that they can tap into any time they want. Aquarius eschews anything like traditional gender roles and loves to live their life floating between masculinity and femininity as it suits them. Here's what to expect on a day when they are landing more to one side than the other.

AQUARIUS DARK MASCULINE

Cold, condescending, and emotionally unavailable—an Aquarius who woke up on the dark masculine side of the bed is the epitome of all three. They hardly have time for things as mundane as human emotion, and will rarely come down off their high horse long enough to consider what those on the ground have to say. Totally convinced of their own superiority, these loners would much rather spend the day wrapped up in their own thoughts than with another human. Some may say that makes them a robot. They'd take that as a compliment.

AQUARIUS DARK FEMININE

An Aquarius that's situated in its dark feminine side pushes back hard against any attempt by an outside force to impose its will, even if it's something as simple as a "no dogs allowed" sign outside a café. These thoroughly unpredictable menaces to society love nothing more than to show up late, wreak havoc, and leave without saying goodbye. The dark feminine Aquarius is all about shaking up institutions just to see if they hold, regardless of whether or not that shakeup is warranted or helpful. They're basically the prototype for the "manic pixie dream girl" that dominated 2000s rom-coms. Unfortunately for everyone, the schtick is a lot less charming in real life.

Aquarius cusp

AQUARIUS–PISCES CUSP
(FEBRUARY 15–FEBRUARY 21)

You call yourself dreamy. Others call you an unfocused mess.
Those born on the cusp between Aquarius and Pisces live
their life with their head in the clouds, floating from unfinished
project to unfinished project without the discipline to even
clean their paintbrushes in between. These deeply sensitive
cusps take everything deadly seriously and are known for
bursting into tears at inappropriate times. You love to
claim that you're an "empath" who feels other people's
emotions. But if that were true, why can't you tell
when everyone is getting annoyed with you?

Hello Pisces...

Of all the signs we've roasted so far, we're pretty sure you're the most excited to get to your chapter. Why? Because it means you get to engage in one of your all-time favorite activities: playing the victim. Poor, misunderstood Pisces can always find a reason to have their feelings hurt. So let's give you some. Your clingy, lazy, gullible sign is basically the poster child for willful naivete. You never seem to know anything about how the world works and love busting out your babe-in-the-woods act anytime someone (i.e. your boss) expects even a modicum of maturity or responsibility. You wear your guilelessness and sensitivity like a badge of honor, constantly lamenting the fact that the rest of the world can't be more like you. Luckily for you, being blissfully unaware of eye rolls is one of your superpowers.

DATES
February 19–March 20

SYMBOL
Fish

RULER PLANET
Neptune

ELEMENT
Water

MODALITY
Mutable

OPPOSING SIGN
Virgo

MORTAL ENEMY
Capricorn

PET PEEVES
Awkward silences, know-it-alls, being asked an ETA, emotional distance

5 NOTORIOUS PISCES

Pisces love gushing about the creative titans in their artistic ranks, from Elizabeth Taylor to Steve Jobs, but this mercurial sign has a dark side better represented by these five notorious names:

1 Anne Bonny (March 8, 1697): One of the only known female pirates, Irish Bonny and her band terrorized the Caribbean until she was captured alongside fellow pirate Mary Read in October 1720. She and Read escaped death sentences by claiming to be pregnant. Bonny's true fate remains unknown.

2 Kurt Cobain (February 20, 1967): 1990s rocker credited with popularizing the Seattle grunge sound as the frontman of Nirvana. He struggled with addiction and tragically took his own life at the age of 27.

3 L. Ron Hubbard (March 13, 1911): Sci-fi writer who founded the Church of Scientology. The subject of numerous documentaries and exposés, many former members say it is actually a dangerous cult.

4 Patty Hearst (February 20, 1954): American heiress kidnapped by a guerilla group only to join their ranks and start robbing banks with them. She later claimed to have been brainwashed and received a presidential pardon for her crimes.

5 Joe Exotic (March 5, 1963): American zoo owner whose wild antics and love of collecting tigers were the subject of the Netflix documentary *The Tiger King*. He was arrested in 2018 for attempting to murder his rival, Big Cat Rescue owner Carole Baskin, and is serving 21 years in prison.

Pisces in a nutshell

Poor little Pisces. All you want is to be able to spend your days swimming from fantasy world to fantasy world in a state of blissful ignorance about the real world around you. You probably already know and love your reputation as the Zodiac's artistic soul, but what about your other claim to fame as the Zodiac's ultimate dilettante? Your moodiness is the stuff of legend, meaning you often go from being totally enthusiastic about an idea one minute to completely over it the next. Friends know to expect at least five potential versions of you to show up to any given event, several of which are in a state of emotional distress. You say you're just sensitive, but those who know you best realize you're also a spotlight hog who loves to use emotional outbursts to be the center of attention. And if anyone dares call you out on your woe-is-Pisces behavior? Bring on the waterworks—and the grudges. For someone so scatterbrained, you sure can hold on to your resentments. In fact, you're probably adding this book to your ever-growing list of personal grievances at this very moment. Sorry fishy. Didn't mean to ruffle your scales. It's just so easy…

LAZY

Pisces are often considered the old souls of the Zodiac, so it's no wonder they act as if they're already retired. Weak-willed Pisces will drop any task the moment they face the slightest hardship, and their work ethic is practically nonexistent. You would rather float along aimlessly going wherever the tide takes you than put forth even the slightest effort to change direction. In fact, just the thought of putting in effort has already left you feeling exhausted. You've never met a deadline you couldn't blow through, for no reason other than that you couldn't muster up the motivation to meet it. Pisces will always take the path of least resistance, even if it means they never quite get what they want. Luckily for you, your laziness means you never really want anything too deeply either.

CLINGY

If you look up the words "insecure attachment style" in the dictionary, you will probably find a picture of a Pisces. Pisces crave external validation. The closer you get to someone, the more constant praise and reassurance you'll need. For Pisces, every moment a text goes unanswered is another sign the recipient secretly hates them, and the only remedy for that is more text messages. Just ask your ex. If, of course, they haven't already blocked your number to stop the near-constant demands for "closure." What these exes don't realize is you've got no problem camping out at their favorite coffee spot for as long as it takes to "accidentally" run into them.

GULLIBLE

Some people might say Pisces is very trusting. We say Pisces is always one email scam away from losing their life savings. When it comes to red flags, your sign is essentially color blind. You love to believe the best of everyone and have no radar for deceit, meaning there is nothing you won't fall for. While at first this trait can seem kind of sweet, eventually your loved ones will grow tired of bailing you out of your latest totally predictable predicament. In an attempt to spare them, repeat after us: No one needs to talk to you about your car's extended warranty, a Nigerian prince does not need your help accessing his inheritance, and that person you haven't seen since high school's message about an "exciting opportunity to be your own boss" is not as good as it may seem.

Pisces placements

Not a Pisces sun sign? That doesn't mean you're out of the deep end. Pisces has a way of pulling you into its moody, mercurial tide from anywhere it appears in your birth chart, especially if it's one of your "big three." If you've always felt like a bit of an overly sensitive space cadet, you can probably thank your Pisces placements.

MOON IN PISCES

If you've got your moon in Pisces, your inner life is a fantasy world of your own design. People are probably used to having a conversation with you only to notice midway through that they've lost your attention to whatever elaborate hypothetical scenario your Piscean brain has conjured up. You're also super-sensitive and often find yourself taking on the emotions of others, aka hijacking their problems to make everything about yourself. Oops.

PISCES RISING

If you've got your rising sign in Pisces, then you are someone the world sees as deeply in need of a reality check. Consider this that check. You spend your life floating from unrealistic goal to unrealistic goal, with zero wherewithal to actually make them come true. Everyone can tell that your ideas are half-baked, but they also get the sense that you're way too sensitive to hear the truth. They're right.

VENUS IN PISCES

If you've got your Venus in Pisces, it means you love love. You're all about the thrill of romantic connection and spend your days fantasizing about your future soulmate. Unfortunately, your rose-colored glasses make it almost impossible for you to see red flags, meaning you often give your heart away to the wrong person and end up hurt. Your friends all told you that the DJ you met on vacation had bad vibes. You were just too love-drunk to listen.

Pisces in love

When it comes to love, Pisces only wants three simple things: constant praise, unwavering support, and everlasting gratitude. Emotionally dependent Pisces needs a partner that is comfortable being the center of their world and is willing to center their Pisces partner in return. Until you find such a person, you're more than happy to indulge in an intense string of fantasy relationships with individuals either real or imagined. You're basically the Zodiac's Snow White, mournfully singing "Someday My Prince Will Come" into a wishing well until the day your soulmate magically appears. It's a lovely dream, but you might find yourself waiting for a while.

SINGLE PISCES

Single Pisces is never really single. In fact, they've probably got multiple make-believe relationships that they are deeply invested in at any given time. Your high-powered imagination can't help but go into overdrive when it comes to your love life, meaning you leave every first date planning a wedding and wondering what your kids will look like. You catch feelings easily, and the intensity of your initial affection can often scare off a relationship before it even begins. This only serves to send you off on another string of fancies in which the person who rejected you shows up ten years from now—preferably at your wedding to a more attractive version of them—to announce they actually loved you all along. It happens in the movies!

PISCES IN A RELATIONSHIP

When Pisces falls in love, they fall hard. You quickly make your partner the center of your world, meaning you're often that friend who totally disappears the moment they get into a relationship. In return for your loving devotion, you expect your partner to shower you with a constant stream of praise and affection. Your need for external validation is never so intense as when you're in a relationship, and you are constantly on high alert for the first sign that your partner's affections might be waning. This insecurity only makes you cling harder, which can end up leaving your partner feeling smothered, so they push away. So you cling, and they push away. Which makes you cling, so they push away—and so on, and so on...

Most compatible

Pisces + Virgo

You may be thinking "messy Pisces and structured Virgo could never make it work!" But you'd be wrong. A Pisces + Virgo match is the perfect example of opposites attracting, as Virgo will love the "project" their chaotic Pisces partner presents, and Pisces will love Virgo's stability, commitment, and attention. Pisces lives in an imagined world, while Virgo is thoroughly reality-oriented, meaning that when these two get together big things might actually get done. Most importantly, Pisces' perpetual rose-colored glasses when it comes to romance makes them uniquely able to see Virgo's nitpicking for what it is: an expression of love.

Least compatible

Pisces + Libra

Noncommittal, self-centered Libra is basically a Pisces' romantic worst nightmare. Libras are far too cool and aloof to ever give Pisces the level of devotion they need. The lack of affection will activate Pisces' insecurities, causing them to cling to their Libra love for dear life. While Libra understands why Pisces would be obsessed with them (who isn't?), they'll always prioritize their independence over Pisces' comfort. These two may find common ground over their love of art and shiny objects, but that's where the connection ends.

Pisces + Gemini

Pisces will run into similar problems with noncommittal Gemini, with the added bonus that Gemini's charm will lead them on to think there really is something there. Pisces will spend their whole life chasing the fantasy of their relationship with Gemini, with Gemini dropping just enough affectionate breadcrumbs to string Pisces along for life. When Gemini inevitably drops them to pursue another (usually Aquarius), sensitive Pisces will be left with a broken heart and a grudge they'll hold onto for life. At least one part of this relationship was built to last.

Pisces + Sagittarius

Simply put, Sagittarius is just too mean and independent to make it work with a Pisces partner. Pisces' delicate self-esteem isn't built to withstand Sagittarius's wit and tactlessness, as they'll always take Sag's off-handed comments to heart. While Sag may love the fun, chaotic, artistic energy Pisces brings to life, they'll chafe at Pisces' constant need for validation and will see all of their attempts at closeness as an attack on their precious independence. These two may make great roommates or travel partners, but they're definitely better off remaining as friends.

PISCES AT WORK

"Work" and "Pisces" are two things that generally do not mix. You're just not someone who is built for traditional employment. Or any employment, really. In the workplace you thrive during a creative brainstorming session, but lose steam the moment it's time to put one of your big ideas into action. Instead of working, you spend most of your time wondering if your bosses and coworkers are mad at you, which in turn makes them mad at you because you haven't been working. Your sluggish sign is no stranger to being called into the boss's office to get put on a corrective course of action that does nothing to stem the flow of missed deadlines or half-finished projects. Coworkers like that you're always available for a good cry in the breakroom (unless you're already in there crying yourself), but know better than to come to you with anything involving the words "ASAP" or "by EOD." Those acronyms are simply not in the Pisces vocabulary. We'd say your best shot at a career would be something in the arts, but even Picasso had to actually produce a painting every once in a while.

PISCES IN THE FAMILY

Pisces loves to oscillate wildly between being the baby of the family and/or the wise elder. One minute you're dispensing sage advice to the younger generation about the nature of life, love, and creativity, the next you're crying at the dinner table because of an old sibling argument you can't let go of. You take familial love very seriously and can get guilt-trippy or needy when you feel like a member of the clan isn't pulling their weight. You're the first person to take it personally when someone opts to see their in-laws for the holidays or can't make the family picnic this year. Pisces also tend to suffer from a lack of boundaries with their family members, often sharing too much with the wrong people at the wrong time. This can be particularly difficult if you ever become a parent, as you tend to treat your kids like they're your friends and overshare. You also totally crumble when it is time for serious decision-making around things like finances or an elderly family member's health. When hard choices need to be made, you're nowhere to be found and will only show up again later when the decisions have been made to cry about how hard it all was for you.

PISCES AT HOME

When thinking about Pisces' home life, only one word comes to mind: chaos. Dreamy, artistic Pisces is someone who makes messes, not someone who cleans them up. Because of this, your home tends to be a shrine to all your half-finished projects and incomplete endeavors. Since your moods are so changeable, the idea of sticking to one color palette or décor style is typically out of the question. If you want to paint your living room lime-green and your bedroom slate-gray, so be it! If you want to pair a mid-century modern couch with a Victorian-era coffee table, then that's what you're gonna do! Sometimes these unusual pairings end up being inspired, other times they'll seem like you're gunning for a spot on the show *Hoarders*. Speaking of hoarding, Pisces' sentimentality means you love to keep everything, from ticket stubs, to tickets for movies you didn't even like, to cords for devices that have been obsolete for decades. Every inch of the Pisces abode is cluttered with knickknacks, baubles, and papers you could have tossed out years ago. But you never know! Those Beanie Babies still might make a comeback.

PISCES AND TRAVEL

When a Pisces travels they let whimsy and romance be their guide. While this may sound like the start of a great novel, their laziness and decision-fatigue kicks in the moment they have to deal with the aspects of travel that conveniently get left out of your favorite "Eat, Pray, Love" adventures. Specifically, booking flights, securing hotel rooms, and doing anything other than dreaming about being swept off your feet by an attractive stranger in a foreign land. Pisces loves to dream about romantic vacations to far-flung locations, but lacks the basic motivation to make these trips a reality. When you do take a trip (usually because it was planned by someone else), you're always at risk of coming down with an acute case of Paris Syndrome (i.e. an extreme malaise brought on by the fact that your destination will never quite match up to the idealized version you built up in your head). The fantasy just never seems to account for things like currency exchanges, flight delays, or figuring out how to navigate the metro.

The two sides of Pisces

Pisces is represented by two fish being pulled in opposite directions, which is a perfect way to describe the influence of their dark masculine and dark feminine sides. Though Pisces is classified as one of the Zodiac's feminine signs, it's dark masculine is always there, pulling Pisces in its own direction. Here's what to expect when one of these two combating fish gets its way.

PISCES DARK MASCULINE

A Pisces that has let its dark masculine fish take the lead is one who will never hold back when it comes to expressing their feelings. They see their self-expression as a God-given right and are prone to emotional outbursts. They prioritize feelings over facts, making them extremely hard to deal with when their emotional response is being challenged. To a Pisces that's swimming in the dark masculine pool, if they feel something is true, it is true, regardless of what anyone else has to say to the contrary.

PISCES DARK FEMININE

When Pisces' dark feminine fish takes the lead, they can often become lost in a sea of reverie. This version of Pisces would rather sit around all day dreaming about their ideal life than take any action to make it happen. In their ideal world, all their dreaming and pining will one day be rewarded by a handsome savior who appears out of thin air to solve all of their problems. It's a nice idea, but it's actually quite hard to meet your Prince Charming when you are locked up in a tower daydreaming all day—no matter what Rapunzel may tell you.

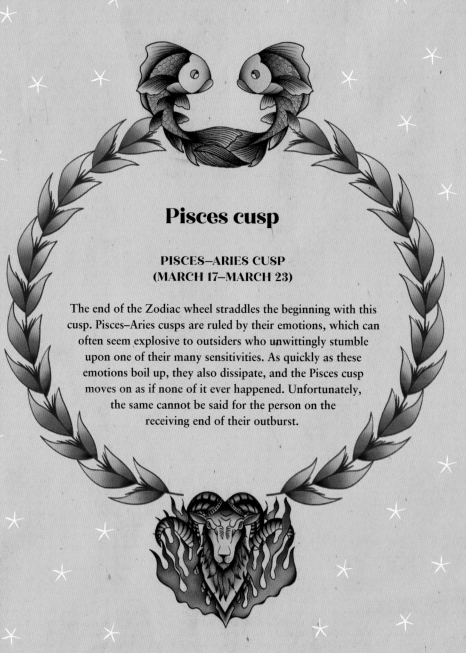

Pisces cusp

PISCES–ARIES CUSP
(MARCH 17–MARCH 23)

The end of the Zodiac wheel straddles the beginning with this cusp. Pisces–Aries cusps are ruled by their emotions, which can often seem explosive to outsiders who unwittingly stumble upon one of their many sensitivities. As quickly as these emotions boil up, they also dissipate, and the Pisces cusp moves on as if none of it ever happened. Unfortunately, the same cannot be said for the person on the receiving end of their outburst.

Index

Credits

Nazarii M/Shutterstock.com; Anastasiia Veretennikova; Shutterstock.com;
Christos Georghiou/Shutterstock.com

About the illustrator

Bruna Carla da Silva is a Brazilian artist and illustrator, based in Liverpool, United Kingdom. Through digital art and paintings on canvas and fabrics, she expresses her passion for the feminine world in a traditional tattoo style. You can find out more about Bruna at sailorbroo.com and on social media @sailor_broo.

Author acknowledgments

I could never have written this book without the wonderful team at Quarto, particularly my editor Charlene Fernandes, who guided me through the process from across the pond. I am forever grateful to my sister Natalie for introducing me to all things woo and for never shying away from a conversation about planetary movements, birth charts, or vibes. I'd also love to thank my wonderful parents, Felix and Deborah, who have never batted an eye at any of my endeavors, astrological or comedic.

This book is also dedicated to my dear friends, Kady Ruth, Bailey, and Tyler, who never got annoyed when I'd send them snippets of the roast of their sign (at least to my face) and my wonderful husband Danny, who, despite being a Scorpio, fills my life with joy, laughter, and lightness every day. And to my wonderful pets, Rusty (dog, Sagittarius) and Biz (cat, Libra) who have never shown any interest in astrology or comedy but are always up for a cuddle after a long day of writing.